The Long Walk

THE LONG WALK

By SLAVOMIR RAWICZ

Lyons & Burford, Publishers

Printed in the United States of America

10   9   8   7   6

Library of Congress Cataloging-in-Publication Data

Rawicz, Slavomir.
The long walk.
1. Rawicz, Slavomir. World War, 1939–1945—Prisoners
and prisons, Russian.   3. World War, 1939–1945—Personal
narratives, Polish.   4. Escapes—Russian S.F.S.R.—
Siberia.   5. Prisoners of war—Poland—Biography.
6. Prisoners of war—Russian S.F.S.R.—Siberia—
Biography.   I. Title.
D805.S65R39   1988   940.54'72'470957   88-534
ISBN 0-941130-86-X (pbk.)

Slavomir Rawicz acknowledges his debt to
Ronald Downing, who helped him write this book.

FOREWORD

Slavomir Rawicz had been in England nearly nine years, a Pole without a country living obscurely in the industrial Midlands, when we first met. My newspaper, the London *Daily Mail*, was launching an expedition into Nepal to seek the yeti, or Abominable Snowman, of the Himalayas. I had flown to Zurich, where the late King of Nepal was under medical treatment, to talk to Nepalese elder statesman General Kaiser. The General, scholar and intellectual, believed the creature existed, but he had never seen one. I talked to distinguished members of previous British expeditions to the Himalayas who had seen mysterious prints in the high snows, but they too had never seen the creature which had made them.

Into the office came a message that a Pole living in England had seen strange animals in the Himalayas which corresponded in many respects with the published descriptions of the yeti. The interview, I was told, would be difficult because the man still had relatives under Russian influence and probably would not allow his name to be revealed. So, without much hope of a story, I travelled north to see Rawicz.

I met Marjorie, Rawicz's English wife, first. They have a young family, for whom they both work extremely hard. She talked to me about him; it was quickly obvious he filled her life. Some of his experiences he had told her many others she would have known only if she understood Polish and Russian, because he talked and screamed in these languages through many tortured nights.

So I met Rawicz. Of medium height but looking taller because of his slim build, he greeted me coolly but courteously. He struck me as withdrawn, taut as a bowstring, a man who had made a virtue of reticence. I had plenty of time and used some of it to put him at ease. I was conscious of the fact that he was appraising me, deciding whether or not to tell me about himself.

After some hours he began to talk—from the beginning. He is a meticulous man and insisted that his encounter with the strange Himalayan creatures should be treated in its place as an incident in the greater adventure. Even in outline it was a great and grim narrative. And the force and sincerity of the man impressed themselves on me. He spoke with quiet authority about the things he had seen. We talked until the fire burned low in the grate in the early hours of the morning.

I went to see him again, to urge him to write a book. He agreed, if I would set it down for him. The deal was made.

It was not always easy. Rawicz had locked so much away in his mind and turned the key. There were happenings he had persuaded himself were better forgotten. For years he had been full up and afraid to talk. Tentatively at first, he began clearing his mind of the memories that had long spilled over into his restless dreams. I sat with him for many hours one weekend in every three for over a year. I came to know him very well. His own picturesque English was often inadequate for our purpose and we worked with Polish- and Russian-English dictionaries near at hand.

Towards the end I marvelled to see Rawicz, as he shed his burden, become relaxed. He smiled more often.

It was not, generally speaking, an emotional chronicle in the actual telling, but three times, I remember, he broke down and was engulfed in tears. I hope that in those rare tears were dissolved some of the sombre memories which had haunted him.

RONALD DOWNING

London, February, 1956

CONTENTS

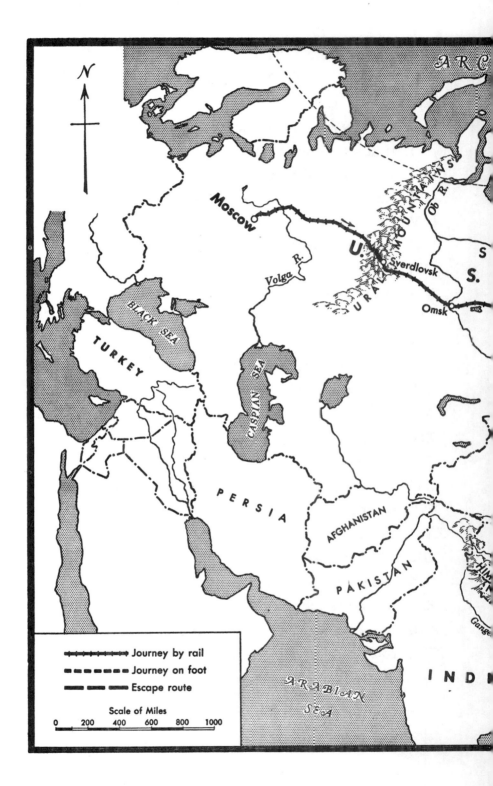

N

Moscow

Volga R.

U.
S.
S.

URAL MOUNTAINS

Ob R.

Sverdlovsk

Omsk

ARC

BLACK SEA

CASPIAN SEA

TURKEY

PERSIA

AFGHANISTAN

PAKISTAN

Ganges

INDI

ARABIAN
SEA

Journey by rail
Journey on foot
Escape route

Scale of Miles

0   200   400   600   800   1000

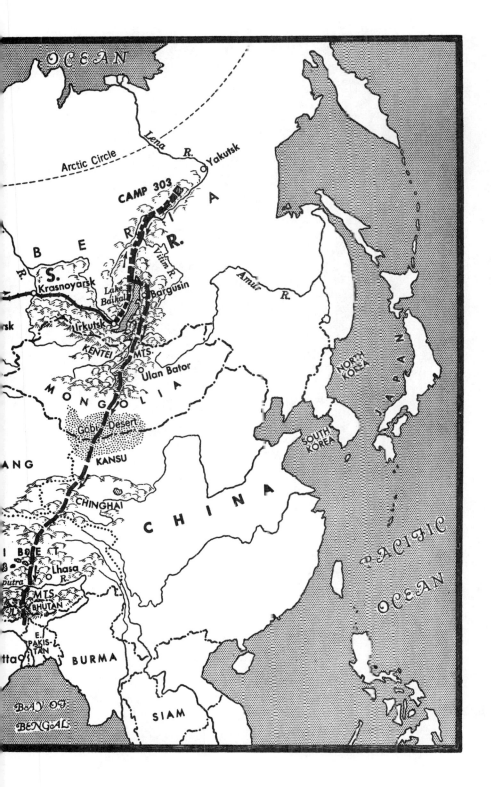

The Long Walk

I

KHARKOV AND THE LUBYANKA

IT WAS about nine o'clock one bleak November day that the
key rattled in the heavy lock of my cell in the Lubyanka
Prison and the two broad-shouldered guards marched purposefully in. I had been walking slowly round, left hand in the now
characteristic prisoner's attitude of supporting the top of the issue
trousers, which Russian ingenuity supplied without buttons or
even string on the quite reasonable assumption that a man preoccupied with keeping up his pants would be severely handicapped
in attempting to escape. I had stopped pacing at the sound of the
door opening and was standing against the far wall as they came
in. One stood near the door, the other took two or three strides
in. "Come," he said. "Get moving."

For me this day—twelve months after my arrest in Pinsk on
19 November 1939—was to be important. I was being marched
off to my trial before the Soviet Supreme Court. Here in Moscow,
shambling through the echoing narrow corridors of the Lubyanka
between my two guards, I was a man almost shorn of identity,
ill-fed, abysmally lonely, trying to keep alive some spark of
resistance in the dank prison atmosphere of studied official
loathing and suspicion of me. Just a year before, when the
Russian security men walked into the welcome-home party my
mother had arranged for me in the family house at Pinsk, I was
Lieutenant Rawicz of the Polish Cavalry, aged 24, slim and smart
in my well-tailored uniform and whipcord breeches and shining
riding-boots. My condition now was a tribute to the unflagging
brutalities and the expert subtleties of N.K.V.D. (Soviet Secret
Police) interrogators at Minsk and Kharkov. No prisoner can forget
Kharkov. In pain and filth and degradation they try to turn a man
into a whimpering beast.

The air struck chill as we turned a last bend in the corridor,
walked down some steps and emerged into a cobbled courtyard.

3

I gave my trousers a hitch and stepped out to keep up with my guards, neither of whom had spoken since we left the cell. On the other side of the yard we pulled up in front of a heavy door. One of them pulled me back a pace by tugging at the loose unfastened blouse which, with the trousers, formed my prison outfit. They stepped up as the door opened, jogging me forward into the arms of two other uniformed men who quickly ran their hands over me in a search for hidden weapons. No word was spoken. I was escorted to another door inside the building. It opened as though by some secret signal and I was pushed through. The recess of the door on the inside was curtained and I was shoved through again. The door closed behind me. Two guards, new ones this time, fell in behind me at attention.

The room was large and pleasantly warm. The walls were cleanly white-painted or whitewashed. Bisecting the room was a massive bench-type table. On this side, bare of the smallest stick of furniture, I and the guards had the whole space to ourselves. Ranged along the other side of the table were about fifteen people, about ten of them in the blue uniforms of the N.K.V.D., the rest in civilian clothes. They were very much at ease, talking, laughing, gesticulating and smoking cigarettes. Not one of them spared me even a casual glance.

After ten minutes or so I shuffled my feet in their canvas shoes (they had lace-holes but no laces) on the polished wooden parquet floor and wondered if a mistake had been made. Somebody has blundered, I thought. I shouldn't really be here at all. Then an N.K.V.D. captain looked our way and told the guards to stand at ease. I heard their boots thump behind me.

I stood there trying not to fidget, and looked round. I surprised myself with the discovery that for the first time in weary months I was faintly enjoying a new experience. Everything was so clean. There was a comforting air of informality all round. I was almost in touch with the world outside prison walls. In and out of the room passed a steady stream of people, laughing and chatting with the crowd behind the table, elbows sprawling over the magnificent red plush covering. Someone asked when an N.K.V.D. major expected to get his holidays. There were happy inquiries about someone else's large family. One man, impeccably dressed in a Western-style dark grey suit, looked like a successful diplomat.

Everyone seemed to have a word for him. They called him Mischa. I was to remember Mischa very well. I shall never forget him.

On the wall facing me on the other side of the table was the Soviet emblem, cast in some kind of plaster and lavishly coloured. On each side of it were the portraits of Russian leaders, dominated by a stern-faced Stalin. I was able to look round now with frank interest. No one bothered me. I switched my trousers grip from my left hand to my right hand. I noted there were three curtained doorways into the room. There was a single telephone, I observed, on the long table. In front of the central position on the great table was an old-fashioned solid brass pen-stand in the form of an anchor and two crossed oars, with a glass inkwell, both standing on a massive marble or alabaster base.

And all the time the everyday conversation flowed across to me from the other side of the table and I, to whom no single kind word had been spoken for a year, who had drifted deeper and deeper into isolated depression under the rigidly-enforced prison rule of absolute silence, felt this was a most memorable day.

Standing there in my dirty, shapeless, two-piece prison rags, I was not conscious of any sense of incongruity before the cheerful and well-dressed Russians. The fastidious pride of the Polish cavalry officer had been the first thing they attacked back in Minsk ten months before. It was a callous public stripping, the preliminary to my first interrogation. The Russian officers lolled around smiling as I was forced to strip off my uniform, my fine shirt, my boots, socks and underwear. I stood before them robbed of dignity, desperately ashamed, knowing fearfully that this was the real start of whatever foul things were to befall me. And when they had looked me over and laughed and finally turned their backs on me, then, a long time afterwards, I was thrown my prisoner's trousers and *rubashka*, the Russian shirt-blouse. Gripping those damned, hateful trousers, closely watching my tormentors, I heard for the first time the questionnaire that was to become the theme of my prison life.

Name? Age? Date of birth? Where born? Parents' names? Their nationality? Father's occupation? Mother's maiden name? Her nationality? The pattern was always the same. The questions at the start came in the order they were set out in the documents flourished in the hands of the investigators. They were quite pleasant at that first interrogation. They gave me coffee and appeared not to notice my awkwardness in handling the cup with my one free hand. One of them handed me a cigarette, turned back in nicely-simulated dismay at the apparent realisation that I could not one-handedly light it for myself and then lit it for me.

Then the other questions. The dangerous questions.

Where were you on 2 August 1939? In the Polish Army mobilised against the Germans in the West, I would say.

But, they would say, you know Eastern Poland very well. Your family lived at Pinsk. Quite near the Polish border with Russia, is it not? Quite easy for a well-educated young man like you to take a trip across, wasn't it?

Careful denials, blacking out of my mind the memories of teen-age trips to the villages across the Russian border. Then the speeding up of the tempo. Two of them firing alternate questions. A string of Russian border village names. Do you know this place or that place. This man you must have met. We know you met him. Our Communist underground movement had you followed. We always knew the people you met. We know what passed between you. Were you working for the *Dwojka* (Army Intelligence)?

You speak Russian fluently?—Yes, my mother is Russian.

She taught you Russian?—Yes, since I was a boy.

And the *Dwojka* were very happy to have a Polish officer who could speak Russian and spy for them?—No. I was a cavalry officer. I fought in the West, not the East.

Then would come the pay-off line. In this first interrogation it was delivered in an affable, we-are-all-good-fellows-together manner. A document was placed before me, a pen put in my hand. "This," said the smiling N.K.V.D. major, "is the questionnaire to which you have given us your answers. Just sign here and we shan't have to bother you any more." I didn't sign. I said I could not sign a document the contents of which were withheld from me. The major smiled, shrugged his shoulders. "You *will* sign, you know—some day you will sign. I feel sorry for you that you do not sign today. Very, very sorry."

He must have been thinking of Kharkov.

6

So opened the battle of wills between Slavomir Rawicz and the men of the N.K.V.D. Quite early I realised they had no specific information against me. They knew only what my Army dossier revealed and what they could pick up in Pinsk about my family background. Their charges were based entirely on the conviction that all Poles of middle or upper class education living on the Russian border were inevitably spies, men who had worked stealthily and powerfully against the Russian day of Liberation. I knew none of the places they mentioned, none of the men they sought to get me to acknowledge as confederates. There were times when I was tempted to relieve the anguish of soul and body by admitting acquaintance with the strangers they mentioned. I never did. In my mind, even in my deepest extremity of spirit, I knew that any such admission would be surely fatal.

The great stone fortress prison of Kharkov opened its grim gates to me in April 1940. Mildly conditioned by the rigours of Minsk I was still unprepared for the horrors of Kharkov. Here the phenomenal genius of an N.K.V.D. major nicknamed The Bull flourished. He weighed about fifteen stone. He was ginger-haired, with luxurious growths on head, on chest and on the backs of his huge red hands. He had a long, powerful body, short, sturdy legs and long, heavy arms. A shining red face topped a bulging great neck. He took his job as chief interrogator with deadly seriousness. He hated with frightening thoroughness the prisoner who failed to capitulate. He certainly hated me. And I, even now, would kill him, without compunction and with abounding happiness.

The Bull must have been something special even in the N.K.V.D. He ran his interrogation sessions like an eminent surgeon, always showing off his skill before a changing crowd of junior officers, assembled like students at an interesting operation. His methods were despicably ingenious. The breaking-down process for difficult prisoners started in the *kishka*, a chimney-like cell into which one stepped down about a foot below the level of the corridor outside. Inside a man could stand and no more. The walls pressed round like a stone coffin. Twenty feet above there was the diffused light from some small, out-of-sight window. The door was opened only to allow a prisoner to be marched for an appointment with The Bull. We excreted standing up and stood in our own filth. The *kishka* was never cleaned—and I spent six months in the one provided for me at Kharkov. Before going to see The Bull I would be taken to the "wash-house"—a small room with a pump. There were no refinements. No soap was provided. I would strip and pump the cold water over my clothes, rub them, stamp on them, wring them and then put them back on to dry on my body.

The questions were the same. They came from the same sheaf of documents which travelled with me from prison to prison. But The Bull was far more pressing in his absorbing desire to get my signature. He swore with great and filthy fluency. He lost his temper explosively and frequently. One day, after hours of un-remitting bawling and threatening, he suddenly pulled out his service pistol. Eyes blazing, the veins on his neck standing out, he put the barrel to my temple. He stood quivering for almost thirty seconds as I closed my eyes and waited. Then he stood back and slammed the pistol butt into my right jaw. I spat out all the teeth on that side. The next day, my face puffed out, the inside of my mouth still lacerated and bleeding, I met him again. He was smiling. His little knot of admirers looked interestedly at his handiwork. "You look lop-sided," he said. And he hit me with the pistol butt on the other side. I spat out more teeth. "That will square your face up," he said.

There was the day when a patch of hair about the size of a half-crown was shaved from the crown of my head. I sat through a forty-eight-hour interrogation with my buttocks barely touching the edge of a chair seat while Russian soldiers took over the duty in relays of tapping the bare spot on my head at the precise interval of once every two seconds. While The Bull roared his questions and leered and, with elephantine show of occasional pleasantry, cajoled me to sign that cursed document.

Then back to the *kishka*, to the clinging, sickening stench, to hours of awful half-sleep. The *kishka* was well named: it means "the intestine" or "the gut". When I came to—usually when my tired knees buckled and I had to straighten up again—I had only The Bull to think about. He filled my life completely. There were one or two occasions when the guard on duty pushed through to me a lighted cigarette. These were the only human gestures made to me at Kharkov. I could have cried with gratitude.

8

There were times when I thought I was there for life. The Bull seemed prepared to continue working on me for ever. My eyes ran copious tears from the long sessions under powerful arc lamps. Strapped on my back on a narrow bench I would be staring direct into the light as he walked round and round in semi-gloom outside its focus, interminably questioning, insulting, consigning me to the deepest hell reserved for stubborn, cunning, bastard Polish spies and enemies of the Soviet. There was something obscene about his untiring energy and brute strength. When my blurred eyes began to close he would prop them open with little sticks. The dripping water trick was one of his specialities. From a container precisely placed over the bench an icy drop of water hit exactly the same spot on my head steadily at well-regulated intervals for hours on end.

Day and night had no meaning. The Bull sent for me when he felt like it, and that could as well be at midnight as at dawn or any other hour. There was always a dull curiosity to guess what he had thought up for me. The guards would take me down the corridors, open the door and push me in. There was the time when The Bull was waiting for me with half-a-dozen of his N.K.V.D. pupils. They formed a little lane, three each side, and the master-mind stood back from them a couple of paces. I had to pass between them to reach him. No word was spoken. A terrific clout above the ear hurled me from one silent rank to the other. Grimly and efficiently they beat me up from one side to the other. They kicked me to my feet when I slumped down, and when it was over and I could not get up again, The Bull walked over and gave me one final paralysing kick in the ribs. Then they lifted me on to the edge of the same old chair and the questioning went on, the document was waved in my face, a pen was thrust at me.

Sometimes I would say to him, "Let me read the document. You can't expect me to sign something I have not read." But he would never let me read. His thick finger would point to the space where I was to sign. "All you have to do is to put your name here and I will leave you alone."

"Have a cigarette?" he said to me on one occasion. He lit one for himself, one for me. Then he walked quietly over and stubbed mine out on the back of my hand, very hard. On that occasion I had been sitting on the edge of the chair until—as always happened—

9

the muscles of the back and legs seized up in excruciating cramp. He walked round behind me as I rubbed the burn and kicked the chair from beneath me. I crashed on to the stone floor.

As a new and lively diversion towards the end of my stay at Kharkov, The Bull showed off with a Cossack knife, of which he seemed very proud. He demonstrated its excellent steel and keen edge on my chest, and I still have those scars to remind me of his undoubted dexterity and ingenuity.

There was a day near the end when he was waiting alone for me. He was quiet. There were none of the usual obscene greetings. And when he spoke the normally harsh, strident voice was low and controlled. As he talked I realised he was *appealing* to me to sign that paper. He was almost abject. I thought he might blubber. In my mind I kept saying to myself, "No, not now, you fat pig. Not now. Not after all this. . . ." I did not trust myself to speak. I shook my head. And he cursed me and cursed me, with violent and passionate intensity, foully and exhaustively.

How much can a man, weakened with ill-feeding and physical violence, stand? The limit of endurance, I found, was long after a tortured body had cried in agony for relief. I never consciously reached the final depth of capitulation. One small, steadfast part of my mind held to the unshakable idea that it was death to give in. So long as I wanted to live—and I was only a young man—I had that last, uttermost, strength of will to resist them, to push away that document which a scrawl of pen on paper might convert into my death warrant.

But there was a long night when they fed me with some dried fish before I was taken to the interrogation room. I retain some fairly clear memory of all the many sessions except this one. My head swam, I drooled, I could not get my eyes to align on anything. Often I almost fell off my chair. The cuffings and shakings seemed not to worry me and when I tried to talk my tongue was thick in my mouth. Vaguely I remember the paper and the pen being thrust at me, but, like a celebrating drunk might feel after a heavy night, there is no memory of the end of that interview.

In the morning when I came back to life I pulled my face away from the wall of my cell and smelt a new and peculiar smell. In the dim light the wall where my mouth had rested showed a wide, greenish stain. I was really frightened as I stood there, weighed down by a truly colossal feeling of oppression, like the father of all hang-overs. They drugged you, I kept telling myself. They drugged you with the fish. What have you told them? I didn't think I could possibly have signed their damned paper, but I couldn't remember. I felt ill and low and very worried.

Quite soon afterwards I was moved to Moscow and the Lubyanka. The guards were chatty and smiling as I left. This was a feature of Pinsk and Minsk, now Kharkov and later Moscow. The guards acted on my departure as if they were glad I was leaving. They talked freely, joked a little. Maybe it was their way of showing a sympathy in which earlier they could not indulge.

Conditions at the Lubyanka were a little easier. My reputation as a recalcitrant had obviously preceded me because I was very soon consigned to the *kishka*. But this *kishka* was clean and the periods I was forced to spend in it were shorter.

The interrogation team at the Lubyanka nevertheless tried out their special powers of persuasion on me. It was possibly a matter of metropolitan pride to try to succeed where the provincial boys had failed. There were the usual questions, the repeated demands for my signature, some manhandling, references to the filthy, spying Poles. But there was only one torture trick of which The Bull might have been envious.

They strapped me with my feet pulled stiffly out under the now familiar "operation table". My arms were stretched out along the table surface, each hand tied and held separately. My body was arched in a straining bow around the table end and the pain grew into searing agony as they hauled taut on the straps. This, however, was preparatory stuff like climbing into the dentist's chair with raging toothache. The operation was yet to come. Over the table was suspended an old-fashioned small cauldron fitted with a spout. It contained hot tar. There followed the usual pressing invitation to sign, with a promise that if I agreed I should be released immediately and returned to my cell. I think they would have been most disappointed if at that stage I had agreed to sign. The first drop of tar was hell. It burned savagely into the back of my hand and held its heat a long time on the puckered and livid skin. That first drop was the worst. It was the peak of pain. The rest were faintly anti-climax. I held on to consciousness and to my will to resist. When they said I should be glad to sign with my left hand at the end of the session, I proved them wrong. I had learned my fortitude in a very hard school.

That was the last major assault. I had been in the Lubyanka only about two weeks when I was led forth to my first and only experience of a Soviet court of justice.

II

TRIAL AND SENTENCE

THE LIVELY buzz of conversation in the courtroom suddenly died down. Mischa, his snow-white collar and shirt and elegant grey silk tie eye-catching among the uniforms and the normal utilitarian Russian civilian dress, said brightly, "Well, I suppose we might as well make a start." I had been standing then for about half-an-hour and for the first time the members of the court looked at me. The guards behind thumped to attention. Sheaves of papers were handed round.

The central seat on the long table was taken by a quiet-voiced, white-haired Russian of about 60. He wore the customary long jacket over his buttoned-to-the-throat blouse, which was black, ornamented at the neck and cuffs with cross-stitching embroidery in green and red. Flanking him were two N.K.V.D. officers in their dark blue uniforms with red flashes on the collar and red hat-bands round their military peaked caps. Mischa's seat was at the end of the table to my left. He, I was to learn, was the chief prosecutor, and as the court prepared to start work he sat coolly looking me over. I hitched my trousers and looked at a point just above the President's head.

It was the President, who, after a whispered consultation with the officers beside him, started the proceedings. The opening gambit was one I now knew by heart. Name? Age? Date of birth? Where born? Parents' names? Their nationality? Father's occupation? Mother's maiden name? And so on through the long catalogue lying before him, complete, I have no doubt, with the answers I had wearily repeated in all my encounters with the N.K.V.D. from my arrest in Pinsk to my arrival in Moscow. If by this repetition they hoped I might vary an occasional answer, it was poor psychology. So often had I answered that any one of these questions produced always the same reply because I had ceased to have to think. It had become habit, a reflex action. The same old questions, the same old answers. . . .

The charges were read over to me. The President (this may not have been his title but it appeared to be his function) took a long time going through the indictment. It bristled with place-names, the names of alleged Polish "reactionaries", and dates covering a period of years on which I was accused of having committed specific acts of espionage against the Soviet Union. Their scope was so sweeping that I have never ceased to marvel that they missed the occasions when, as a teen-ager looking for danger and adventure, I *had* indeed crossed the Polish-Russian border. These charges were completely without foundation and I felt some satisfaction in the thought that if they could not torture me into admission of them in the specially-equipped interrogation rooms of a series of Russian prisons, they were unlikely to get me to change my tune in the comparatively pleasant and civilised atmosphere of this court.

As the questioning really got under way I found myself grudgingly admiring the resolute singleness of purpose of the official Russian mind. All this I had gone through before in a series of appalling nightmares. Now, in the light of day, having emerged from the twisting, horror-filled corridors of frustration and despair, I found the dream persisting. Shortly stated, the indictment might have read: *You, Slavomir Rawicz, being a well-educated middle-class Pole and an officer in the anti-Russian Polish Army, having a home near the Russian border, are therefore beyond any question of doubt a Polish spy and an enemy of the people of the Union of Socialist Soviet Republics.* It remained only for the court to ask, with some asperity, why waste our time with denials?

After two hours the guards behind me were replaced. I found that the changing of the escort every two hours was the regular procedure throughout the trial. I went on answering the President's questions. They afforded me no difficulty because they were the long, routine preliminaries. I had not yet reached the point where I had to think, to recognise a flash of danger and avoid some carefully-baited trap. Although it must have been clearly stated many times in the documents before him that I spoke fluent Russian, the President had meticulously repeated the question "Do you understand and speak Russian?" Thereafter all the proceedings were in Russian and most of the questions were tinged with the special distrust which all Russians seem to have for the foreigner who knows their language. The underlying suspicion is that no foreigner would learn Russian if he did not want to be a spy.

As I stood there I was shaping my plans. I decided it would be to my advantage not to antagonise the court. I freely admitted those facts which were undeniable. Where an accusation was manifestly false I refuted it but asked the court's permission to explain why it was so. They let me talk quite a lot. I agreed with this, partially acknowledged that, denied most things and almost eagerly did my explaining. The atmosphere was hostile but faintly interested in my methods. The rigid nature of the questions left me under no illusion that I could change the official attitude, but at least I felt I was not worsening my position by appearing anxious to co-operate with the court.

The informality of the proceedings impressed me. The members of the court smoked cigarettes endlessly. The stream of visitors I had noted while I was waiting for things to start continued while the hearing was on. There was a constant mutter of behind-the-scenes talking, little murmured exchanges with the men on the long table, smiles, hands laid on shoulders in a friendly and confidential way. As I listened and talked I observed all the new sights and sounds. Like a man at a theatre, I tried to assess the importance and significance of each character in order of appearance.

Most intriguing was a distinguished-looking man in uniform, tall, with white-streaked hair, who strolled through one of the curtained doors when the trial had been in progress about three hours. The President was half-way through a question when one of his flanking N.K.V.D. officers nudged him and inclined his head towards the door. The newcomer, his hand still holding the curtain, was looking round the court. His glance took me in, paused on my two guards and swung to the judicial bench. The President leapt to his feet. All the officials stood with great haste. There was a great scraping of heavy chairs He had a nervous look, this distinguished visitor, a tense jerky gait as he walked over towards the beaming President. There were polite murmurs as he passed all the way down the table, of which I picked out repeatedly the greeting "Comrade Colonel". The President shook hands warmly with Comrade Colonel and Comrade Colonel listened in a detached way to the President's few remarks. Then he turned about, gave a smiling nod to the elegant Mischa and stood against the wall near the door through which he had arrived.

Comrade Colonel made some gesture and the court resumed its seat. The questioning was resumed. The visitor listened with apparent boredom, glanced up to the ceiling, appeared to be wrapped up in thoughts of things far more weighty than the trial of a mere Pole, and then, after about ten minutes slipped quietly out the way he had come.

About two o'clock in the afternoon the President yielded his place to a younger man and went off, presumably to lunch. There were changes among the officials in other parts of the long table. In this type of court it was apparently not necessary to preserve continuity. Anyone who had read the depositions could take over to give the principals a rest. The deputy-President had an air of efficiency which the older man lacked. His questioning was quicker, left less time to think. But he was not unpleasant, and soon after taking over he astonished me by offering me a cigarette. There was no catch. An official brought me a cigarette and lit it for me. I drew the smoke in and felt good. Before the end of the day they gave me another. Two cigarettes in a day. I felt that perhaps the signs were auspicious.

Comrade Colonel looked in once more during the afternoon, walked along the long table, picked up documents, laid them down, nervously exchanged words with two or three of the top men, and slipped out again. The examination went on.

The second change of guard at my back marked the passage of another two hours. Mischa now put in some rather leisurely cross-examination. Occasionally he smiled. I answered with a show of great willingness. I thought what a welcome change it was to be dealing with a man who seemed to have brought back with his stylish Western clothes some of the niceties of another civilisation.

It almost seemed to me that there was even a remote touch of sympathy when they asked me about my wife. It was a brief enough story. I married Vera at Pinsk on 5 July 1939, during a forty-eight-hour leave from the Army. My mother called me from my place at the table during the wedding feast on the pretext I was wanted on the telephone. She handed me a telegram which ordered my immediate return to my unit. I packed my bags. Vera cried as I kissed her goodbye. The tears streamed down as she stroked my hair and face. So I went away, and most of the wedding guests did not know I had gone. A fortnight later I was able to get permission for her to come and stay near me at Ozharov. She stayed for four or five days and I was able to see her for about three hours a day. They were glorious, wonderful hours, in which we almost succeeded in banishing the sense of doom which hung heavily over us and over all Poland. It was all the married life I was to know with Vera. When I had fought the Germans in the West and the Russians had pushed in from the East I went back to Pinsk. The N.K.V.D. moved very swiftly. I had barely time to greet Vera, to answer her first eager questions, when they walked in. That was the last time I saw her.

About mid-afternoon when I had been standing before the court for well over four hours, the deputy-President asked me if I would like a cup of coffee. I said "Yes, please." That was when I was also given my second cigarette. The coffee was excellent—hot, strong and sweetened. When I had drunk and smoked—the coffee first and the cigarette afterwards because of my clumsy one-handedness—there were a few questions from a burly civilian at the opposite end of the table from Mischa. This man, I gathered, was my defence counsel. He showed every sign of irritation at the rôle he was forced to play and gave me the impression of being barely able to conceal his contempt for me. He took very little part in the trial and certainly his intervention at any stage did nothing to advance my cause. He was, at best, a most reluctant champion.

The day's proceedings ended rather abruptly at about four o'clock. One of the two centre-of-the-table officers whispered to the deputy-President. An officer called my guards to attention and I was turned about and marched back to my cell. Food was brought me and I sat down to ponder the events of the day. I decided that my trial must be over, that there remained now only the formality of being told the sentence of the court. I did not think I had done badly this day. I even cherished a slight hope that the sentence would be light. That night I slept very well. It was the most restful night I had enjoyed for many months.

The guards came for me at seven the next morning. The weather was misty and the damp chill struck through my clothes and caused me to shiver as we walked across the cobbled yard to the court building. There was the routine search at the entrance inside the big doors and again I was pushed through the curtained door to my place facing the long table.

But things inside were much different from yesterday. The tribunal, all of them with a sour-faced, early-morning look, were ready and waiting for me. There was none of yesterday's badinage. The Soviet Supreme Court was showing me a very cold and businesslike face. The tribunal was the same as that which had sat at the end of yesterday—the younger deputy-President in the middle, his two N.K.V.D. advisers on right and left. This is it, I thought. They are going to announce my sentence. I stood up straight and waited. The gentlemen of the court stared at me.

A quick shuffling of papers and the trial restarted. The deputy-President whipped out the questions. Name? . . . Age? . . . Where born? . . . The same routine. It was as though I had never before seen this white-walled courtroom. Yesterday might never have been. There was a new and forceful insistence about the catechism, as though my answers of the day before had been shrugged away, wiped off the slate. For the first half-hour I fought with waves of engulfing depression. I felt utterly miserable, downcast almost to breaking point. I told myself bitterly what a hopeful and stupid fool I had been to delude myself into thinking they would let me go so easily. I had relaxed and now I had to fight again, and the fight was all the harder for having allowed myself to weaken. These men and the men of Minsk and Kharkov were all Russians, motivated by the same hatreds, working along the same lines, one-tracked.

I was bawled at, my answers were cut off half-heard, the table was thumped until the heavy inkstand leapt up and rattled back. Polish spy. Polish traitor. Polish bastard. Polish fascist. Insults were thrown in with the questions.

A new and tense, unsmiling Mischa rose to continue the questioning. The court was for a moment quiet as he stood there eyeing me. Behind the presidential chair stood three young civilians I had not seen before. Each had a little notebook. They looked expectantly towards the chief prosecutor. I remember thinking back to The Bull and his coterie of apprentices.

"Now, Rawicz, you Polish son of a bitch," he said, "we have

finished pandering to your stupidity. You know you are a dirty spy and you are going to tell us all about it."

"I have told you all I know," I said. "There is nothing more to tell. I have nothing to hide."

Dramatically, Mischa walked from behind the table, took about ten steady paces and pulled up in front of me. "You," he said, "are a professional liar." Then, very deliberately, he smacked me across the face with the full fling of his arm, once, twice, three times, four times. And as I shook my head he added, "But I will *make* you tell the truth." He turned abruptly, strode back to his place at the table. The young observers behind the presidential chair jotted furiously in their little notebooks.

I stood there shaking, hating him and them and all the Russians, all they were and all they represented. For fully fifteen minutes I shut my ears to a barrage of insults and questions and, tight-lipped, refused to answer. My cheeks burned from the face-slapping, a cut inside my mouth bled and I could taste the salt blood. Finally I talked because I knew I must go on fighting them to the end. I chose my moment to break silence when Mischa spoke three names—all unknown to me—of men he claimed to be self-confessed spies against Russia and who were witnesses of my own treacherous activities.

"Why don't you bring them here and confront me with them?" I asked. "Maybe we will, maybe we will," said Mischa. But no "witnesses" were ever produced against me. There was no real case against me. Except, perhaps that I was a Pole. That indeed seemed to be a grave offence against the Russians.

I cannot remember all the questions, but I do remember Mischa's skill as a prosecutor. He was adept at leading me along a clear path of places and people I knew so that I could almost anticipate the next question and have my answer half-formed. Then, abruptly, with no change of tempo there would be another town mentioned, another name. I would pause to get on to the new track and Mischa would shout in triumph, "So, you Polish dog, that question stops your lying mouth! *That* was where you handed over your spy reports!" A torrent of abuse and accusations would follow as I kept repeating that I knew neither the town nor the man he mentioned.

The day before, when I had been expansive and friendly, I had talked about the happy days when I went duck-shooting with my father in the Pripet Marshes. Today, Mischa used this as a theme for a blistering, blustering attack on my character as a spy and saboteur. Beyond the Pripet was Russia and Mischa did not intend that either I or the court should forget it. Yesterday I had quietly boasted of my prowess with a sporting gun. Today I was not only the most despicable of spies but also a well-trained potential assassin, a crack-shot hireling of Polish Army Intelligence. And so it went on.

It was a crazy trial, run by madmen. It became in the end a test of endurance between one weak, half-starved, ill-used Pole and the powerful, time-squandering State machine. I had been given no food before I came in and I received nothing throughout the long day's trial that ended, astonishingly, at midnight. Seventeen hours I stood there. There were no cigarettes, no coffee. Mischa would occasionally step out and punch or slap me, especially when I looked like keeling over or nodding to sleep on my feet.

Everyone else in the court, Mischa included, took a break at intervals during the day. Other people took over the examination. The composition of the court was constantly changing. During the afternoon the President came in for a few hours to allow his deputy a rest. The guards were regularly changed every two hours. Only I went on standing there, dry-throated, swaying, wondering dully if this day would ever end.

When I stumbled back into my cell there was still no food for me. At 7 a.m. the next day when I was led back again I still was without food and again, hungry, aching and deathly tired, I survived another marathon madmen's session of Soviet justice. Why do they do it, I kept asking myself. Why do they waste all this time on one Pole? Why don't they just sentence me and have done with it? For myself, I could have admitted all the things they charged me with and ended it all. But I still did not want to die. For me it was a struggle for life.

They did not break me down. They even re-introduced the Kharkov trick of taking me off my staggering feet and sitting me on the edge of a chair for a few hours. It got painful, but it was at least a change from trying to stop my knees buckling under me.

The fourth day was the last. There seemed to be many more

people there than at any previous stage. I imagine all those officials who from time to time had acted as stand-ins for the principals wanted to be present for the last act. The atmosphere was much the same as it had been on the first day. The President was back in his accustomed position, riffling through his sheaf of papers. Everybody talked and Mischa was in laughing conversation with an N.K.V.D. captain.

The old preliminaries were gone through. Again I identified myself. I was tired, sick and still unfed. There were some more questions, which I answered automatically. They were straightforward and unbaited.

The President then asked me if I would give the court a specimen of my signature. When I hesitated, he made it clear that I was not being asked to sign any document. Someone came forward with a small piece of paper, a slip only big enough to take my name. I turned it over in my hand. Someone said, "We only want to see how you sign your name." I took the pencil held out to me and wrote my name. The President glanced at the slip, passed it along to the two N.K.V.D. men. All three remained in a huddle for a couple of minutes. The President looked at me, held up the slip in his right hand, screwed it up and threw it away.

The President held up a document. A court official took it from him and brought it over to me. "Is that your signature?" asked the President. I looked closely for a full minute while the court waited. It was my signature. Wavery and thin. But unmistakably my signature. Kharkov, I thought. That night at Kharkov.

"Is that your signature?" repeated the President.

"Yes," I said. "But I do not remember signing and it does not mean I admit anything contained in this document."

"That document," he continued, "is a full list of the charges against you."

"I know it well," I replied. "But no one would ever let me read it. I never knowingly signed it."

"It is your signature, nevertheless?"

"It is my signature, but I cannot remember writing it."

There were whispered consultations up and down the table. The President stood, the court stood. He read the charges at length. He announced that the court had found me guilty of espionage and plotting against the people of the U.S.S.R. It took quite a long time to get through all this and all I was waiting for was the sentence. It came at last.

"You will therefore be sentenced to twenty-five years forced labour."

"And that," said the blue-uniformed major on the President's right, "should be ample time to restore your shocking memory."

I stood there for a moment looking down the table. I caught the eye of Mischa, the elegant, well-groomed Mischa. He was standing back slightly from the table. He smiled. There was no malice in that smile. It was friendly, the smile of a man who is stepping forward to shake your hand. It was almost as though he were encouraging me, complimenting me on the show I had put up. He was still smiling when one of the guards tugged at my blouse to turn me round. I passed through the curtain and was taken back to my cell.

Food was brought to me, a big meal by prison standards, and drink. The guards talked again. I felt a great weight had been lifted from me. I slept.

III

FROM PRISON TO CATTLE TRUCK

THERE WAS evidence the next day that the prison authorities had taken immediate note of my change in status from having been a prisoner under interrogation and trial to that of prisoner under sentence. I was restored to full rations—coffee and 100 grammes of the usual black rye bread at 7 a.m. and, in the evening, another 100 grammes of bread and a bowl of soup. The soup was merely the water in which turnips had been boiled, without salt or any seasoning, but it was a welcome change of diet.

I was awarded, too, my first hot bath since my arrest. The wash-house to which I was escorted by my two guards was about twenty yards from my cell and differed from the others I had used only in having two taps in the wall instead of one. Off came my *rubashka*, I stepped out of my trousers and canvas shoes and stood in the shallow sink let into the stone floor. I turned on the right-hand tap and the hot water gushed out. There was no towel, no soap, but this was luxury. I jumped about, bent down against the tap and let the water run over me from head to foot, rubbed myself until my pale skin began to glow pink.

The two guards, one armed with a Nagan-type pistol in an unbuttoned holster, the other with a carbine, lounged one each side of the door watching my antics. Said one, "You will be all right now. You are going away from here." "When?" I asked quickly. "Where to?" Both guards ignored the questions. I carried on with my bath, making it last as long as I could. Then I turned off the tap and danced about to get dry. I dabbed at myself with my blouse and finally ran some water over my clothes and kneaded the prison dirt out of them until it flowed away in a dark stream down the hole in the sink. I rinsed them, wrung them, shook them and put them back on my body, the steam still rising from them. "You look a nice clean boy now," said the man with the carbine. "Let's go."

Back in my cell I was given a cigarette. One of the guards rolled the cigarette, lit it and then put it down on the floor. As he walked back I moved forward and picked it up. This was always the procedure when I was given a smoke. No guard would directly hand the cigarette to me, and if it went out before I took my first puff a single match would be thrown to me. The used match would be picked up and removed from the cell. Most of the many rigid security measures had obvious significance, but I could never quite appreciate the need for this elaborate care over a cigarette in the presence of two fully-armed men in the heart of a prison like the Lubyanka.

In spite of the fact that a prisoner was hopelessly equipped to attempt escape, the security drill was unvarying. A prisoner leaving or returning to his cell was always escorted by two guards. When a man was being taken out the guards took up position one at each side of the door. The prisoner would advance between them and halt a pace ahead of them. The instruction would then be given, to quote a typical example: "You will walk down this corridor on the left, turn right at the end and keep going until you are told to stop. Keep to the middle of the corridor all the way." These instructions were usually ended by the recital of an ominous little jingle which went:

> "Step to the Right,
> Step to the Left—
> Attempt to Escape."

I must have heard that warning hundreds of times during my captivity. All guards used it, all prisoners knew it. The Russians took great pains to explain to a prisoner exactly where he was to go and the prisoner was left in no doubt that a deviation off course to right or left would mean death from the carbine or pistol of the guards marching two paces behind him. In the Lubyanka it seemed to be an excessive and almost ridiculous precaution, but later, when thousands of captives were being moved from one end of Russia to the other and escape became at least a possibility, the warning sounded sensible enough from the Russian point of view.

On the morning of the fourth day after my sentence an N.K.V.D. lieutenant entered my cell. "Can you read Russian?" he asked.

"Yes," I answered. He handed me a document which I found was a movement permit. Even convicted men apparently needed a permit to change their place of residence, although it might be a move only from prison to prison. The officer handed me a pen and I signed my name on the paper. He pocketed the permit and left.

Towards dusk on this mid-November afternoon in 1940 I quit my Lubyanka cell for the last time. I was marched out into the prison yard. Snow was drifting down and the cold had an edge which made me draw in my breath. Around the yard were a number of small buildings. At one end were the massive main gates, near which were two red brick storehouses. I was led to one of these and handed a brown paper parcel. The man who gave it me said, "This is for your journey," and smiled.

As I stood in the yard, one hand holding on to my trousers, the other gripping my parcel, I felt myself shivering with cold and with excitement. There was a great sense of freedom. I told myself, "Slav, my friend, this is goodbye to prisons. Wherever they take you, it won't be to another stinking prison." I felt faintly elated. Whatever was ahead of me, here I was already breathing in good, clean, cold air and knowing I was going somewhere—not from cell to cell, from prison to prison, from one interrogator to another, but to a new life, a chance to work, to use my hands again, to meet and talk with other men. . . .

Those other men, my fellow prisoners, were even now being escorted in small batches into the yard. I could feel my heart thumping as I watched each one of them arrive. I stared and stared. They eyed me and one another in the same way. We were all looking for someone we knew. But the odd thing borne in on me was that recognition was impossible. We were all in complete and uniform disguise. We were all long-haired and heavily bearded—I had not had a haircut or shave for nearly a year, but it had never occurred to me that all the others would have been treated alike. Our clothes were the same. When we had all been herded into the yard there were about 150 men like me all holding on to their trousers. One hundred and fifty lost souls turning up in the same pitiful costume at some devil's fancy dress ball, each with a neat brown paper parcel in one hand and a pair of trousers in the other. The corners of my mouth twitched and I could almost have laughed, but suddenly I felt a choking wave of pity for us all that they should make such fools of us.

This was my first encounter with any other prisoner. In Kharkov and the Lubyanka I had heard noises. I had heard men being shot. I had heard the awful howling of a man who is going mad. I had listened to scrapings and tappings as though someone was trying to communicate with me through a cell wall. But I was never allowed to meet any of the other unfortunates. Isolation was part of the treatment and I got it in full measure.

The business of assembling us, checking names against documents and counting heads took about two hours. During this period we were all made to squat in the snow—another security rule. Two groups of about a dozen armed soldiers kept watch on us. There was little daylight left when we were ordered to our feet and loaded standing into five canvas-topped Army lorries. One lorry-load of soldiers headed the convoy and another followed in the rear. Tossed about and flung from side to side, we were driven at breakneck speed for what seemed to be about ten miles before the brakes were slammed on and we pitched forward in mass. The convoy had stopped.

In that short, jolting ride, I could feel a tense, bubbling excitement all round me. It was an odd and powerful experience to be with other men again, to feel the thump of another shoulder, the sharp prod of an elbow in the ribs, to be reminded again of the smell of men in a packed crowd, to hear exclamations in rich, colloquial Polish. But that great surge of talk one might have expected did not come. We were to find it took some little time to recover the habit of conversation. It came back slowly by way of shouted little questions and short, jerky answers.

The place where the lorry convoy stopped was a small station on a branch line which I estimated to be about five miles outside Moscow. Someone later professed to know the place, gave it a name and said it was a suburb of scattered villas much favoured by the well-to-do Soviet official. As I jumped down from the lorry I saw in the distance the lights of houses, well spaced out, which might support the theory, but there were no civilians around and the prisoners and soldiers had the place to themselves. Drawn up on the railway was a train of cattle trucks of the type which normally accommodated eight horses or cows in stalls, four each side, tails against the front and rear ends and heads pointing inwards to a small central gangway between the two truck doors. There was an engine with steam up at each end of the train.

The loading was carried out quickly. As the name of each man was called he stepped up to the door of the truck and two soldiers hoisted him in. Inside, two more soldiers packed the men around the truck walls, gradually filling the available space towards the centre until they were themselves inched back towards the door. When they had finished there were sixty men jammed immovably in my truck. All the cattle fittings had been removed except the steel rings to which their safety harness had been made fast, and the four barred ventilation openings had been covered from the outside by metal plates solidly bolted into position.

Two soldiers with some special armbands on their uniform looked in at the door and called out, "We are first-aid men. If any of you feel ill during the journey, just call for us and we'll put you right." The door was slammed shut and barred from the outside just when it seemed that those near the entrance were in danger of being forced out by the press like corks from a bottle. In the stuffy darkness someone raised a laugh about the first-aid men. "How shall we attract their attention—ring 'em up on the phone?" And, in fact, in the weeks ahead no one in my truck ever saw the experts with the armbands exercising their first-aid skill. It was just one of the many ironies of Russian organisation.

I was rammed hard against one end of the truck, my parcel still under one arm. Both arms were pressed into my body. It was impossible to sit and when I wanted to lift a hand I had to have the co-operation of the man next to me, who would lean back against his neighbour on the other side to squeeze out the extra space I needed. It was this anonymous friend who advised me to open my parcel and eat some food in case it might later be stolen. I explored the contents by feel and smell—and it was a rich and rewarding experience. There was a loaf of special bread, oval in shape, about nine inches long and about five inches across at the middle. There were two excellent dried fish of a kind known in Russia as *taran*. And there was an ounce of *korizhki*, the coarse tobacco made from the veins of tobacco leaves, with a sheet of newspaper (I later found it was dated 1938) to use for rolling cigarettes. I ate half the loaf and one of the fish and stuffed the rest into my blouse, wrapped still in the brown paper.

It was not until the train moved off that the talk began to flow. Voices began to speculate on where we were going. Some expressed the fear that we might end up in Novaya Zemlya, that bleakest of islands in the Barents Sea, or in the Kamchatka salt mines of Eastern Siberia. Everyone agreed that our destination was Siberia.

One of the parting instructions as the door was slid home was that we were to make no noise. But as the train lumbered slowly into some kind of speed and the wheels began to rattle more loudly, we began to shout. Someone would bawl, "Anyone here from Lvov?" A voice would answer from the other end of the truck, "I come from near there," but any attempt at sustained conversation died in the general hubbub. There were calls for men from this regiment and that regiment. Then the yelling quite suddenly subsided and men began hopefully to engage the attention of their immediate neighbours. Some of the excitement of the occasion was still with me but I could not join in the general free-for-all of question and answer. It always took me time to thaw out. Up against the cold wall of that truck I listened to the others but still hugged my thoughts to myself, reluctant as yet to open out, to seek a friend, but happy just to be one of the crowd, to know I was not alone any more.

Later I found myself inquiring of those near me if anyone knew Pinsk. From my left came a voice which eagerly replied, "Yes, I know Pinsk." We tried each other with the names of people we knew, of streets, of surrounding villages. But his Pinsk was not my Pinsk and we could find no common ground. The effort died away. I felt disappointed, irritated at his failure to know the people and things I had known. I think he made another attempt to continue talking, but I could not bring myself to answer. It had been a half-hearted effort on my part anyway and I felt vaguely sorry I had started it.

The train stopped several times that first night and at each stop there were the sounds of men being unloaded from lorries and stuffed into the trucks in their hundreds. Men favourably placed against the long platform side of the truck found chinks in the planks through which to watch the proceedings in the light of searchlights shining down the train from the two engines and reported what they saw to the rest of us.

That first leg of our journey eastwards soon developed into a nightmare. We stayed locked in throughout the first night and all through the following day. There were, of course, no toilet facilities of even the crudest kind and men relieved themselves standing up, unable to move. The smell was foul, the air stank. When the train drew up at a signal check, men would shout for food and water and the guards would race along the train hammering on the truck sides with their gun butts and ordering silence, promising the trucks would be opened soon. It was bitterly cold for the prisoners around the truck walls. Even if those towards the middle would have changed position it was impossible to move. Twelve hours or so after my first meal on the train, I wormed my hand into my blouse and slowly ate the remainder of the bread and fish.

Those of us who had first joined the train had been locked in for nearly twenty-four hours when the train finally drew up on an isolated section of branch line and the truck doors were at last slid back. It was late afternoon and all we could see around was undulating, snow-covered country, with clumps of trees near the line and others dotted around in the distance. Some of my companions were too stiff from the long standing to get down unaided. All of us stretched and yawned and rubbed at our aching limbs to restore circulation. An old grenade wound in my ankle had started to open and the back of my right hand, on which the Lubyanka specialists had dropped hot tar, was puffed up and sore. There were ex-soldiers with much more serious untreated wounds than mine. I could only admire their courage. We could do nothing for them and the Russian first-aiders contributed not even an aspirin for their relief.

A knifing east wind whistled around the train. The snow had stopped falling and the wind seemed all the colder as a result. Russian soldiers were strategically placed in a flat arc around the open side of the train and there were patrolling guards on the blind side.

The first move was for security. We were ordered to squat in front of our truck and then were issued with the familiar lump of black bread. There was also a water issue which tasted of steam and train oil. Afterwards we were allowed to walk in a carefully prescribed area and the request that a few men be allowed to walk a little farther afield to gather branches to clean out the truck was granted—on condition it was understood that "Step to the right, step to the left" would be treated as an attempt to escape. The wind outside cut through our flimsy clothes and there was no lack of volunteers for cleaning the truck. They worked awhile inside and then jumped down to gulp in the clean air. Standing against the truck door a little later I saw that the steel bar used to lock us in was itself finally secured with a loop of wire and a lead seal. Not only locked in, I thought, but sealed. A finishing touch of absolute security.

The pattern of the journey became clearer thereafter. The general plan was to move us stealthily through sleeping towns at night and to halt on some branch line out in the country during the day. Signal delays and long stretches of inhabited country meant over-running the schedule until well into the daylight of a following day. On those occasions there was near panic among the soldiers and train staff. I often wonder what civilian Russians standing on station platforms made of the low murmur of voices which came from the long line of cattle trucks almost stopping or slowly crawling past them during these out-of-schedule morning runs.

Towards the end of the first week our sixty men had organised itself with rough community rules. A rota system was started to enable everyone in turn to enjoy the close-packed body warmth of the middle of the truck. Everyone in turn experienced the numbing cold of the truck walls. It was getting colder and colder and those perimeter positions were grim. This meant, too, that the favoured daylight spot of observer at the cracks and knotholes in the truck sides also went round. A good, loud-voiced look-out with his eye to a hole in the wood helped greatly to relieve the general boredom. Some of them could turn in a really entertaining commentary.

Shut in this dark travelling-box it was difficult to get any clear idea of the actual course of the journey. From the disjointed reports of men who may or may not have known the route followed I formed the idea that we must have made a number of fairly substantial detours in the progress through Western Russia.

These may have been necessitated by traffic conditions and the points chosen for picking up prisoner road convoys. During the second week, however, when we approached the Urals and a third engine was coupled into the train, it became clear we were on the Trans-Siberian Railway and there could be no doubt that our destination lay somewhere in the vast reaches of fabulous Siberia. We clanked through nearly all the big towns and rail junctions at night. We always knew the junctions by the break in running rhythm as the wheels crossed a succession of points and by the noise of other trains and shunting engines.

One incident sticks vividly in my mind, especially since it was daylight and I had my eye to one of the wider cracks in the truck side. The train had been moving for nearly a fortnight and this was one of the occasions when there had been a number of hold-ups and we had not reached our prearranged hiding-place when dawn came. It was a junction, a big place. The city beyond was remarkable only for the fact that all the buildings seemed to be in red brick. The train had been creeping tentatively at something like ten miles an hour. It shuddered to a heavily-braked halt. A minute or so later it jerked off again, barely moving. And then I saw, drawing slowly alongside, another train of trucks, just like ours, on the parallel track.

I called out. Others at vantage points called out. "A train like ours," I shouted. "The windows are not covered. There are people in it." Our train halted. The other was already stationary. "Women. Women. There are women in it. And children." I don't know if it was my voice telling the news or some of the others. I think we were yelling against each other. There was pandemonium. The men in the middle surged towards the outside and we look-outs were pressed flat against the woodwork. We hardly noticed the additional discomfort. The women looked startled. They could see nothing but the big blank sides of the trucks. The noise from our train became a swelling roar. Some-one screamed, "They are Polish women. They are our women," and the men went almost mad. Perhaps they were Poles, or Latvians, or Estonians. I don't know. If they made any sound I could not hear it with the yelling of the mob all round me.

Russian soldiers ran distractedly from their quarters at each end of the train, thumping on the trucks and ordering quiet. It was hopeless. The whole train was in the grip of hysteria. I can only imagine how the engine-driver of the leading locomotive was being ordered to get going, signals or no signals. That stop lasted seven or eight minutes and men who did not know where their wives and families might be were sobbing as we got under way again. The disturbing influence of that one incident lasted for days. It was the worst piece of organisation of the whole rail trip.

There was an ironic postscript. When we finally reached the secluded stretch of branch line that was our stopping-place for the day, the Russian train commandant—tall, smooth-faced and easily spoken—addressed us in batches on the need for obeying the rules of silence in transit. He wagged his head in grave admonition and told us, "The trouble with you is that you have no culture." He was quite serious, as far as I could see. Whenever he had occasion to warn us about breaches of rules he always reminded us of this cultural failing.

Behind our flowing beards and our long, matted hair, we were beginning to know one another. It was not a question of names. Names did not count. Nobody bothered with them. Men became identified by character and characteristics. There were the leaders, the organisers, the men who automatically assumed some kind of command to make the rules so that as many as possible might survive. There were men, like me, who were determined not to die. There were the others in whom the spark of hope had already been almost crushed when they were first herded into these travelling coffins. They died without a whisper in the long nights when their turn came to stand out of the warmth of the ruck. They died standing and we did not know they were dead until the door opened in the light of morning. They had no graves, the ground was iron-hard and impossible to dig. They were taken away and snow was heaped on them. They were names crossed off an official list. At least eight were taken out, stark and stiff, from our truck.

The men I most admired were the jokers. They saved us often in our blackest moments. There were maybe four or five of them in our lot. They would joke about anything. Their quips were frequently macabre, almost always earthy and pungent with the good strong language that men use. They were irrepressible. Nothing stopped them. I bless their memory for the gusty belly laughs they gave us as they aped the train commandant, the Russian guards, anything and everything Russian. When there was speculation about the possibility of our working in the Eastern Siberian gold-mines, one of the jokers announced his plans for escape.

He was a powerful, short, thick-set fellow with a magnificent black beard. "Gentlemen," he announced, "I shall eat handfuls of gold dust with my black bread, run like hell for Kamchatka, cross to Japan. I shall s——t Russian gold and live happily ever after on the proceeds." We laughed at the absurdity of it, laughed loud and long, without restraint, as men near despair will laugh.

There was a bitter, hard edge to their humour when they watched the Russians stripping the trousers and blouses off the pathetic corpses before they shovelled the snow on them. "After all," said one, "Father Stalin only loaned the poor bastard the clothes for the duration of his stay in the U.S.S.R. He won't need any for the next journey; he goes out as he came in. . . .'

Men, bound together by common misfortune, were talking together more freely. The outcome was not always comradely. Nerves were often taut and it needed only the wrong topic to start a violent flare-up. Politics were dynamite. I heard two men start arguing the rôle of Polish Foreign Minister Beck in the events leading to the German invasion of Poland. The argument simmered with barely suppressed passion and then one exploded the word "traitor" to describe Beck. In a moment they were screaming with rage that knew no bounds. As other voices called to them to "cut it out", they impotently struggled to raise their hands, tried vainly to use knees and feet, and then attacked each other with teeth. Somehow, the mass heaved itself to separate them. One man had the lobe of his ear almost bitten off, the other had deep teeth marks in his cheek. Tears of frustration rolled down their cheeks. For some time afterwards they mouthed threats. Then they were quiet and forgot all about it.

Once, in the dark, the train stopped and all was quiet. Most of us were in that dozing, half-awake state which comes with long hours of travelling. A voice started speaking, in a dreaming tone, slightly above ordinary conversational level. Men stirred, shifted, began, in spite of themselves, to listen.

"My wife," said the voice, "was quite a small woman. A happy

little lady, she was. We got on very well, we two. She was a
wonderful cook. Her mother was, too, you know, and she taught
her. Let me tell you about the cake she baked for my birthday,
this wife of mine. She knew I was crazy about her cakes. . . ."

The voice went on. It was throaty, the words came slowly and
very clearly. We were fascinated, listening in on another man's
waking dream. He described it all exactly and lovingly. We
followed the mixing of that cake in the big white earthenware
bowl, the breaking of the eggs, the care of the whisking, the
precise quantity of flour and baking powder and all those extra
touches of candied peel and raisins and God knows what, the art
that went into the rich almond icing. "It was," said the man, "a
most beautiful, beautiful, rare, wonderful cake, this cake my wife
baked for me. The smell of it cooking was like something from
heaven."

Suddenly another voice howled—yes, it was a howl that
shocked us, like the douche of freezing water that awakens a
dreamer from his sleep. "Stop it, stop it! For the love of Jesus
Christ Almighty, stop it!" Other voices joined it. "Do you want
to make us insane? Shut up, you bloody fool." The man with the
dream cake said no more. I longed for that damned wonderful
cake for days afterwards. I just could not remember what cake
tasted like.

IV

THREE THOUSAND MILES BY TRAIN

THERE WAS time and to spare for a powerful amount of individual thinking as the endless-seeming ride entered its third week, with the train well into Western Siberia. We had been losing interest in the names of stations, each with their white-painted bust of Stalin prominently displayed. The stopping-places all looked alike, stretches of bleak, snow-covered country sometimes wooded and sometimes not. They varied only in the degree of cold they offered. The further east we went, the lower became the temperature. We debouched on more than one occasion into the teeth of a shrieking, snow-laden north-easter and were not sorry to huddle back into the communal half-warmth of the truck.

We went on gleaning things about one another. I discovered that no one in this crowd had a lighter sentence than ten years hard labour. My own sentence of twenty-five years was fairly common and there were a few even longer. Quite half of the men had one crime in common: they had served in the Polish armed forces. They talked, as soldiers will the world over, of their experiences and the places they had served in, of their regiments and their friends. It set me thinking back and to taking stock of myself. I did not want particularly to bring my mind back to Poland, but there was nothing else to do. I think it was an escape backwards to the memory of freedom.

It was the little Jew who started me recalling it all. He posed me an odd question—for a Jew, a most odd question. When the Germans came through in the West and the Russians in the East, this little man with his little shop in Beloyostok realised on his stock and bought diamonds. He had relatives in Zyrardow, the textile centre near Warsaw, and a shoemaker friend who made him a special pair of boots into which he built the diamonds. So, his preparations made, he set out to flee Poland. Where was he going? Why, *to Germany*. Because, he said, he did not trust the

35

Russians. But, I argued, the Germans would have killed you; they hate Jews. "Maybe, maybe," he answered. "But at least I was right about distrusting the Russians. Just look at me now." Perhaps it was well for him that he never was given the chance to test the Germans. The Russians caught him trying to cross the border and that meant an almost automatic sentence of ten years. Trying to escape from your liberators can be regarded as very anti-social behaviour.

By going home to Pinsk after the collapse of Polish Army resistance to the Germans, I had virtually chosen to let myself fall into the hands of the Russians. Would I have fared better as a prisoner-of-war of the Nazis? It was an unanswerable question now, but it got me thinking of the Germans and the futile fighting of cavalry against tanks, the chaos, the bravery of a foredoomed army in those crowded, desperate weeks of September 1939.

I was originally called up in 1937 while I was studying for my certificate as an architect and surveyor at the Wawelberea and Rotwanda Technical School in Warsaw, and served for twelve months at the infantry training school at Brest Litovsk. After seven months they asked for volunteers for training as cavalry reconnaissance. I could ride well and leapt at the chance. At the end of the year I passed out in the highest cadet rank. I went back to college and passed my finals in 1938, returning the same year to the Army for the big six-weeks manoeuvres in the Wolyn area near the Russian Ukrainian border. I became a second lieutenant and went home, fit, bronzed and pleased with myself, to help my mother run the estate at Pinsk. Mother was the bright and practical element in our family. My father thought the function of the estate was to provide the means for him to pursue his hobby— landscape painting. The house was full of his canvases, none of which he ever allowed to be sold, although dealers had made approaches to him.

I followed my calling as estate manager for only a few months. On 1 March 1939, I was called up under an order of "unofficial mobilisation". Just six months later, on 31 August, on the eve of my twenty-fourth birthday, as I sat reading letters from my wife and my mother and was preparing to open the parcels they had sent me, a messenger rode into our cavalry camp near Ozharov to announce that the Germans were on the move. It was war.

My active service lasted just about three weeks but they were weeks packed with movement and incident. I went through again, in that rocking Russian railway van, my impressions of those days. I remembered ducking for cover with my horse as the Stukas screamed on their road-strafing missions, the blocked roads, the baulked horse-drawn Polish artillery toiling to get within gun range of the enemy. Often we were shelled and no one seemed to be quite sure where the Germans were. Near Kutno we found the main force of the Polish Cavalry, nearly ten thousand horses and their riders, their main retreat route to Modlan blocked by well-positioned and dug-in Germans.

Here, at least there was some kind of unified command. The order went down the lines that we were to break through. Between us and the Germans were woods about a mile and a half in depth. From unit to unit the bugles sounded the advance and we moved off. Men who were unhorsed in the first wave never got up again, horses went down squealing and the mounts behind jumped over them. As I broke cover I saw horses staked on the steel barbed-wire supporting stakes, horses disembowelled on the wire. A cavalry charge induces a form of madness. Riders and horses alike are infected. Its fury, its weight and its pounding impetus can only be stopped by the most awful and concentrated heavy gunfire. The Germans who stood up to surrender were mown down. The cavalry in a charge cannot take prisoners.

Harassed by dive-bombers, threading our way along the choked roads, we fell back on Warsaw to reorganise, as we were told, for the defence of the capital. Foot soldiers climbed on to our riderless horses and rode back with us—there was even a Polish sailor on horseback as we straggled into the outskirts of Warsaw. We found no organisation for defence and when, after carrying out some transfer of stores from military quarters in Praga across the Vistula to the old Warsaw cadet school, I heard there was an organised defence force in the outer suburbs on the Warsaw-Piastov road, I saddled up, provisioned myself, and rode out. I was welcomed. I became leader of an eight-man cavalry patrol.

So it was that I came to see probably the last cavalry charge in modern warfare. We had left the horses in charge of four patrol-men in the outer fringe of some woods and had crawled to a hillock topped by a clump of small trees from which we had a clear view down the main Piastov road, intercepted about a hundred yards from us by a four-road junction. There was a gaily-painted roadhouse in the angle of the main road and one of the side roads. It was untenanted now, but there was still a large multi-coloured umbrella over an outside table. Then we saw two German patrols cautiously probing the area on each side of the main road. One patrol passed between us and our horses. We froze quite still and kept our eyes on the two miles of clear main road ahead.

Not long afterwards we saw the reason for the scouting parties. Away in the distance swinging along with rifles slung over their shoulders came a platoon of German soldiers, followed by about half-a-dozen officers on horseback. Behind them was a company of infantry and then some horse-drawn guns. The column was half-a-mile from the crossroads when I heard horses on the road behind me. Emerging from the woods on to the road was a force of about 150 fully-equipped Polish Cavalry—I learned later they were the 12th Uhlans.

The cavalry formed up immediately and were thundering down the road, swords flashing, before the marching Germans knew what was happening. The horses smashed through the whole column with hardly a shot fired against them. As the frightened artillery horses reared, the guns slewed across the road and there were Polish casualties as riders were unhorsed against the guns. They formed up again and charged back to complete the havoc. They swung off along one of the side roads and it was all over. We crept away and found our horses, mounted and returned to report. The date was either the 15th or 16th of September. Warsaw capitulated soon afterwards.

The problem posed by the little Jewish shopkeeper just could not be answered, I decided. Germans or Russians? For the Pole in my position in 1939 there was little choice. There were plenty more like me on this train, who had thought that fighting the Nazis might be a passport to Soviet clemency.

The days of comfortless tedium went dragging by. We dozed in numb misery, we dreamed racking nightmares which stayed with us as we woke again to realisation that we were still in this awful train and there seemed no end to the grinding of the wheels. We talked of wives and families. Some of the men would describe their babies in loving detail. We railed against the Russians and we cursed Hitler and his Germans. We lived through long hours in which no man spoke as we huddled together against intense cold. Sometimes we were locked in for thirty-six hours on end. That was when men moaned with the abject frustration of it all and called down searing curses on the architects of our degradation.

But we were moving, moving all the time. Men died and their names were written off, but the long snake of sixty or more cattle trucks went on eating up a staggering total of miles. The vastness of Russia is appalling. We reached and identified the important Siberian centre of Novo Sibirsk, eighteen hundred miles from our starting point outside Moscow, and still the train went on. We had covered over two thousand miles eastwards in an almost straight line when we passed slowly through Krasnoyarsk and saw grain piled high in the open, deteriorating and throwing out green shoots because there was either no labour or no transport to move it. A big place, this Krasnoyarsk, seen through the spyholes in our wooden cells. A place of huge granaries and red brick buildings and the activity normally associated with a busy rail junction.

About eight miles beyond Krasnoyarsk we pulled up at a long siding well out of sight and sound of the town. A brisk, well-wrapped team of wheel-tappers wielded their hammers down the length of the train. These wheel-tappers must be among the most assiduous of the world's railway workers. At every possible opportunity during the long ride they banged away at the wheels. They were obviously workers of the greatest importance. A breakdown on one of the stretches of snowy wilderness between towns would have been disastrous. This time they found defects in some of the wagons and we spent the hours from mid-morning to dusk in the open trying to keep circulation moving while repairs were carried out from materials taken from a couple of brick shacks at the side of the line. There was, by now, one slight improvement in our condition. Following the example of one unknown minor genius, we had made trouser-fasteners from twigs threaded through the waist bands. Now we had both hands free. Now we could flail our arms about to stop freezing.

It was the end of the third week and some thought that Krasnoyarsk might be the end of the line for us. At dusk, however, we were loaded aboard, locked in and sealed again. The wheels turned and thudded into the old rhythm. There were six more nights of travel, six days or parts of days in the open, stamping around to stay alive. Then, incredibly, one month and over 3,000 miles after the start, we reached the end of the train journey. The place was Irkutsk, near the southern tip of the great Baikal Lake.

The soldiers walked down the train removing the seals and unbarring the trucks and ordering, "All out. The trip's over."

We stumbled out and a shrieking, whipping wind, and a sub-zero temperature made us gulp and gasp and cling to the small shelter afforded by the trucks. In a few minutes ears became icy cold, noses purple-red and eyes streamed tears. We shivered, all of us, uncontrollably. It was the second week in December and Siberia was already fast bound in winter. We met it still clad only in a pair of trousers, canvas shoes and a thin cotton blouse. The soldiers inspected each wagon to make sure it had been cleared. Some men, seized with cramp or worse, had to be lifted down. There was some milling about, a shouting of orders, repeated again down the line to each group and we formed into a long, untidy column—a crowd of perhaps four thousand prisoners, headed, tailed and flanked by soldiers. We shambled off, heads bent against the wind, trousers soaked to the knees in the snow and slush churned up by those ahead.

The march took us five miles across country, out of sight and sound of the railway. It was typical of the whole enterprise that our resting-place was to be no haven for drooping travellers. We stopped and broke out of ranks in a vast, wind-swept potato field. Nowhere, as far as the eye could see in any direction, was there a building of any sort. The field lay under two feet of crisp snow. A few wood-burning *kolhoz* lorries stood around. There was a single mobile field kitchen which seemed grossly inadequate for the needs of such a mass of prisoners. The wind had jagged teeth that made me feel quite naked to its attack. Men stood in the snow and looked bleakly at one another. All the tears were not caused by the cutting wind.

The period of aimless standing around did not last long. It was urgently necessary to do something to get out of the paralysing blast of the wind. One group near me started to scrape heaped snow into a windbreak. The idea spread rapidly. Soon there was feverish toiling to make little snow-ringed compounds. Men scraped and scratched away with numb fingers down to the rock-hard black earth and when their work was done crouched down behind the windbreak.

Outside the barbed wire, about a quarter of a mile away from the edge of the field, were some woods. When the transport commandant, that apostle of Soviet culture, walked round later in the day, spokesmen from some of the groups asked him if we could be allowed to gather branches to cover the freezing ground. He gave permission. The prisoners had automatically held together in their truck communities. A few volunteers from each group were formed up and under armed escort made several trips to the woods, returning with armfuls of small twigs and branches which were carefully spread out on the ground. Men were then able to stretch out below the level of the snow heaps and escape the full impact of the wind. Even so, it was only a barely tolerable position as we huddled tightly together. Food was doled out, about one pound of bread per man per day, and, remarkably, the food kitchen managed to produce two steaming tin mugs of unsweetened ersatz coffee a day for each man.

We spent three days in the potato field, in the course of which batches of hundreds more prisoners joined us. Some of these were Finns. Now and later they were unmistakable. They always clung tenaciously together in a solid racial group. When the assembly had been completed there were not fewer than five thousand men in the field, all wondering what was going to happen next and fearfully speculating on what might be in store. Events were to justify the worst of our fears.

On our camp followers, the lice which had lived on and with us from the prisons of Western Russia, the potato field inflicted heavy casualties. Their warm hiding-places on our bodies exposed to the lash of that all-pervading blast, they dropped off or were easily picked off, and died. We did not mourn them. We were in little shape to act as hosts. They might have fared better if they could have stuck it out until the third day—a memorable day indeed.

41

The *kolhoz* lorries, with their wood-fuelled gas-generator engines, drove in on that third day and the soldiers ran round. We felt something unusual was about to happen but we could never in our most hopeful dreams have guessed what it was. The word rippled out from those closest to the lorries, "Clothes! New clothes."

And new clothes it was. It took hours to make the distribution, but when it was over each man had exchanged his flimsy *rubashka* for the Russian winter top garment, the *fufaika*, a thigh-length, buttoned-to-the-throat, kapok-padded jacket.

With the jackets came a pair of padded winter trousers and stout rubberised canvas boots, laced to a point a few inches above the ankle. The boots were available in three sizes only—small, medium and large. No attempt was made to give a man the size he needed. If he were lucky they fitted. If not, he exchanged his too-small or too-large boots with someone else who had the opposite kind of misfit. I was one of the lucky ones. My issue fitted. Our old blouses and trousers were all carefully collected. The excitement was wonderful. Men's faces glowed. They hurried and fumbled to get into their handsome new jackets. They called out to one another, parading around. And those dear old jokers, who had been almost silent since we came to the potato field, gave us a mannequin display, hands on hips and beards flying in the wind. It is a laboured truism that all things and experiences are comparative. By all normal standards we were still abjectly dressed for a Siberian winter, but the additional warmth we felt from our *fufaikas* was extraordinary.

On the fourth day of our stay in the potato field, the issue of winter clothing was completed. We were each handed two pieces of linen which the soldiers explained were for wrapping up the feet inside our boots. A few of the men in our truck group knew about these "socks" and how best to wind them, not too tightly, around the feet to stave off frostbite. There were little demonstrations all over the field.

Into the compound drove a whole convoy of some sixty powerful lorries, each with an Army driver accompanied in the cab by another soldier as driver's mate. They were heavy duty vehicles requisitioned from the collective farms for hundreds of miles around and had painted on their sides the names of the various *kolhozi*. Just behind the cabin they carried tall, cylindrical gas generators, the fuel for which was eight-inch lengths of birch and ash, known to the Russians as *churki*. This wood, plentifully available throughout well-forested Siberia, was a cheap and efficient substitute for precious motor spirit and solved one of the many Russian transport and distribution problems. Clipped into brackets on the lorry sides was an assortment of spades and pickaxes. The load-carrying bodies were open to the weather. Apart from their odd-looking gas generators, they looked like the normal commercial Western three-tonner.

As we watched them bumping and rolling in, the orders started to fly and we knew that the last stage of our journey was about to begin. For many of those jostling around it would be the last stage of any journey they would know on this earth.

V

CHAIN GANG

O N THAT last day in the potato field there was an air of some big—and for the five thousand prisoners, ominous—event ahead, some major Russian transportation enterprise. The soldiers were in battalion strength, hooded in balaclavas, wearing warm sheepskin gloves and each carrying his distinctive khaki sack slung across the back and held in place by a piece of string. There were at least fifty lorries parked in a long, well-spaced line. They were open and mounted machine-gun platforms against the drivers' cabins. If the issue of new warm clothing had not been enough warning, the presence of so many troops and vehicles removed any doubt that a fresh ordeal lay ahead.

The troops arrived about 11 a.m. after the morning issue of bread and coffee had been completed. They started work immediately re-checking the list of prisoners' names. At times the checking became chaotic. Some names had to be shouted out several times before the men concerned recognised them in their mispronounced Russian form. As each batch of one hundred names were ticked off on the lists, the men were led away in a column towards the waiting lorries. Whether by design or not, the truck communities were split up. I found myself with an almost entirely different bunch of men as we moved away. We were led to the space between the sixth and seventh lorries and there we stood for some hours while the paper work and the marshalling went on throughout the afternoon in the field.

The light of a clear, cold, December day was fading as the preliminaries ended. The soldiers were detailed into sections of about twenty, each in charge of an N.C.O. or junior officer. Each section was disposed to guard one hundred prisoners, strung out two abreast behind each lorry. We watched the proceedings with interest, chilled and hoping there would soon be a move.

There had been a low buzz of talk all the way down the great line of men. Suddenly it was stilled, cut short in shock and appalled surprise, as from each lorry was uncoiled a length of heavy steel chain of about one inch diameter. A soldier in my detachment walked between the two men at the head of my column, forcing them apart, and then walked through the middle cleaving us into two single lines. Other soldiers followed him, running out the chain. On shouted instructions, we picked up the chain with the hand nearest to it. I was about halfway along with my left side to the chain. I remember thinking I was lucky not to have to use my right hand, which was still open, raw and painful. The chain was brand new, still coated with some dark, sticky, anti-rust compound, and its coldness struck the hand almost like a burn. Then, fifty men a side, we were handcuffed to the chain by one wrist. Three guards took station on each side, spaced along the line, the section commander climbed into the cab alongside the driver and the remaining troops piled quickly into the back of the lorry. We were ready to start. The prisoners remained very silent.

Like some great, slowly-walking reptile, the long procession began to move, the lorry at the head setting the pace, a fair walking speed of about four miles an hour. The forward end of the chain was secured to a strong spring-closed hook, a fixture normally used for towing jobs. As our lorry moved and the chain took up the strain, we strode out, automatically falling into step. There was just enough room between the man ahead and the man behind for me to to step out without hindrance. When the leading lorry struck a deeper drift of snow, the whole convoy piled forward and then stopped, vehicle by vehicle, prisoner group by prisoner group, until the full marching speed was resumed.

We trudged non-stop through that first dark night at the beginning of the third week in December for twelve hours or more. The leading lorry lighted the way with the beam of bright lamps. We struggled on in the blackness, obeying the insistent pull of the chain, still wondering where we were going, fearful of how long we should have to march on in this killing cold. The road was obviously well known and I had no doubt that this first long drag by night was intended to take us clear of any inhabited places near Irkutsk, unseen by the Russian civilian population.

In the following days the programme was one of day marches and night halts, but the route was chosen still to avoid places where we might be seen. So vast and thinly-populated are these stupendous areas of Siberia, that I saw not a single native in the length of Irkutsk province.

A halt was called about half-an-hour after dawn in a wooded depression between two hills. We were all stiff, weighed down with heavy-limbed fatigue, cold and hungry. In my group were men of all ages, from lads of 17 to men of over 60, and from many different civilian backgrounds. Some of the older men were moaning already with misery. They were for the most part professional types, lawyers and architects and the like, who had reached that stage in life before the coming of the Russians when they drove in their cars from home to office and back again— men who had given up the physical caperings of youth and could look not too far ahead to a well-to-do, respected and comfortable retirement. They were skirmishing with death and they had such paltry weapons left for the fight. Then and later we younger men did what we could to help them along, but casualties among them were heavy indeed.

That first stop lasted only a couple of hours, long enough for the field kitchen which had accompanied us to brew up hot coffee and for the soldiers to distribute the bread ration. The heat of the coffee was like a breath of warm life, and we ate ravenously of our bread. We were not unshackled from the chain and in all too short a time we were on the move again, this time in daylight.

The six flanking guards were regularly changed every two hours. They jogged forward to the lorry, six reliefs jumped down, and a new turn of duty started without slowing the march of the winding, toiling column of prisoners. Over the exposed places on high ground the wind howled like a chorus of demons, our feet slipped in the churned up snow, tips of fingers, ears and noses felt the insidious attack of frostbite. And, even this early, the toll of death started. A shout, passed from a contingent well behind us, was relayed along by the walking sentries until it reached the transport commandant in the leading lorry. The leader stopped, the rest stopped. Some poor prisoner was unshackled, his body removed. The same method of disposal was followed as for the dead of the train. The clothes and boots were removed, the corpse was left behind under a mound of snow. This was the first of many. Taking my own section as typical, the death-rate was to reach between ten and fifteen per cent before the long trek was over.

It was difficult to appreciate that we were following any kind of regular road. Everything was blanketed with thick snow. But every hundred yards there would be a stout stake about eight feet tall topped by a well-lashed-on clump of dried hay or small twigs, like a succession of witches' brooms. These, I guessed, were route markers. They were with us for miles, up steep hills, down into forested valleys, across the fording places of hard-frozen rivers. There were times when even the chain-bound lorry wheels began to slip and then the soldiers would jump down and put their shoulders into a helping heave and we prisoners, motivated only by a desire to get to our resting-place as soon as possible, would close up behind and add our considerable weight to the effort. It was hard going, and it got worse as we progressed.

Few of the marchers had any doubt of our direction. We were pushing north—almost due north—out towards the upper end of Irkutsk province towards the great sprawling area of Yakutsk. We were probably following a course roughly parallel with the western shore of Lake Baikal, that mighty, banana-shaped expanse of inland water stretching over four hundred miles north from its southern tip where the town of Irkutsk lies across the Trans-Siberian Railway. We were headed north from Latitude 50°N. to Latitude 60°N. and beyond, up towards the Arctic Circle, and the Siberian weather got worse as we went forward.

The march continued on the second day until late afternoon. It might, I feel, have ended earlier if we could have reached a sheltered position before this, but, as was to be the practice from then on, there appeared to be an order requiring the Commandant to find some unexposed place, usually in the lee of woods, for the night's halt. The consideration was almost certainly one of expediency rather than a humanitarian one. Since so much time, effort and money was being spent in getting this considerable free labour force from one end of Russia to the other, there must have been some pressure on the Commandant to bring through as many men as possible still capable of work. Now, outside the settled area of urban Irkutsk, we were unshackled for the night and allowed to light fires. As in the potato field, we dug into the snow to get some warmth and clung close together, dozing in the light of fires for which, with cramped and frozen hands, we had eagerly foraged the wood from the trees about us. There we had our second mug of coffee of the day, and those who had been careful enough to save some bread from the morning issue ate as they drank.

I have grateful memories of the general efficiency of the lumbering field kitchen. It baked the bread issued to us each morning and which was our only sustenance throughout and it produced two hot drinks a day. Only once did it fail, and that was after we had been buffeted and bogged down for hours by a blizzard. On this day we received an emergency issue which proved to be a most welcome and palatable change of fare—rye bread which had been soaked in honey and partially dried to form an easily stored and transported form of iron ration. How well I remember any change of diet on the long road from Pinsk to Northern Siberia. I struggle sometimes to remember in sharp detail some of my experiences but small incidents concerning food come back to me clearly and unbidden. There was never enough of it and the thought of it nagged at us always. Men would have given a handful of diamonds for an extra slice of bread in these circumstances and counted themselves the most fortunate of beings, because only food had value. It was beyond price.

We were hit by three tearing blizzards in the course of our march. The first one. which struck towards the end of the first week was the worst because it was our first experience of the full fury of one of these freezing, high-velocity winds hurling with it a concentrated, driving weight of snow. The sky had been heavy, the clouds low and lead-grey, when we got under way soon after dawn, and the blizzard shrieked down on us about two hours later. It slowed the convoy almost immediately until we were creeping along, heads well down, at only a slow shuffle. It was almost impossible to open the eyes to it. The snow packed on our matted hair and beards, coated the lorries and the taut chains, mantled the soldiers exposed to it ahead and above us, crouched forward near their whitened machine-gun. The blizzard met us almost head on and its impact was such that I wondered how for the next few hours the leading lorry still succeeded in keeping the convoy crawling on. We found some kind of comparative shelter

48

about two o'clock. This was the first time I saw the Russians wearing their *bashliks*, a larger super-type balaclava in a kind of camel-hair material, the use of which required a special order from the commanding officer.

The storm blew for the rest of the day and well into the night. We could light no fires while it continued. When it abated before dawn into thin flurries of snow we all, and this must include the soldiers too, felt at our lowest ebb. At dawn, looking like a collection of snowmen, we turned with desperate hope towards the field kitchen. The mute appeal was answered. The hot coffee came round. There was a bread issue.

Little opportunity existed for striking up any kind of friendship with one's fellow sufferers. Everyone seemed preoccupied with his own troubles, grappling in his own fashion with the overriding necessity of keeping going. One man, however, I did get to know, because he was my partner on the chain, handcuffed at the same point and abreast of me. He was a young man, thick-legged, strong and with big, muscled shoulders. It was days before we spoke, although we had been taking stock of each other from the beginning. For my part, I liked what I saw and I think the feeling was reciprocated on his side. We talked first during an enforced stop to unshackle a dead man from a place on the chain just ahead of us. "They won't kill me like that," he said quietly. "Me neither," I answered. "We'll get there . . . wherever we're going."

His name, he told me, was Grechinen, and he came from Lublin. He was—although the description is a little too grandiose for the actual job—the stationmaster at a small station outside Lublin. In fact, he did what work was required almost on his own, including the portering. A boy of modest ambitions, content with his own small sphere of importance, happier working with his hands than carrying out the modest amount of clerical work that went with the title of stationmaster. The Russians came, and for no logical reason relieved him of his appointment and sent him to one of the motor transport stations they were setting up to deal with the repair of tractors. Grechinen, born a Ukrainian, was one of those who became Polish in the great Central European rearrangement of boundaries after the first World War. He was philosophical about his changed occupation. In fact he quite liked "messing about with tractors".

Some of those tractors, Grechinen told me, were beyond repair, but he and his workmates nevertheless were expected to get them in running order to be sent back to the farms. Grechinen spent nearly a week on one of them and then watched it go with misgivings. One day he was called to the superintendent's office and gravely informed that this particular machine had broken down soon after it returned to its farm. Grechinen, a stolid lad and slow to temper, said his piece forcefully and pointedly about the impossibility of turning scrap-iron into farm tractors.

Mechanic Grechinen was arrested and charged with sabotage. A few other charges were thrown in as well. His previous unexceptionable career as stationmaster supported the accusation that he had been a willing worker for the Polish police state and therefore an enemy of the people. Grechinen tried to explain, but no one took any notice, so he shut his mouth after the first interrogation and resolutely refused to say another word. "What can you say," he asked me, "to a crowd of bloody fools who ask questions and get mad at you because you won't give them the answers they want?" They manhandled him, pushed him round, yelled at him. Grechinen kept his mouth shut. They thought he was a bit simple in the head, and eventually stopped the treatment and put him on trial. He got off lightly with ten years hard labour.

When the sentence was announced, Grechinen was so surprised that he forgot his vow of silence. "Ten years!" he exclaimed. "What for?" The prosecutor jumped to his feet. "Oh," he said menacingly. "So now you start to talk." Grechinen shut his mouth again. He had kept silent, he said, until he met me. Talking in the wrong places, he warned me, could get a man into a lot of unexpected trouble. This, I realised, was advice from a friend. I thanked him. There was a strong bond between us for the rest of the trip. I liked honest Grechinen.

Somehow someone learned during the second week of the march that it was 24 December. Maybe a prisoner had guessed we must be near that date and had had the day confirmed by a guard. The news went up and down the long, struggling line like the leaping flames of a forest fire. It's Christmas Eve, went the whisper from man to man. "It's Christmas Eve, Grechinen," I said. Grechinen half-smiled through his cracked lips. "Christmas Eve," he repeated. Away back behind us there was suddenly a thin, wavering sound. It was odd and startling. It grew in volume and swept towards us. It was the sound of men singing, men singing with increasing power in the wastes of the Siberian wilderness.

I thought the soldiers would have been ordered to shout us down, but the mounting song reached us unchecked and engulfed us. I was singing and Grechinen was singing. Everybody who had a voice left was joining in. A marching choir of nearly five thousand male voices drowning their despair in a song of praise for the Child who would be born on the morrow. The song was "Holy Night", and those who did not sing it in Polish sang it in the language in which they had learnt it as children. Then a few voices started the Polish Christmas carol, "Jesu's Lullaby", and I choked on it and fell silent. And half-way through it, others broke down and wept quietly. The Lullaby died abruptly and there was no more singing. Our hearts were full to bursting with the bitter-sweet memories of other Christmases.

Christmas Day came and went like any other of the dreary succession of marching days. We walked into our second blizzard and walked out of it. Grechinen and I between us supported the man directly ahead of him for hours during this second storm, calling on the guards to do something to help him. "He'll manage all right," said one of them. He died barely half-an-hour before we reached the night's stopping-place.

The soldiers were not always so indifferent to the appeals of exhausted prisoners, but it became clear that they were under orders to discriminate. The gasping, flagging, floundering older men from the original train party were never helped, in spite of the advice given out by the guards frequently before the start of a day's march to "call out if you are taken ill". We were reminded, too, that there were still with us specially-trained first-aid men, but I never saw them about their business.

Back at the assembly point near Irkutsk the train prisoners had been joined by a small crowd of Russians. They seemed to be nearly all youngish men and I suspect they were not, like us, political offenders but ordinary Soviet criminal types, consigned to Siberia to work out the expiation of their crimes. There were three or four of them on our chain and these were the only ones who were helped along on their journey. The procedure when a man began to stumble and fall about and mumble in his misery was for his nearest colleagues on the chain to call one of the walking guards. The name of the unfortunate was shouted ahead to the soldiers in the lorry. A list would be consulted. More often than not the sick man was out of luck. He was told to keep going and his friends heaved and strained to keep him on his feet until the next halt. I saw men collapse into the snow and cry to be unchained and to be allowed to lie down and sleep. It would have been release by death and they begged for it. But the soldiers pulled and kicked them to their feet and the awful struggle went on.

We were surprised indeed at what happened the first time one of the newcomers keeled over, his hand dragging at the chain. There were the usual shouts between the walking guards and the soldiers ahead. The list of names was brought out. The guards roughly hauled the man erect. There was a bit of heavy banter from one of the soldiers as the prisoner was unshackled. "You are a fine, strapping young fellow," he said. "We'll give you a little rest and then you'll be able to do some work for us later." The man was taken off to the lorry and helped up to join the soldiers. He rode with them for two hours or more and was then brought back to resume his place in the marching column. I suppose we should have been happy that one of our number had had his burden lightened, but, remembering the men who died unaided, we hated him and bitterly distrusted him. We never had anything more to say to a prisoner who had received the favour of a lift in the lorry. Our suspicions even went so far as to conjecture whether such men were planted among us as informers, although, in all reason, it would be difficult to imagine what reward could be offered for their services which would compensate for a winter trip through Siberia. The only discrimination by the military escort might possibly have been on the grounds of age—a quite practical expedient to bring through alive as many young men as possible—but I saw no Pole get a lift and we were not existing in conditions congenial to logical thinking anyway.

The days dragged on in much the same pattern through January. More and more we looked forward to the nightly halt, the fires, the bread and the hot coffee. Some of the old hands among the soldiers said we were lucky that this was not one of the worst Siberian winters, but it was as cruel and bleak as any weather I ever want to experience. The snowdrifts piling high along the track slowed us down increasingly each day. The occasions when we had to help get the lorries out of difficulties became more frequent until we began to wonder how long any progress at all could be maintained. The cold steel of the handcuff burned into my wrist. I was always cold, wet and wolfishly hungry. Stolid Grechinen plodded along beside me day after day. We said little but we derived strength from each other, from our mutual determination to see it through alive. Grechinen would go for days in silence but occasionally he would smile through his beard at me and I would give my own face-frozen smile back to him.

VI

END OF THE JOURNEY

IT MUST have been in the last week in January 1941, when we
had spent over forty days on the march, that the third and
most violent blizzard hurled itself out of the north and at last
bogged down the lorries. The convoy had covered well over
eight hundred miles from Irkutsk. We had crossed two great
rivers, the Vitim first and, but a few days ago, the mighty Lena,
both of them solid frozen and looking like broad smooth roads
winding away on their long courses through the vastness of
Siberia. After all this, it seemed incredible that the lorries would
ever stop their slow thrusting northwards. With the dry, powdery
snow thrown stingingly into their faces by the howling wind,
soldiers and prisoners together worked to keep digging the leading
vehicle out of drifts, but there came a time when no expenditure
of human effort could prevail. The long line of trucks and men
piled forward on itself and raggedly came to a standstill.

It had been the practice throughout the journey for the heavy
duties of leading lorry to be taken in rotation. When the order was
given for a change of leadership, the first driver would pull his
truck out of line with his chained men behind and allow the rest
to move past him, taking up position behind the last truck. The
duration of duty at the head of the convoy depended on the type
of road and the weather. Now we were on some kind of main
road alongside which ran telephone poles, their wires sagging
under the weight of the snow, but the advantage of being on a
fair road was outweighed by its position on high ground completely exposed to the weather. Apart from the pile-up of snow it
must have been almost impossible for the drivers to see ahead into
the white wall of swirling snow.

The position of my group at this stage was fourth or fifth in line
and it was here, almost alongside me, that the Commandant and
his junior officers, after inspecting conditions ahead, got together

for an anxious conference. Whether a complete forced stop had ever been envisaged I do not know, but these Russian officers were obviously a very worried lot. They talked, their backs to the wind, for a few minutes and then a signalman climbed precariously up one of the telephone poles and plugged in with a portable hand-set. He came down and reported. There were nods of rather taut approval and the officer group broke up to their various emergency duties. We stood around while a small patrol of troops struck off along the road ahead to reconnoitre for a sheltered place.

About half-an-hour after the breakdown the chains were unhooked from the lorries and the prisoners marched off ahead, crunching into the fresh snow, beating out a track and laboriously treading down the snow. The lorries crept after us. We struggled on for a mile until we came to the blessed haven of a belt of woods. Somehow we got the fires going, hundreds of them, and all through the raging night tended them for our lives. We felt the storm was trying to blot us out *en masse*. Prisoners dourly struggled and inched their way in towards the inner ring around the blazing timber. Some fools, ignoring advice that had been given since the start of the march, warmed their numbed hands close to the flames and then shrieked with the agony of returning circulation, beating their arms about and contorting themselves with the fierce pangs of it. Within range of the heat we kept turning ourselves about because the blizzard froze one's back even while the fire was giving out some little warmth to hands, face and the front of the body. No one was allowed to sleep. Those in the inner ring who began to doze off were shaken roughly awake by their friends. To sleep, as we all knew, might mean no awakening.

For twenty-four hours we lived out the full force of the blizzard, the lorries hopelessly snowed in. Only the fires and the still-functioning field kitchen preserved us. The tufts of hardy broad-bladed grass, a roadside feature all through the march, bent over, swung and gyrated under the whiplash of the wind with a constant swishing and whistling. The snow hissed and sizzled as it drove against the fires. We stamped around to save our frozen feet from frostbite, huddled our hands in our *fufaikas*, damned the storm and wondered how we were to get out of this place.

When the wind eventually abated and the snow began to thin,

the first impression I had was of the silence. It was possible again to hear clearly ordinary camp noises, to pick up the murmur of low conversation. There was still a sharp wind, keening quietly through the trees, but its sound was nothing to the hammering whine of the blizzard which had assaulted us through the long hours. I do not remember just how long we stayed under the lee of the woods. It seemed a long time. Maybe it was no more than two days. At any rate, there came a morning which was clear with that extraordinary clarity one gets on a fine Siberian winter day, a very cold day when the breath is expelled in clouds of steam, when the eye can see for vast distances. A knot of Russian officers stood talking, occasionally looking back in the direction whence we had come, from time to time glancing at their watches. There was an air of waiting for something to happen and because we had not the remotest idea of what the next move could be, we were all stirred with curiosity and a growing excitement.

We heard before we saw what we were waiting for—the sound of men's voices yipping and yelling in the distance. Everyone turned in the direction of the sounds. We stood looking for perhaps five minutes before the first of them came over the ridge about a quarter of a mile away. We shouted our surprise and excitement. Reindeer! Reindeer and sledges! Dozens of them. Reindeer, two, three and even four to a sled in line ahead, driven by little brown men, barely five feet tall, with smooth Mongoloid faces, the nomadic Ostyaks, the primitive herdsmen of the Siberian steppes. The novelty of it all was like a tonic. Men came out of their discomfort and apathy with shouting and laughter. Near me was a man who jumped up and down and kept saying over and over again, "Well, I'm damned. Look at that lot." New faces, new sights, new sounds. The cries of the Ostyaks, the unharnessing of the reindeer, the hobbling of the forefeet and the setting of the animals free to feed and look for their staple diet of moss under the covering of the thick snow—all these activities absorbed our interest. It was all new in surroundings and conditions where we thought there could be nothing new. The man near me was still talking to himself in a tone which suggested, "What will they think of next?"

It took the Ostyaks only a short time to release their reindeer from the primitive harness, a neck collar of reindeer hide, thong-fastened to two long, curved shafts which swept down and back to form the runners of the simple, wood-platformed sled, on which were sable and other skins. The little men had brought food with them in small sacks and they joined us round the fire as we received our morning issue of bread and coffee. They wore warm skin clothing. They looked at us with pity, their sharp, twinkling eyes puckered into slits as is the manner of men who spent their lives facing hazards of the world's worst weather.

I spoke to one of them in Russian. He might have been sixty, but it is difficult to tell with these Mongol types. He told me they had been visited at their winter camp by the Red Army men and they were not pleased to be sent on this trip. He thought they had made a fast journey of nearly a hundred miles to meet us. They had brought soldiers with them, a couple to each sledge. He told me about reindeer, that you could not ride on their backs because they were weak there, but their necks and the humps of their shoulders were very strong and an Ostyak could vault up there with the help of his long pole, the gentle goad they used in driving the sledge, and ride without strain or fatigue to the animal. He told me his name, but to a mind used only to Western and Russian names it left no impression on the memory.

On several occasions I was to talk to this little man. He would quietly seek me out. He had not a great deal to say. He would think hard and with obvious effort to put over any idea. But he called us, as did all the Ostyaks, the Unfortunates. Traditionally, from the time of the Czars we were, to his people, the Unfortunates, the prisoners of a régime which always sought to wrest the riches of Siberia by the use of unpaid labourers, the political prisoners who could not fit in the framework of successive tyrannies.

"We are your friends always," he once said to me. "Since a long time ago, before me and my father and his father before him, we placed outside our dwellings at night food for the wandering Unfortunates who had fled away from their camps and knew not where to go. In my time, too, because I am becoming an old man, I remember the placing of food."

"These men like us," I said, "have they always tried to escape from the Russians?"

"Always men who are young and strong and hate slavery have

tried to escape," said the Ostyak. "Perhaps you will try to escape, I think."

Escape. I turned the word over in my mind and knew that it had been with me as an idea since the day I left the Lubyanka. Yes, old Ostyak, I thought, all men who are young and strong and do not want to die must think of escape. Step to the right, step to the left . . . the Russians knew it too. But only a madman could entertain any serious hopes of a break on this wintry trek to the North. If a man were not shot—and there *were* chances of getting away as security slackened in the last stages, with the soldiers as preoccupied as anyone in keeping fit and alive and completing the march—there could only be death in attempting to live off this country in winter, weak and half-starved as we already were. Nevertheless, the old reindeer man left me with one thought I was to cherish later: men did attempt to escape.

The old man talked of the way of life of his people, the animals whose skins were so valuable to them, about the reindeer which they looked after with such care. "Once," he said, "we were allowed to shoot animals with a gun, but now the Soviets will not let us use guns and we catch all our animals in traps."

The day we moved off behind the sledges there was some laughter at the protests of the Ostyak whose four-reindeer team had been selected to draw the field kitchen, which was only a wood-fired steel boiler and oven combined. He swore that his animals and his light sledge would never be able to cope with so difficult a load. The Russian cooks went stolidly on with the job and we watched with amused sympathy for the Ostyak but with a tinge of concern lest his fears became justified. It was all right, though. We trudged off, our chains now fastened to the sledges, and the field kitchen, to our relief, came too. Some of the soldiers stayed with the lorries and I was sorry to see those big, dependable vehicles left behind. What happened to them I do not know. Perhaps they were able to turn back, or the *kolhoz* tractors came to their rescue.

The novelty of marching behind the wagging rumps of reindeer and watching their antlered heads swinging along the trail never quite wore off. We learned that by gently leaning back on the chain all together we could slow the pace considerably. We picked up that trick in a somewhat disorderly crossing of a small river bounded by steep banks. The reindeer made a great scramble of it, the guards bawled at the drivers to hold their charges to a reasonable pace and we, half-enjoying the confusion, threw our combined weight back against the speeding sledges. We got down one bank at a rush and then tore up the opposite side at a shambling trot. It took the best part of an hour to get the crazy circus back into line and ready to move again.

The hazards of the journey did not diminish and exhaustion claimed more victims, some of them soldiers. The troops were now coping with difficulties as great as our own, although they were still getting better food, their basic rations fortified with tinned meat and vegetable soups, and were, of course, better clothed against the cold. But none of them—except the Commandant and the sick—was allowed to ride. We were still being helped along by the chains, but they had to break their own trails on the flanks through thick snow, an effort which all except the leading prisoner groups avoided. For many of these guards, men from the southern autonomous Soviet republics, this was their first experience of the harshness of a northern winter, and they suffered accordingly.

The Ostyaks were the least affected. The only thing new about the situation to them was the job they were doing. They pitied us, but seemed to realise the only help they could give was to get us to where we were going as quickly as possible. Over all kinds of terrain they managed to average about fifteen miles a day. They acted towards the soldiers with an almost jaunty independence. They coveted from the Army only the empty tins which, by order, were always carefully preserved. Their interest in metalware revealed their primitive background. Metal was scarce but skins and timber were plentiful. So there was a good deal of surreptitious bartering between them and the Army cooks of skins for tins. A sable for an empty meat tin was a bargain for both sides and a lesson for the rest of us in relative values. The tins, they told us, were for use as cooking utensils and would be highly prized by the women when they returned home.

The fantastic procession wound its way onwards for over a week, mostly through open country, still keeping away from inhabited places. The length of chain dragging in the snow at the end of each section of prisoners told the tale of the men who had fallen out on the way. At each death the men behind the vacant space were moved up and the varying lengths of spare chain were an indication of the casualty rate in each group. The two end-of-the-line prisoners hugged the chain to their bodies under their armpits to ease the strain and we took turns in this least favoured position, sparing, however, the older and weaker men.

On the eighth or ninth day after leaving the lorries we entered a vast forest which, from high ground some hours before, we had seen stretching ahead of us unbrokenly as far as eye could range. We walked along quite a wide track between the trees, grateful to be out of the sharp cut of the wind and to know our nightly shelter was assured. We noticed, too, that the soldiers were showing some signs of cheerfulness and guessed, rightly as it turned out, that this must be a landmark near the end of the journey. The progress through the forest lasted two days and there was a sense of drive and urgency about the second day's march that convinced men who were almost dead to hope that the great trial was finishing. It was a long march, starting at the first light of dawn and continuing through the short winter day to dusk. We emerged in the failing light into a big, man-made clearing carved out from the surrounding forest. There were lights ahead and voices calling.

This, then, was our destination—Camp Number 303, on the north side of the Lena River, which I estimate to have been between 200 and 300 miles south-west of the Northern Siberia capital, Yakutsk. I do not remember in any sharp detail the scenes of arrival that night in the first week of February 1941. I remember how we moved, reindeer team by reindeer team up to a massive main gate in a stout palisade of rough-hewn logs, of being freed of my chains, the odd feeling of security as I milled about inside the compound, the meal enhanced by turnip-water "soup", the lighting of fires on what appeared to be a big parade-ground, the hearing of my name called in the checking of the lists. Sitting shoulder to shoulder with Grechinen round a crackling pile of logs, I talked a little, dozed often, stood up to ease the pain in my aching legs. Over a thousand miles of marching from Irkutsk and we had got here. I found myself marvelling. In spite of my physical misery I had a feeling that was almost happy.

The awful strain of two months on the road was over. Nothing the next day could bring could be worse. I think I must have been a bit light-headed.

Aching, heavy-eyed and weary, we were astir, by habit, at dawn. Some of the men were very sick and their companions had to lift them to their feet. The Ostyaks and their reindeer had gone in the night. The first day of my life in a Soviet labour camp was before me.

VII

LIFE IN CAMP 303

A FAINT early-morning haze dissipated and in the cold, clear light of day I looked round at the place to which I had been consigned to spend twenty-five years of my life. Camp 303, lying between 300 and 400 miles south of the Arctic Circle, was a rectangular enclosure about half-a-mile long and about 400 yards broad, at each corner of which stood a guard tower raised high on solid timber stilts, manned by machine-gun crews. The main gate, around which were built the troops' quarters, the kitchens, storehouses and administrative huts, faced west in one of the shorter sides of the oblong. Roughly in the centre of the enclosure was an open stretch of ground which served as the security no-man's-land between the soldiers and the prisoners.

Between us and the surrounding forest were the typical defences of a prison camp. Looking from the inside, the first barrier to freedom was an unbroken ring of coiled barbed wire, behind which was a six-feet-deep dry moat, its inner side cut downwards at an angle of about thirty degrees and its outer wall rising sheer and perpendicular to the foot of the first of two twelve-feet-high log palisades presenting a smooth surface inwards but strongly buttressed on the far side. Both outer sides of the two wooden walls were protected by rolled barbed wire. The space between the two provided a well-beaten track giving access from the main gate guardroom to all four control towers, and was regularly patrolled by armed sentries accompanied at night by police dogs, who shared kennels near the west gate with a pack of sled dogs.

Mingling diffidently with us that first morning were about a thousand men, a large proportion of them Finns, who were already installed when our bedraggled crowd of some 4,500 arrived. They came from four big huts at the eastern end of the compound. These log-built prisoner barracks were about eighty yards long by ten yards wide conforming in situation with the general plan of the camp itself, the doors, facing west, in the narrow end and protected from the direct blast of wind and snow by a small covered porch with a southerly opening. It was obvious that there was no accommodation for us newcomers.

Speculation was cut short by orders from the troops to line ourselves up for food. We shuffled along in line to the open window of the kitchens, one of the buildings to the left of the main gate. There was the usual issue of ersatz coffee and bread. Each man drank up as quickly as he could and returned his tin mug through another window. There was plenty of hot liquid but a shortage of utensils. This shortage remained all the time I was in the camp and applied also to the wooden bowls in which soup was dished out.

Into the middle of the parade ground soldiers carried out a portable wooden platform. Around it, under orders from junior officers and N.C.O.s, they formed a ring. We prisoners were then hustled to form ourselves in a big circle around the troops, facing inwards towards the platform. Accompanied by a small armed guard, two Russian colonels walked through the ranks to the foot of the platform. One of them stepped up. From my place in the front row I eyed him closely. He was tall, slim and distinguished looking, his hair greying at the temples, a typical example of a professional soldier in any army. His small grey moustache was carefully trimmed, his lean face showed two deep lines etched from a firm mouth into a strong chin. He carried his head slightly forward and I was struck by his air of detachment, that indefinable quality of effortless authority that any man who has served in armed forces will have met in professional commanders. He was facing a hostile audience, a mob of ill-treated humans whose bitter hate of all things Russian was almost a tangible thing, but he gave no sign. He stood perfectly relaxed with no movement of hands, feet or body. From the assembled prisoners there was a hum of comment. The Colonel turned his head slowly to look at us all. There was perfect silence.

He spoke clearly and crisply in Russian. "I am Colonel Ushakov," he said. "I am commandant of this camp. You have come here to work and I expect from you hard work and discipline. I will not talk to you of punishment since you probably know what to expect if you do not behave.

63

"Our first job is to provide shelter for you. Your first task, therefore, will be to build barracks for yourselves. How quickly you get inside out of the weather depends on your own efforts. It is up to you. In all communities there are those who will let others do the work for them. That kind of slacking will not be tolerated here and it will be to the benefit of all of you to see that everyone pulls his weight.

"I expect no trouble from you. If you have any complaints I will always listen to them, and I will do what is in my power to help you. There are no doctors here but there are trained soldiers who can administer first-aid. Those of you who are now too sick after your journey to work will be accommodated in the existing barracks while the rest of you get on with the new buildings. That is all I have to say."

He stepped down. Immediately the other Colonel took his place. He did not step up so much as leap forward in eagerness. There was nothing relaxed about this man. If there was a sense of restrained authority about Ushakov, this fellow wore his power like a flaunting banner. He was better dressed than the Commandant. He wore a sheepskin jacket, his well-made high boots were of soft leather, brightly polished. He was young enough to have been Ushakov's son.

If I ever knew his name, I do not remember it. He was the political officer and we never called him anything but the Politruk, the short title by which all such officials were known. He stood for fully a minute just looking at us, faintly smiling, eminently sure of himself, a picture of well-being and arrogance. The men stirred uneasily and stayed quiet.

He spoke like a sergeant-major, strongly, harshly and insultingly. "Look at you," he said, hunching his shoulders and placing his gloved hands on his hips. "You look like a bunch of animals. Just look at yourselves! You are supposed to be the highly civilised people who fancy they can run the world. Can't you now appreciate what stupid nonsense you have been taught?"

Fortified by his anonymity in the restless crowd, one brave man had the temerity to answer back. His voice shocked the silence of the pause which the Politruk had allowed himself for dramatic emphasis after his opening onslaught. "How can we look any different? You won't let us shave, there's no soap and no clean clothes."

64

The Politruk turned in the direction of the voice. "I'll get your food ration stopped if I am interrupted again." He was not interrupted again.

"After a time here," he went on, "and under the guidance of Comrade Stalin, we shall make useful citizens of you. Those who don't work don't eat. It is my job to help you to improve yourselves. It won't all be work here. You can attend classes to correct your way of thinking. We have an excellent library which you can use after working hours."

There was some more in the same vein. Then, briskly, "Any questions?" A prisoner asked, "When does spring come here?" Replied the Politruk, "Don't ask stupid questions." The meeting ended.

The first few days of building the new prisoners' barracks were chaotic. All were willing enough to work but it was most difficult to direct to the work for which they were effective the men with the best qualifications. The position sorted itself out smoothly enough after about three days. There were teams of architects and surveyors to plan out the ground and mark with stakes the plots for each hut. There were teams of young labourers hacking away at the frozen earth to make deep post-holes for the main structural timbers. There were builders, men skilled in the use of axes to rough-shape the virgin wood from the forest. The main labour force issued forth from the camp gate every morning at eight, in charge of armed soldiers.

I joined the forest workers. The camp was awakened by a bugle at 5 a.m. and there was an early morning procession of half-asleep men to the latrine trenches inside the wire behind the building site. Then would follow the line-up for breakfast. Tools were issued from the store on the left side of the gate, carefully checked out and as scrupulously checked in again at the end of the day. As we marched out of the gate a tallyman checked our names against his lists.

The forest was mainly of pine, but there was also an abundance of birch and larch. I worked in a felling team, handling one end of a heavy, cross-cut, two-man saw. Occasionally I was able to get some variation by lopping with an axe the branches of the trees. Since the days of my boyhood on the estate at Pinsk I had always been handy with an axe and I enjoyed the work. I found my

65

strength coming back daily. I became absorbed in the bustle and activity. There was a glow of pride and satisfaction in being able to use my hands again. At 1 p.m. we went back to the camp, man-handling the timber we had cut back to the builders. We received a midday issue of soup and returned to the forest to work until the light faded. Each day the line of huts increased in length.

A fortnight after our arrival the huts were finished. They lay in two lines with a wide "street" between each line of ten huts. I was allocated a bunk in one of the last half-dozen to be completed and I well remember the wonderful feeling of shelter and warmth, protection and comfort I felt the first night I came in out of the chilling night into my new home. The air smelt deliciously of fresh-cut pine. Down each long side wall of heavy timbers were fifty three-tier bunks, simply made of planks laid out within a strong, four-post framework. Three square, sheet-iron stoves equally spaced out down the length of the room blazed red into the gloom, fuelled by short pieces of sawn log, of which a supply was brought in daily by the forest working parties. Following the example of those already installed in their huts we had brought in as much moss as we could carry in our *fufaikas* to spread on the hard boards of our beds. There were no chimneys for the stoves; the smoke issued from a short length of stackpipe and curled away through vents in the roof. The smell of wood-smoke mingled with the scent of the pine. I lay on my top bunk, hands clasped behind my head and listened to the talk of the men around me.

Lying on his side facing me on one of the adjoining top bunks was a man of about fifty. We talked about the huts. We complimented the builders on the excellence of their workmanship, we were magnanimous enough to compliment the Russians on their efficient stoves. We talked about each other. He told me he had been a schoolteacher in Brest Litovsk and a sergeant in the Polish Army Reserve. The Russians came and he lost his job to a Communist who had taken a fortnight's "short course" in teaching in the Soviet style. The mothers still brought their children to him, someone complained, he was arrested, interrogated and sentenced to ten years. I sympathised, even as I thought, "Ten years; you're lucky, my friend." He was still talking as I fell asleep, my first real sleep for months.

We had to spend many hours in our huts. After 6 p.m. all

prisoners had to be back in their own quarters. A certain amount of movement in and around the huts was allowed as long as there was no standing about in large groups. Both lines of barracks were under close supervision from the towers at the eastern end of the compound, but as long as prisoners obeyed the strict order to keep well away from the wire, the guards took no action. There was nothing much to do in the huts. There was nothing to read and no light to read by. The only permitted activity after the 6 p.m. deadline was a visit either to the Wednesday night lecture by the Politruk or to the library, the other Politruk-controlled enterprise. I began to think a browse among the books would commit me to nothing and would break up the long nights. On an impulse I sought permission to go to the library one evening. It was readily granted.

The library was housed in half of one of the administrative buildings on the left of the gate and farthest away from it, about twenty yards from the wire on the long south side. About two hundred books were set out on plain wooden shelves along one side of the room and I moved about picking them out at random. There were a number of works by a man named Mayakovski. Some fifty books were all of a series of *Russkaya Azbuka*, illustrated primers for children. On this and other nights I spent some time reading the *Azbuka*. It was an ABC, the text in simple verses, extolling the virtues of Soviet aeroplanes and pilots, Soviet tanks and tankmen, the Red Army, Soviet heroes like Voroshilov, Soviet statesmen like Lenin and Stalin, Soviet tractor-drivers and *kolhoz* workers, and all the rest of the glories of the U.S.S.R.

But the pride of the collection was the *History of the Great Communist Party of Bolsheviks* in two well-bound volumes, and a complete version of the Russian Constitution. I spent some interesting hours with both works and concluded there was little danger that, even in twenty-five years, I should be converted to Communism of the Russian or any other brand.

It was a lively, cynical and entertaining Czech occupying a bunk near me who persuaded me to go along to one of the Politruk's Wednesday night talks, compulsory for all off-duty troops. The Politruk made no secret of his pleasure at seeing us and addressed a few special remarks to us before proceeding to deal with his military class. He spoke of the might of Russia, of her dominating place in the world (with asides at us on the decadence of the evil Capitalist system). Soldiers asked questions and the Politruk answered with the dogma of Marx and quotations from the speeches and writings of Lenin and Stalin. He was smiling as we left. He would not have been smiling a few minutes later had he watched the Czech put on a magnificent show for the benefit of the prisoners in our hut of the Politruk's education of the Red Army. I joined in the uproarious laughter. The Czech was a born actor and mimic. He wound up by asking for questions from his vastly entertained audience and answered them in an acidly-clever distortion of Marxisms, Leninisms and Stalinisms. The rest of the prisoners agreed that our visit to school had been well worthwhile.

There was a diversion of a different kind a few nights later. In our hut was one of the handful of prisoner priests, mostly Roman Catholic, but with a few Russian and Greek Orthodox also. We were lying and sitting about late in the evening when our cleric, a Roman Catholic, walked slowly down the long aisle between the beds asking quietly if anyone objected to his holding a short service. Some did not answer, no one objected. He stood in the middle of the room and carried through a simple service, the Latin words striking strangely in this place. I peered at him through the faint light given out by the stoves and thought it odd to see a Catholic priest in a long black beard. Then he prayed for our deliverance and I climbed down from my bunk and fell on my knees. Many others did the same. Holding in his hand a silver birch crucifix, he called a blessing down on us. He was beanpole thin, tall and slightly stooped, his black hair tinged with grey, although he was probably not more than 35. I never knew what brought him to Siberia. He never talked about himself. His name was Gorycz, which means in Polish "bitterness". No man could have been more unsuitably labelled.

By the end of the first month the camp had settled into a disciplined rhythm of life and there was a general feeling that, harsh though existence was in this remote, winter-bound spot, conditions could have been much worse. All working prisoners were given 400 grammes of bread (some 14 ounces) a day and those too sick to work received 300 grammes. The bread was issued with the early morning coffee, part was eaten then, another portion went down with the midday soup and the rest was taken with the hot drink handed out at the end of the day's work. There was an occasional treat on Sunday when we were given dried fish, but bread remained our staple diet and the most important single factor in our lives. Tobacco, too, was important in a lesser degree. There was a fairly generous issue once a week of the coarse *korizhki*, with a sheet of very old newspaper to act as cigarette paper. Bread and tobacco were the only commodities of value in the camp. They were the currency of the camp, the only means of payment for services.

The mortality rate continued high in that first month. Many of the men who survived the death march wrecked in body and mind never did any work. They were given bunks in the existing huts when we arrived and, worn out beyond endurance, just lay there day after day until they lost their feeble grip on life. Volunteer burial parties from among their friends carried their bodies under armed escort to a clearing about a quarter of a mile from the camp, laboured to hack shallow graves out of the hard-frozen earth, and committed them at last to rest.

Twice I went out with burial parties and in so doing discovered that the Commandant was provided with an aeroplane. Our way took us past what seemed to me to be an inadequate runway cut out of the forest at its highest point. The plane, protected by tarpaulins, stood under the shelter of some trees. It was a small, Tiger Moth trainer type. One of the guards said Ushakov piloted it himself to attend conferences at area Army headquarters at Yakutsk.

The Russians interfered very little with our lives outside working hours. Inspection of our quarters was infrequent and perfunctory. Prisoners working in felling teams in the forest found new friends and at first sought permission to change from one hut to another to bunk near their team-mates. The authorities offered no objection and let it be known that such moves could be made as a mutual arrangement between prisoners. Most men could be persuaded to switch places from one hut to another by a bribe of tobacco, and there was therefore a constant movement in those early weeks as men sorted out themselves and their friends. I knew none of my companions particularly well, although I still occasionally saw Grechinen, my companion of the march. Apart from him there was only the Czech, whose wit and gaiety I admired but who was never a close friend. The various national groups tended to hold together and we Poles, for instance, used to start the day with the singing of that little traditional hymn of praise, "When the Morning Light Appears". The Russians did not care for our singing, but they never took active steps to stop us.

I used to lie on my bunk in the long evenings looking up to the smoke vent twenty feet above me and think about it all. There would be men talking quietly, some of them visitors from other huts. Words and disconnected sentences would reach me . . . names of places, and prisons and Army regiments. . . . "She said, 'Darling, don't worry, it will all be over soon, and I will still be here'." . . . A snippet of conversation about the guard who didn't get out of the way as the tree groaned and broke and fell the wrong way. . . . "Poor bastard, he won't get any real treatment for that smashed leg of his." . . . There was talk of somebody who had got his ribs bruised. "He's doing all right for himself— light duties cleaning out the officers' mess and plenty of tobacco to be picked up." . . . It would flow around me, a half-noticed background to my own thoughts. The pine smell and the warmth and the movement of men clanging open the tops of the stoves to stoke up with bright-burning wood. And all the time my mind juggling with pictures of the stockaded camp and Ushakov and the Politruk and the soldiers (how many of them died?) and always the men about me, the young ones like me who were resilient and quick to recover, the forty-year-olds who surprisingly (to me, then) moved slowly but with great reserves of courage and strength, and the over-fifties who fought to stay young, to work, to live, the men who had lived leisured lives and now, marvellously, displayed the guts to face a cruel new life very bravely. They should have been telling tales to their devoted grandchildren, these oldsters. Instead they spent their days straining and lifting at the great fallen trees, working alongside men who were often half their age. There is a courage which flourishes in the worst kind of adversity and it is quite unspectacular. These men had it in full.

My mind revolved them round, these crowding impressions. And then, unfailingly, until I dropped off to sleep on the moss-covered planks, I would grapple with my own problem. The

70

insistent, hammering thought always was, "Twenty-five years in this place." Many of these men I now knew would die as the years passed. There would be fresh entries. And I would get older and older. Twenty-five years. Twenty-five years. As long to go as I had already lived. But how to get out? And having beaten the wire, the moat and the formidable wooden fences, where would one escape to? I would think of the little Ostyak and his talk of the Unfortunates. Did any of them ever get out of Siberia? No man could ever hope to fight his way out alone against the crushing hazards of this country with its immense distances. Where, having planned an escape, could one find resolute men to make the attempt? These, and other questions, I put to myself. And I had no answers.

I fell in with Grechinen on the way to the latrines one evening. "Grechinen," I said, "if I could one day think up a plan of escape, would you come with me?" A frown creased his forehead. "Are you serious?" I nodded. Grechinen ran his fingers slowly through his beard. "Rawicz," he answered finally, "I will think about it tonight and tell you tomorrow."

Cautious Grechinen. I saw him the next day in the wide space between the two rows of huts. "No," he said. "I would come with you if there was a chance, but the snow and the cold would kill us before we could get anywhere, even if the Russians didn't catch us." I shrugged my shoulders. "I still don't want to die young," added Grechinen.

I put the same question to the Czech. He thought at first that I was joking. Then he sat down on the edge of his bunk and motioned me down beside him. He put his hand on my shoulder. Quietly, in a voice just above a whisper, he said, "Yes, I would come with you, but you want strong and healthy men. My stomach plagues me and I think it will eventually kill me. If I came with you I would die that much sooner out there and you would suffer for having me with you." We sat there in silence for a few minutes after that. Then the Czech spoke again. "If you get the chance, clear out, my boy. Keep your eyes skinned, pick your men. I shall wish you luck, anyway."

We worked hard for six days and had an easy day on the seventh. Sunday was the day when the Commandant addressed the prisoners. He would talk of the work target for the following week, draw attention to any infringements of camp rules and make any announcements necessary affecting the life of prisoners. He would also call for suggestions and questions. We had been there a month when the Commandant called for volunteers for a new job. He wanted men who had experience of making skis. There was no response at first. Said the Commandant, "Volunteers will receive an immediate increase of one hundred grammes on their daily bread ration, and there will be more if the skis turned out are of good quality." Sixty men volunteered, and I was one of them. I had once made a pair of skis. I could not claim to be an expert, but for an extra three or four ounces of bread a day I was willing to try my hand.

The ski shop was the other half of the building occupied by the library. Half-a-dozen of the volunteers were real experts at the job and by common consent they divided the rest into a team of handymen for the actual process of manufacture and an outdoor crew for felling the birch trees, sawing the wood into the right lengths and keeping up a steady supply of the right timber to the shop. My achievement in having once made a pair of skis earned me a job inside the hut on the last stage of steaming and shaping. And the very first day, before a single pair of skis had been produced, we all received our new ration of 500 grammes of bread.

On the second day we turned out our first two pairs of skis. They were each in turn placed with their ends on two upturned logs, the middle unsupported, and Ushakov himself tested them by treading down on them until they touched the floor in the shape of a letter U. Two soldiers then took them away and tested them on a run through the forest. They passed both tests. At the end of the week Ushakov came to the shop and announced that samples sent away to Yakutsk had been accepted as up to the standard required by the Red Army. Our bread ration would go up immediately to a kilogramme a day—over double the normal ration—and there would be more tobacco for us. At the end of a fortnight we were turning out 160 pairs of skis a day.

There was considerable bad feeling among the forest gangs over our new privileges. I was asked more than once how I could allow myself to make skis for Russian soldiers, but I never entered into arguments. My own feeling was any work one did in a Siberian camp was bound to benefit the Soviet in some degree, so one might as well take the most interesting job available. Interesting, of course, and well paid. With bread occupying the exalted position it did in our lives, it would have been surprising had there been no adverse comment from the less favoured majority. I shared my extra tobacco and I took some of my extra bread to the sick. So did many others of the ski-making prisoners. But the dissatisfaction persisted. It is odd to reflect that the prime advocates of a classless society had this early succeeded in making two classes of workers and in marking the difference so clearly with substantial rewards to one class.

Working all day in the warmth of the ski shop, with the big stove roaring all day for the steaming of the wood, I felt I was getting back towards my full strength again. It should have made me resigned to my sentence, but instead it turned my thoughts more and more to escape. I began to wonder how I could preserve and hide some of my extra bread. I still had no workable plan and I could not know then that I was soon to get help from a most unexpected quarter.

VIII

THE WIFE OF THE COMMISSAR

I HAD volunteered once and struck lucky. I volunteered again one cold blustery Sunday morning in mid-March as flurries of snow swept about the hunched-up prisoners at the weekly parade.

"In my quarters," said Ushakov, "I have a radio set. It is called a Telefunken. Is there any one of you who knows this make of set well enough to do a repair job?" I knew the Telefunken, because we had one at home—a German make, I think, made under licence in a factory at Wilno for the Polish market. Men turned their heads to see who might step forward. There was a full minute of silence and nobody made a move. I knew the set, but could I repair it? If I could, there was the exciting prospect of hearing some news from the outside world, from which I had been cut off for nearly eighteen months. I had a sudden panic that somebody else would get the job. I stuck up my hand and called out. An N.C.O. stepped up and took my name and my place of work. "I will send for you when I want you," said the Commandant.

It was to be a fateful decision, launching me into the last and most extraordinary phase of my stay at Camp 303. In this isolated community of between five and six thousand men under sentence and a battalion strength of officers and men, there was but one woman. The defective Telefunken was to be the means of my meeting her, and, so far as I knew, I was the only prisoner who ever talked to her.

The following afternoon as I worked in the ski shop, the Commandant's messenger, a moon-faced private named Igor, called for me. "The Commandant wants you," he said. "Come with me." As we left, the other men in the shop called out, "Find out how the war's going," and "Get us some news from Poland," and so on. I waved my hand. I confess I felt nervous as I walked

74

away from the ski shop, across in front of the big gate, past the officers' mess to the Commandant's house standing on the other side of the camp at the north-west corner of the parade ground. It was, like all the other buildings, built of logs with the typical porch opening south to keep the wind and snow away from the front door. As I stepped inside I saw it differed only from the style of the prisoners' barracks in having an inner skin of smooth plank walls, a wooden ceiling and floor, and a stove stackpipe that went all the way up through the roof. For windows it had, not glass, but the same peculiar tough fish-skin stuff which was fitted in all the other buildings. The most that could be said for this skin was that it was windproof and let in light. It could not be seen through.

Igor ushered me in. Ushakov stepped forward towards the door, dismissed Igor and motioned me in. "I have come to look at the set, *Gospodin Polkovnik*," I said in Russian, using the old Russian style of respectful address to a Colonel.

"Yes, of course. I will show it to you." He stepped past me and out through the door I had just entered, looked around and came back in.

The woman sat in front of the stove, which had been placed so that it protruded through the partition which divided the home into two rooms, so heating both halves. The Colonel murmured a conventional introduction to his wife. I bowed and said something formal and she smiled with a small inclination of her head. I found myself staring at her. She was the first woman I had met since I left my wife and my mother in Pinsk. I felt awkward and ill at ease, painfully aware of my ugly clothes, my beard and my long hair which curled over the neck of my jacket. I could not take my eyes off her.

She stood up and I saw she was tall for a woman. She wore a long thick skirt and a dark woollen cardigan over a white, flower-embroidered cotton blouse. Her brown hair, tightly plaited and wound in the Russian style halo-wise around the head, had a live, well-brushed sheen, and I was struck by the clearness of her skin. I was never much good at guessing women's ages, but I think she would have been nearing forty. She was not beautiful but she had that quiet quality of essential womanliness, a way of holding herself, an ease of moving, a way of looking at one, that would

75

demand attention anywhere. I came out of my fleeting trance to find her blue eyes regarding me in a look of frank pity and sympathy. And I turned my head away and saw Ushakov standing in the doorway between the two rooms looking at me in that preoccupied and detached manner of his. "Let me show you the radio," he said.

The inner room was their bedroom and his office combined. Along one wall nearest to the stove was a heavy wooden bunk, at the head of which was a cupboard in which I could see his uniforms hanging. Near it, against the wall farthest from the door, was a solid wooden chest. The bed was to my left as I walked in through the partition door, the chest immediately in front of me. The part of the room to my right was Ushakov's office. Hanging on the wall was a big contour map of Eastern Siberia—an extraordinary production in that instead of place-names there were only numbers. There was also a plan of the camp and a coloured portrait of Joseph Stalin. On a bench under the all-seeing eye of Stalin was the radio, a brand-new, battery-operated Telefunken.

Ushakov gave me a Pushki cigarette, fetched over a kerosene lamp and set it down on a bench near me. I took the back off the set and began running my fingers along the leads, suspecting a loose connection somewhere. Ushakov asked me questions about the set, where it was made, what it cost, how it worked. Hesitantly, I inquired where he had got it. "I happened unfortunately," he answered, "to be in charge of troops in Poland in 1939, and I acquired it there." My mind seized on the use of the word "unfortunately". It tied in with the theory which the prisoners expressed that even to be commandant of a camp in Siberia was in the nature of a punishment. I had the impression then, later to be strengthened, that Ushakov owed his appointment to Siberia to some indiscretion during the Polish campaign.

He went back to the fire and sat down on the polished bench with his wife. I worked on, unhurriedly checking the circuit. After about half-an-hour, I was aware that she was busying herself in the next room, and then he called me to the fire, while she poured out two mugs of tea, saccharine sweetened. The Colonel drank first and then gave his mug to me. I went back to the radio, and as I worked I surprised myself with the thought that I was not going to rush this job, that this was my most pleasant experience

76

since my arrest and that I must make it last. When Igor came to collect me, I explained that checking all the leads and valves was a slow business. "Very well," said Ushakov, "you must come again. I will send for you." He gave me another cigarette and I went off with my escort.

"What's the news?" they called out to me when I got back.

"I haven't got it going yet," I said, "but I'll tell you what's happening when I do."

Igor fetched me again the next day. As I fiddled with the set, they both talked to me. Ushakova was interested in my family, impressed by the fluency of my Russian. I told her my mother was Russian.

"What did you do to get sent here?" This was the Colonel
"Nothing," I said.

"You have twenty-five years, haven't you?"
"Yes."

There was a pause and then she spoke. "Twenty-five years is a long time. How old are you?" I told her I was 25.

The three-cornered conversation was interspersed with odd silences. They sat close together on the bench, I was on my haunches looking over the top of the Telefunken. Surprisingly, Ushakov asked me if I thought Russia would be involved in another war. The last war for Russia, as far as he was concerned, was that of 1914. I mentioned Finland and Poland. "Ah," he replied, "that wasn't war; it was liberation." I wondered if he believed it. I popped my head up over the top of the radio and looked at him. He was looking up at the ceiling and his face was expressionless. He returned to the question of Russia being involved in war.

"In Poland," I said, "it was common knowledge that Goering came to us to get us to give the Germans a corridor through which they could attack Russia. Germany is ready and the attack is inevitable." I gabbled it out fast. I expected to be told I was talking too much. But neither Ushakov nor his wife made any comment.

"Did you find the war very cruel?" she asked me eventually. I told her about the roads choked by fleeing Polish women and children and old men, and how the Stukas came screaming down and blasted them. "That is war," said the Colonel. "When you

77

chop wood somebody is always liable to be hurt by splinters."

It occurred to me that they did not seem very anxious to hurry the repair of the radio. I had found what I believed to be the fault, a loose battery lead. But I just did not want to put the back on the set, connect up and switch on. I thought my visits must then end.

She asked me about pre-war Poland. What were the women's fashions? They were often elegant, I said, straight from Paris. And high-heeled shoes? Yes, I said. They, too, were very attractive.

Two days went by before I was summoned again and meanwhile my workmates chaffed me that I couldn't mend the set anyway and that the Commandant was going to get fed up with the delay.

On this third visit I started straightaway to get the Telefunken working. Ushakov was busy at his desk and the woman did the talking. She asked me about the films I used to see and was surprised to hear that Russian films were banned in Poland. As she talked I switched on. The radio hummed into life and I began to turn the dials. Ushakov left his work and came over beside me. We heard a concert from Moscow. I went from station to station, picking up fragments of news and finally we heard the voice of Hitler, ranting in his own unmistakable fashion, at a youth rally in the Ruhr—I think it was Düsseldorf.

Ushakov gave me a whole packet of *korizhki* tobacco and a sheet of old newspaper. As Igor stood in the doorway waiting to escort me away, he said, "If the set needs any attention, I will send for you again. I am afraid we do not understand how to work it very well." I went back and I told the men all I had learned from the wireless. Their greatest interest was in Germany and the Hitler speech. They wanted to know when I would be going again. "When the set breaks down," I said.

It was now nearing the end of March. I worked uninterruptedly for several days in the ski shop and began regretfully to think that the Telefunken episode was over. Just about that time I came to know a remarkable man named Anastazi Kolemenos. I had seen him come in occasionally to warm himself at the big fire. He was one of the finest physical specimens I have ever seen, over six feet tall, blond-haired and blond-bearded, with curious grey-green eyes. In spite of the privations he had endured, he must have weighed fourteen stone. He was a kind and helpful giant of a man, whose job was to carry the birch logs and split them for use in the ski shop.

I was standing outside the ski shop door watching him this day. I walked across to where he had piled some logs and went to lift one to take it over to him. The end came up easily enough. I tried to get a grip round the middle to hoist it up. It defied my efforts. Then, suddenly, Kolemenos was beside me. "That's all right, friend," he said, "I'll do it." He bent down and swung the log on to his shoulder in one powerful movement. I did not regard myself as a weakling, but this man's strength was phenomenal. I spoke to him, spontaneously told him who I was. Kolemenos told me his name, volunteered the information that he had been a landowner in Latvia, that he was now 27 years of age. The old escape idea came surging into my mind, but this was no place to talk of it. "We will have a talk some time," I said.

"I shall be glad to," answered the giant.

Over the clatter of workshop activity they called out to me, "Your friend has called for you again." Igor stood stolidly inside the door and beckoned. I put down a ski I was testing, dusted myself down, and walked out with him.

Ushakov was there and she was there. He told me the set was not working as well as it did. I tested it and it seemed to function, although the signal strength was down a little. I said he would be advised to get spare batteries. He said he would arrange that. He put on his greatcoat, murmured something to her about having to attend an officers' meeting and went out. There was great understanding between these two and they were completely devoted to each other.

"I will make some tea for you," she smiled. "You can find me a station with some good music." She talked on for a while about the music she liked, praised Chopin but declared her favourite composer to be Tchaikovsky. She told me she played the piano and that having to leave her piano behind was one of her greatest hardships here in Siberia. I looked at her hands, which she had spread in front of her. The fingers were white, long and capable, the hands well-shaped and cared-for. "Those are artist's hands," I ventured. "I sketch, too," she told me. "It is a hobby of mine."

I found her the kind of music she wanted and she talked about herself with a symphony orchestra as the background. She talked

79

to draw me out, to get me to tell her about myself. It was as though she were saying, "This is me, this is my life. You can trust me." I didn't quite know why this was happening to me. I said to myself that in spite of his exalted position here, these are really exiles and outcasts. She, especially, is almost as much a prisoner as I am. She is here only because he is here, and probably the real ruler of Camp 303 is the Politruk.

We sipped hot tea and she kept her voice low. This was the story she told me. Her family had been Army officers for generations before the Revolution. Her father had been a Colonel in the Czar's personal guard and had been shot by the Bolsheviks. Her young cadet brother died of wounds received in the defence of the Smolny Institute. Her mother had fled with her from their home near Nijni Novgorod and when, later, the mother died, she had adapted herself to the new order of life, got herself a work-card and found herself a job. She did well and earned herself a State holiday with other favoured workers at Yalta. And there she met Ushakov. I gathered that from then on he was the only man in her life.

She was very loyal to Ushakov. She did not tell me why he had suddenly been posted from Poland. He went first to Vladivostock and she had no word from him for six months. Ushakova knew some Party people with the right influence. They told her he was going to Siberia in charge of a camp and she strove unceasingly until her friends got her a travel permit to join him.

All the time I was telling myself: She talks to me because I am a prisoner and she is sorry for me and because she cannot talk these kind of things to her own people. Yet, amid lingering doubts, there was the conviction that this was an intelligent, sensitive and most compassionate woman, and this camp, which surrounded her with the evidence of cruelly wasted lives, had shocked her. It was no place for a woman. Ushakova was a Russian, she believed passionately in the great destiny of Russia. But she was also a woman and I don't think she liked what she now had to see, day after day, month after month.

What made me talk about the Ostyaks? I do not know. I think I was embarrassed at her complete acceptance of me and I seized on another topic to steer the conversation away from ourselves. They used to put out food for the Unfortunates, I said.

Those clear blue eyes held mine. 'Do *you* ever think of escape?"
The question panicked me. There was awful danger in it. I had
my mouth open and could not speak. I put the cup down with a
clumsy thump. And her eyes, wide open and blue and candid,
held me still and watched my flutterings of fear.

The quiet voice was going on. "You do not answer, Rawicz.
You do not trust me. I thought you might want to talk about it.
There is no danger in talking to me about it. . . ."

Escape. Escape. It was though she had looked into my mind
and plucked out that one word of danger and longing and hope.
Yes, I wanted to tell her about my perilous dreams. But she had
shocked me into silence. The words would not come.

Then came Igor and I turned to go, disconcerted and miserable,
like a man who has turned his head from the extended hand of a
friend. She spoke coolly and formally. "You will come again if
the set wants adjusting?" My words came in a rush. "Yes, yes, of
course I will. I shall be glad to."

I felt a slow burn of excitement as I waited through the next
few days to see if I would get another call. I met a man named
Sigmund Makowski, a thirty-seven-year-old captain in the Polish
frontier forces. A precise, clear-thinking fellow, fit, active and
bearing the stamp of the Regular Army officer. I marked him
down, as I had marked Kolemenos, but I said nothing of
my plans at this stage. I do not know what I expected of
Ushakova, but at least I thought she would be in a position to
advise.

Call for me she did, and when I had tuned in the radio, dallying
round the dial to pick up some news items for my friends, she
started casually enough to talk of the approaching short Siberian
summer. I took the plunge. "I am sorry about the last time," I
said. "Of course, I do think of those things, but the distances are
so great, the country so difficult and I have no equipment to face
such a journey."

"You are only 25," she answered. "You need not have been
afraid to admit that you do not look forward to the next twenty-
five years in these surroundings. It was something to talk about
between us. I am reasonably well looked after here. We have
comfortable quarters, much better food than yours and as many
cigarettes as we need. But I couldn't spend twenty-five years

here. So escape must be an idea close to your heart and it may do you good to tell me what you think."

So we talked of it as an abstract thing, as though it were being contemplated by some third person. We posed the question: Supposing a man could get out of the camp, where could he head for? The only possibility for such a man, I thought, would be to dash due east the short six hundred miles to Kamchatka and from there find his way to Japan. The attempt would be a failure, in her opinion. The Kamchatka coast was a Number One security commitment and would be heavily guarded. Could he smuggle himself on to a westbound train, maybe find himself a job in the Ural mines and possibly make his way out of Russia later? There would be difficulties of travel and work permits and other vital papers, she said. That was all the exploring we did that day, and it was not until I lay thinking things over on my bunk that night that I realised the one escape route she appeared deliberately to have ignored—south, past Lake Baikal. Whence from there? Afghanistan was the name that popped into my mind. It sounded sufficiently neutral and obscure.

It was the Colonel himself who next sent for me. He genuinely could not work that simple radio set, a fact which greatly surprised me, for he was an intelligent man. He seemed to be a little in awe of it and liked to have me find the stations for him. He wanted news, and as I got it for him in various speeches and bulletins, he said he now felt certain that Russia would soon be involved in war. I don't think he wanted war but in war obviously lay his chance to get out of Siberia and back to the real job of soldiering for which he was trained.

There was no fanciful talk of escape when the Commandant was there. I imagine he would have been horrified to know his wife had ever broached such a topic with a prisoner. When the time came for me to go, he stayed near the radio and she walked behind me to the door. "Don't worry," she said. "You will be all right."

That night I spoke to Makowski. I walked him over to the latrines. "What would you think of an escape?"

"Don't be crazy, man. We have nothing to escape with, even if we got outside the camp."

"I might get a little help."

"If you can, I'm with you. To hell with this place."

Ushakova appeared to be actively enjoying her rôle as conspirator-in-chief. I have been unable to decide whether she ever believed I would really attempt an escape. It might be that all this was an intriguing exercise for the sharp wits of a woman bored by depressing camp life. Some things, even at this distance of time, I cannot answer.

The business had emerged from the abstract. This was Ushakova planning away as the radio gave us one of her favourite Tchaikovsky symphonies. "You will want a small number of the fittest and most enterprising men. You, from your extra rations, will save a quarter of a kilo of bread a day and dry it at the back of your ski shop stove and you will hide it every day. I will find some sacking to make into bags. Skins you will need for extra clothing and footwear. The soldiers trap sables and the officers shoot them. They hang them on the outer wire. The men working outside must grab one a day. No one will miss them. Plan your own way out and then head south. Wait for a night when it is snowing heavily, so that your tracks are covered."

And then, almost as an afterthought, "Colonel Ushakov will be leaving for a senior officer's course at Yakutsk shortly. I would not want anything to happen while he was in command." A very loyal wife, this Ushakova.

I sought out Makowski immediately. "We are getting out," I said. "There will be a little help for us."

"How many men will you want?"

"About half-a-dozen," I said.

"Good. We'll find them. I know one I can personally recommend."

I thought of Kolemenos. "I know one, too. We'll start rounding them up tomorrow."

IX

PLANS FOR ESCAPE

"THERE HE is now." Makowski, standing beside me at the midday break the next day indicated a prisoner standing a little apart from the rest. "Let us wait here a couple of minutes so that you can look him over." The man's shoulders were squared and the shapeless clothes could not disguise that ramrod back.

"You are a cavalry man," said Makowski at length. "You should recognise the type."

"Who is he?"

"He's a Pole. Sergeant of Cavalry Anton Paluchowicz. He's 41, but strong and fit, well-trained, experienced. I'd go anywhere with him. Shall we talk to him?"

We went over and talked. I liked the look of Paluchowicz. He accepted the proposition like a good soldier undertaking a mission of war. He was glad to know I was a Lieutenant of the Polish Cavalry. "We shall do it together," he said. "It won't be easy, but we shall do it."

That evening I came up behind Kolemenos. I tapped him on the shoulder and he turned. He smiled. "Oh, it's you again."

"Kolemenos, I am getting out of here with some others. Would you like to join us?"

He put one big hand on my shoulder. "You mean it? Seriously?" I nodded. "Yes, seriously. Perhaps very soon." The big man smiled happily through his blond beard. "I shall come." He laughed aloud and brought the weight of his hand down twice on my shoulder. "I could carry you on my shoulders if necessary. If we could come all that way from Irkutsk hanging on those bloody chains we can go a long way further without them."

Now there were four of us. We began to plan with a sense of urgency. It was the end of March and I felt we had not a great deal of time. We began to watch things closely. We noted, for instance, that the starting of the dog patrol around the perimeter at night was always signalled by the yelping and whining of the sledge dogs showing their annoyance at being left behind. That signal came only once every two hours. We discovered the patrol always went round anti-clockwise, covering the long south side first. We decided the escape must be through the southerly defences and that therefore we must get ourselves established in the end hut on that side. We began to bribe and cajole ourselves bunks in that hut.

Paluchowicz brought Zaro into the scheme. Eugene Zaro came from the Balkans, a Yugoslav I think. He was 30, and, before the Russians had caught up with him, had been a clerk. "If you want some fun on the way," said our Sergeant, "Zaro is the man." Like an inspection committee, Makowski and Paluchowicz and I stood back and watched him in the food queue. He was a well-built man, below average height, and his almost black eyes had a constant gleam of laughter and mischief. The men around him roared in joyous gusts and Zaro stood there, his eyes twinkling in a mock-serious face. "All right,' I pronounced, "we'll have him."

"I've always wanted to travel, and this sound good," was Zaro's answer to my approach.

"It's going to be the worst trip you ever had," I told him.

"I know," he replied, "but I'm coming with you anyway." There was a pause. "The Russians have no sense of humour. It will do me good to get away from them."

So Eugene Zaro came in and we were five. And we talked about making the number up to ten so that outside we might split into two parties and take different routes to make the job of pursuit more difficult and confusing.

But it was not to be as easy as that. Two likely-looking fellows I approached in the ski shop shied away even from the mention of the word escape. To talk about it was dangerous enough, in their view. To attempt it would be suicidal. They were content with their new-found riches, the daily kilo of bread and the extra tobacco. Why invite disaster and death in a crazy bid to break out? "You are probably right," I said. "It was just an idea that passed through my head." And I went on with my daily chore of drying a quarter of a kilo of my bread behind the big stove to add to the growing store hidden beneath the pile of rejected skis in the far corner of the shop.

Escaper Number Six was brought in by big Kolemenos. He was a twenty-eight-year-old Lithuanian architect named Zacharius Marchinkovas. He was tall, spare-framed, with alert brown eyes. I was impressed at the manner in which he had already weighed the odds against us, and, having found them formidable, decided that the slightest hope of success was worth the attempt. An intelligent, likeable type, this Lithuanian.

When Sergeant Paluchowicz brought into our hushed deliberations the name Schmidt, I thought this must be one of the Russo-German colony who had joined our prison train at Ufa in the Urals. These Russians with German names were the descendants of German craftsmen brought in by Peter the Great. I had read that they settled on the Volga. "Is he German?" I asked the Sergeant. "His name is Schmidt, but I do not know," was the answer. "He speaks Russian very well and easily. He stands apart from the others. He does a great deal of thinking by himself and he gives me excellent advice on everything. I recommend him to you." Makowski and I announced our intention of meeting Mr. Schmidt the next day. "I will point him out to you, then," said the Sergeant with a smile.

He was coming up to the window of the kitchen for his coffee, the last issue of the day, when Paluchowicz indicated him with a jerk of the head. Makowski and I strolled over. My first impression was that he might be too old for the rigours of the adventure we were planning. I judged him to be about fifty. He was well built, wide-shouldered and slim-waisted. His thick hair and beard were tinged with grey. He had seen us coming and, probably because the Sergeant had warned him of the meeting, showed no surprise when I spoke. "We would like to talk to you."

I spoke in Russian. He answered in Russian, "Walk towards the huts and I will join you." He moved on and we walked away.

Holding his mug of coffee, he fell in with us and, clear of the crowd, we stopped. He faced us and smiled. "Gentlemen, my name is Smith. I understand you have a proposition."

Makowski and I stood there, mouths agape. "*Smith?*" We repeated the name together.

"I am Smith, Mister Smith. I am an American." He grinned

happily at our astonishment. "You are surprised, gentlemen."
We just could not believe our ears. His Russian was impeccable.
I could detect no trace of an accent.

"Forgive me," I said at last. "It is hard to believe. How did you
get here?"

He had an easy, patient, almost professorial manner of speech.
"Let me repeat, I am an American. By profession I am an
engineer and was one of a number cordially invited by the Soviet
Government to help build the Moscow Metro. There were about
fifty of us. That was nine or ten years ago. They arrested me in
1936, convinced themselves I was a professional foreign spy and
gave me twenty years." He drank off his coffee. We were still
looking at him like a pair of fools. "Now I'll take my mug back
and we shall walk together to the huts."

Makowski and I followed his retreating back. Poles,
Ukrainians, Latvians, Estonians, Czechs, Finns, the flotsam of a
European upheaval, these we expected to meet in the hands of
the Russians. But an American. . . . Said Makowski, with heavy
humour, "Maybe if we look around a little more we shall find
some English and French." Paluchowicz came over to us. "What
do you think of him?" Makowski shrugged, still following with
his eyes the figure of Smith as he handed in his mug and turned to
walk back. "Herr Schmidt," he told the Sergeant, "is *Mister
Smith.*" Paluchowicz furrowed his forehead in puzzlement. "And
Mister Smith, my dear Sergeant, is an American." It was all over
Paluchowicz's head. He opened his mouth to speak and then shut it.

The four of us walked slowly back to the huts and, as was
the custom, exchanged sentences. That is to say, we introduced
ourselves by name as Smith had done. And he, in accordance with
camp etiquette, asked us in turn, "How long are you in for?"
This question always had its place in first meetings. It was a form
of introduction.

By now, the beginning of April, Makowski and I had got
ourselves bunks near the door of the end hut. Kolemenos had
also managed the switch and the others hoped to join us within
a few days. Telling the Sergeant we would see him later, we
invited Mister Smith into our hut. Sitting on Makowski's bottom
bunk, I cautiously outlined our plans. I told him I had sound
reasons for believing that only the long road south held any

chance of success, although some of the others were still reluctant to drop the idea of the short route east to Kamchatka.

He did not rush to answer. He asked a few shrewd questions. We sat silent as he thought things over. And then, "Gentlemen, it will be a privilege to join you. I agree that the south route is the best. You can count on me."

We sat long with Smith. All our histories, our Russian dossiers, followed a similar pattern. Smith was different. He was the odd man out, and he intrigued us. He told us much, but neither then nor ever did he tell us his Christian name. Later, when we six Europeans addressed one another familiarly by first names, the American was always, as he first introduced himself, Mister Smith to us all, the "Mister" somehow being accepted as a substitute for the name we were never told.

He had a ridged scar curving lividly from right to left from the crown of his head to the nape of his neck, some eight or nine inches long. He received it, he explained, when some scaffolding fell on him during the Metro building.

"Apart from the accident that gave me this scar," he told us, "I had a good time in Moscow for a few years. The work was interesting, I was highly paid, and I found the Russians easy to work with. They had skilled engineers themselves, but key positions went to foreigners like myself. The reason, I think, was that this Metro scheme was a great prestige prospect and if anything went wrong national pride would be saved by having a foreigner as the scapegoat. I was quite happy. I had wanted to see Russia and I was being financially well rewarded for the experience."

In a Moscow obsessed between the wars with its Five-Year Plans, Smith and his friends, installed in well-appointed flats and with money to spare to buy luxuries in those shops where the entry permit was either a Party membership card or a foreign passport, must have been conspicuous. Smith had a car and travelled around freely—a circumstance which must have earned him an underlined report in secret police records. He had a Russian girl friend; the police would not have liked that, either. But they let him go on, working hard and playing hard.

"I never saw the blow coming," he went on. "After a year's work, the Russians, without any move from me, doubled my

88

salary, which had been fixed by contract, to show their appreciation of the steady progress that was being made with the work. From then on I thought I was well in with them."

Smith was in his flat with the girl after midnight one night in 1936 when the N.K.V.D. called in force. They were quiet, determined and most efficient. Smith and the girl were both arrested. He never saw her again. Other occupants of the flats probably never saw or heard a thing. When dawn came Smith was occupying a cell in the Lubyanka—it was to be his home for the next six months. Repeatedly they brushed aside his demands to be allowed to see someone from the United States Embassy.

"What a transition," mused Mister Smith. "One day a successful engineer, the next a professional foreign spy. It seems that apart from keeping a general watchful eye on my activities they had been opening my mail home. The main charge against me was that I had been sending out information about Russia in my letters to my folks in America.

"The trial was secret and farcical. I got twenty years, as I told you. They confiscated my car and all my possessions, so perhaps they got back most of the extra salary they had so generously awarded me.

"I was digging for diamonds in a mine in the Urals. I told them I could, by modern engineering practice, substantially increase efficiency and output. They weren't interested. They kept me on manual labour."

Makowski broke in. "Have you ever thought about escaping?"

"I have been thinking of how it could be done ever since I was first sent to the Urals. I decided I could not do it alone."

Then he questioned us closely about our plans. He wanted as clear and detailed a picture as we could give at this stage. He questioned shrewdly about the distances involved. Had we realised it would be a thousand miles of foot-slogging to the borders of Mongolia alone? We talked, almost in whispers, for a long time, as other occupants of Hut Number One came in past us, stamping snow off their boots, calling out to friends, standing in groups round the three red-hot stoves. I told him we would help him make the move from his hut in the middle of the line to this one. I urged that time was short.

He stood up, nodded thoughtfully. "Goodbye for now," I

said. "Goodbye, gentlemen," he answered, and walked out.

The others readily accepted the seventh and last recruit to the party. There was the practical consideration that he would be useful when we got to the English-speaking world. And Zaro told him, "I would like to go to America when we are free." Said Smith, "I would like to have you all come to America."

By the end of the first week in April we were all in the same hut—a triumph of preliminary organisation. We were gathering an impressive store of skins, most of them pulled off the wires by Kolemenos on his frequent trips to pick up the birch logs for the ski shop. On the grindstone in the ski shop I flattened and sharpened a six-inch nail into an instrument that could be used to cut and pierce holes in the tough pelts. Our final collection included sable, ermine, Siberian fox and, a real prize, the skin of a deer which one of the officers had shot for the pot. We cut long thongs of hide for lacing up the simple moccasins we fashioned in the nightly gloom of the hut. We plaited thongs together and used them as belts. Each man made and wore under his *fufaika* a warm waistcoat with the fur inwards to the body. To protect the legs, we made fur gaiters.

Our acute fear at this time was that we might be betrayed. Our feverish efforts were bound to attract some attention. Had a word been dropped to the Russians, the informant would have been well paid in extra bread and tobacco. But there was no Judas. Those who suspected what we were up to probably thought us mad and left us alone to the disaster they were sure we were inviting. For the more casual observer there was nothing odd about pilfering skins from the Russians and using them to the best advantage. We kept apart as much as possible in the hut and most of our serious planning was done on trips to the latrine trench.

I told Ushakova that I had found six friends. She did not ask me who they were and I do not think she wanted to know. She handed over to me a gift that was to be of inestimable value—an axehead. "That will be on my conscience all my life," she said. "It is the first thing I have ever stolen." I made a handle for it and Kolemenos wore it for safe keeping inside the back waistband of his trousers.

One other priceless article I made in the ski shop was a fine three-inch-wide and foot-long knife. It was originally a section of broken saw blade which I heated in the workshop stove, hammered into shape and ground on the grindstone. The handle was two pieces of shaped wood tightly thonged together by long strips of deerskin. As Kolemenos became the keeper of the axe, so did I take over the custody of the knife. These were perilous possessions inside the camp. The discovery of either would have wrecked the whole scheme.

The problem of making fire was one we already had the answer to. Here, where matches were counted a luxury, there existed an effective, if primitive, method which made use of a thick fungoid forest growth which the Russians called *gubka*, literally sponge. It could be tugged off the trees in sheets. It was then boiled and dried. The fire-making equipment was completed with a bent nail and a piece of flintstone. The dry *gubka*, a supply of which we all carried stuffed into our jacket pockets, readily took the spark from the flint and could be blown into a red smoulder. We all became experts in its use.

The word reached us that in a week's time it would be Easter Sunday. It fell in 1941 on 13 April, I have since discovered. The Sunday before, 6 April, marked the end of our preparations. Our escape wardrobe was then complete with the making of seven balaclava caps of fur with an extension flap down the back which could be tucked into the neck of our jackets. We were all tense and ready to go, worried about our valuable new possessions— the skins, the axe, the knife, the store of dehydrated bread—and fearful that at this point some of them might be stolen.

And on that day Ushakova sent for me and said, "My husband has gone to Yakutsk. That is why he did not attend the parade today. I have made seven bags out of provision sacks. You will have to take them out one at a time." She was perfectly calm. My heart was hammering with anxiety. When she handed me the first of these bags I saw that she had provisioned it, too, and I wondered how possibly we could hide it. I tucked the bag under my arm inside my jacket, stuck my hands in the deep pockets and walked back to the prisoners' lines hunched up and bending over like a man in deep thought. Six times more in the next few days I made that hazardous trip, knowing each time that if any Russian discovered what I was carrying disaster would be sudden and complete. We made pillows of them, covering them with bits of animal skin and moss, and every hour that we were away from the hut we sweated in apprehension.

We acquired in those last few days a discarded and worn soldier's sheepskin jacket. I told the others of an old poacher's trick in which a sheepskin was dragged along behind to put the gamekeeper's dogs off the human scent. We could try the trick ourselves, I suggested. The others agreed.

We watched the weather, so essential a part of our escape plan. We wanted snow, big-flaked, heavy-falling snow, to screen our movements. Monday was cold and clear. On Tuesday there was wind-driven, icy sleet. Mid-morning on Wednesday a lead-grey and lowering sky gave us the boon we sought. The snow thickened as the day went on. It began to pile up round the untrodden no-man's-land between us and the wire. At the mid-day break the seven of us met briefly. The word went round. "This is the day." At about 4 p.m. I left the ski shop for the last time with my *fufaika* bulging with my hoard of bread and the knife-blade cold against my leg in my right boot. We drank our evening mug of hot coffee, ate some of the day's bread issue and walked back to the hut in ones and twos.

There were frequent walks to the latrines as we tensely talked over the final plans. It was Smith who advised that we must not start our break too early. The camp must be allowed to settle down for the night before we moved. Midnight, he thought, would be a reasonable time to run for it. Meanwhile we must try to keep calm. And the blessed snow kept falling in big, obliterating cotton-wool flakes, covering everything.

Zaro it was who had the preposterous idea of attending the Politruk's Wednesday evening indoctrination. We laughed at first and then Makowski said, "Why not?" So we went, all seven of us, leaving our precious, moss-camouflaged bags on our bunks and telling ourselves that now, on this last night, nothing could go wrong. We sat ourselves at the back and the Politruk beamed a faintly surprised welcome at us. We smiled right back at him and tried not to fidget.

It was the most exciting political meeting I have ever attended, although the element of excitement owed little to the speaker. The Politruk, now the camp's senior officer in the absence of Ushakov, was in good form. We heard again about the miracle of the Soviet State, about the value of toil, of self-discipline within the framework of State discipline, of the glorious international ideal of Communism. And what did Comrade Stalin say to his comrade workers on the State farms in 1938? An eager soldier leaps to his feet and quotes word-for-word two or three sentences of this epic appeal. The Politruk gave us it all—Soviet culture, capitalist decadence and disintegration and the rest of it. It was, as far as we were concerned, his farewell speech, and we enjoyed it accordingly.

There was about an hour and a half of it before we stood up to go.

"Goodnight, Colonel," we chorused.

"Goodnight," he answered.

Back in Hut Number One the men were beginning to settle for the night. Smith and Zaro, in the bunk nearest the door, were to give us the starting signal. We all broke up and climbed on to our bunks and lay there. Six of us lay wide awake and waiting, but big Kolemenos in the bunk below me was gently snoring.

I lay thinking and listening to the bumping of my heart. I remembered I had not said goodbye to Ushakova. I decided she would not have wanted me to. The hours dragged by. Gradually the hut grew quiet. There was a loud snoring from someone. A man babbled in his sleep. Someone, barely awake, got up and stoked the stove near his bunk.

Smith tapped my shoulder. "Now", he whispered. Gently I shook Kolemenos. "Now," I repeated.

93

X

SEVEN CROSS THE LENA RIVER

WE SWUNG our bags off the bunks by the rawhide straps which we had fitted for slinging them across our backs. We piled the moss coverings back in pillow form at the head of the beds. "Everybody well?" I whispered. From all around me came the hissed answer, "Yes." "Anybody changed his mind?" There was no reply. Said Makowski, "Let's go."

I dropped my bag near the door and stepped outside. The camp was silent. It was snowing as heavily as ever. I could not see the nearest wire. In the south-east guard tower, our nearest danger, they could not have had twenty yards visibility. We could be thankful that in this place of no piped water supply and no electricity, there were no searchlights to menace us.

The inner wire was a hundred yards from the hut door and the success of the first part of the operation depended on the observation that the frost-stiffened coils did not faithfully follow the contours of the ground. There was a dip in the ground straight ahead of us which we reckoned would provide a couple of feet of clearance if we burrowed through the snow and under the wire.

We went out one by one with about a minute's interval between each. Zaro went first and I prayed he found the right spot at the first attempt. Then the Lithuanian. Then Mister Smith. Then Makowski and Paluchowicz. Kolemenos turned and whispered to me, "I hope they've made a bloody great hole for me to get through." I watched him run off into the night like the others, carrying his bag in front of him, ready, according to plan, to shove it through the gap ahead of him. Then it was my turn, and the palms of my hands were moist with sweat. I took a last swift look round. The men in the hut were sleeping on. I turned and bolted.

When I reached the wire Smith was under it and slowly wriggling forward. Two were through. The rest of us crouched down and waited. Agonising minutes passed as first the Sergeant and then Makowski squirmed and grunted, bellies flat pressed against the earth, under the wire. The big bulk of Kolemenos went head first into the gap and I held my breath. He was halfway through when the barbs took hold on the back of his jacket between the shoulder-blades. He shook himself gently and little pieces of ice tinkled musically down the coils of the wire.

"Lie still, Anastazi," I hissed. "Don't move at all." Someone on the other side had pulled his bag through and was reaching through over his neck to try to release him. The minutes ticked by. I was aware that my jaws were clamped tight and I was trying to count the passing seconds on my fingers. Kolemenos lay very still as the hand worked over between his shoulders. Someone spoke on the other side and the big man went forward again. I let my breath out in a long sigh and followed through. The first obstacle was behind us. It had taken a full twenty minutes.

We knelt down along the edge of the dry moat and looked across to the loom of the first tall wooden fence as Kolemenos slithered in and braced himself against the steep-sloping near side. We used him as a human stepping stone, and as we clambered over him he took our feet in his linked and cupped hands and heaved us one by one on to the ledge at the base of the twelve-foot palisade. More vital minutes were lost in pulling Kolemenos out of the ditch. By standing on his shoulders and reaching out at full stretch, we were able to haul ourselves over the top, and standing on the lateral securing timber on the other side, lean over and help up the later arrivals.

Anchor-man Kolemenos again posed us a problem. Straddling the top of the fence, our legs held firm, Makowski and I leaned head downwards and arms outstretched to haul at him, one arm each. Three times we got his fingers to within inches of the top and three times we had to lower him down again. We paused, trembling with exertion and near-despair, and tried again. His fingers scrabbled for a hold on the top, gripped. To our straining he began to add his own tremendous strength. He came up, up and over.

To beat the coiled wire at the foot of the fence we threw ourselves outwards, landing in a heap in the deep snow. One or two failed to leap quite clear and were scratched as they pulled themselves away. We were in the patrol alley now between the two fences and time was running out. If I had heard the sound of the sledge dogs announcing the start of a patrol now, I think I might have been physically sick.

We ran the few yards to the outer fence and this time shoved Kolemenos up first. We were probably making little noise, but it seemed to me the commotion was deafening. This time I was last up and it was Kolemenos who swung me up and over. In a final mad scramble we leapt and tumbled over the last lot of barbed wire at the foot of the outer fence, picked ourselves up, breathlessly inquired if everyone was all right, and, with one accord, started to run. Round my waist was tied the old sheepskin jacket. I tugged it free, dropped it and heard it slithering along behind me attached to the thong looped on my wrist.

We gasped and choked and wheezed, but we ran and kept running, into the great forest among the looming, white-clothed trees. We ran south, with the camp at our backs. One and then another stumbled, fell and were helped to their feet. The first headlong rush slowed to a steady, racking lope. We jogged along for hours, into the dawn and beyond it to another snow-filled day, our packs bumping and pounding our backs as we went. When we stopped to draw air into labouring lungs, I made them start again. And I made them struggle on until about 11 a.m. when hardly one of us could have moved another pace. I picked up the old sheepskin and held it under my arm. We looked round at one another. Paluchowicz was bent over double with his hands on his knees, his shoulders heaving, fighting to get his breath back. Two of the others were squatting on their haunches in the snow. All of us were open-mouthed with wagging tongues like spent animals.

This place was a shallow, bowl-like depression where the trees grew more widely spaced. We had stumbled down into it and could not, without a rest, have attempted the slight climb out of it. We stood there for about ten minutes, too breathless to speak and in a lather of sweat in spite of the sub-zero temperature. The snow still came down, thinning a little now, and there was a moaning wind through the trees that made the gaunt branches shake and creak miserably. Like hunted animals we were all straining our ears for sounds of the chase. In all our minds was the thought of the dogs. But there was only the wind, the falling snow and the stirring trees.

Up the slope to our left the trees grew more closely together. "We will get up there," I said, finally. "There is more shelter and we shall be better hidden." There were groans of protest. Smith joined in, "Rawicz is right." So we laboured our way out of the hollow and picked on the broad base of a great tree as the location of our shelter. We scooped the snow away down to the tree roots and cleared a space a couple of yards square. We built up the snow around into a solid low wall. Kolemenos cut branches with his axe and we laid them on top in a close mesh, piling on more snow to complete the roof. It was a lesson we had learned the hard way in Siberia: Get out of the wind, because the wind is the killer. The old Ostyak had told me, "Snow? Who worries about snow? Just wrap it around you and you'll sleep warm as though you were in a feather bed."

Here it was that we had our first real look at the contents of our packs. Each man had a flat baked loaf, a little flour, about five pounds of pearl barley, some salt, four or five ounces of *korizhki* tobacco and some old newspaper. All this in addition to the dried ration bread I had managed to save. On the top of each pack were the spare moccasins we had made and the left-over pieces of skin. We crawled into the little snow-house, all jammed closely together, and talked in low voices. There was a discussion as to whether we should smoke. We decided the additional risk was slight and the benefit to jangling nerves great. So we smoked and lay close together in the warm blue fug of burning tobacco.

There was, this relatively short distance from the camp, no question of lighting a fire, so we wolfed some of our bread. And in so doing we made a discovery about Sergeant-of-Cavalry Paluchowicz. He had not a tooth in his head. Eating this hard bread was agony to him. The only way he could cope with it was by soaking it—in this case, where there was no water, by painstakingly kneading it with snow.

"I had a nice set of dentures when they took me prisoner near Belystok," he explained. "Then those bastard N.K.V.D. fellows knocked them out of my mouth and they smashed on the floor. They laughed at that trick but it was no bloody joke to me, trying to get my gums round that prison bread, I can tell you. First thing

97

I do when we get to where we are going will be to treat myself to another set of teeth."

"And have them gold-plated. You'll deserve them." This from Zaro. We laughed, and Paluchowicz joined in, too.

We slept through the remaining few hours of daylight, only one man remaining awake at a time to keep a listening guard near the small opening. Kolemenos went off like a tired child and snored gently and musically. No one had the heart to stir him for guard duty. The Lithuanian Marchinkovas roused us as the light outside began to fade. We ate some more bread, smoked one cigarette each and crawled out. The snowfall had diminished to light flurries and the wind was getting up. It was very cold and we were stiff and sore.

All seven of us knew it was imperative that we should get clear out of the camp area as soon as possible. All through that second night we alternately ran and walked. The stiffness began to leave me after about an hour but I acquired new aches as the bumping pack chafed my back. I swung it round at intervals and held it against my chest. Kolemenos found the axe in his waistband was rubbing him raw, took it out and jogged on with it under his arm. It never seemed to be completely dark but the going was nevertheless difficult through two and three feet of crisp snow, the undulations of the ground masked by close-growing trees. Near morning we crossed a frozen stream, steeply banked on the other side, and when we scrambled up and got away from it into the continuing forest, we made our camp.

For the first four or five days we stuck to this night movement and daylight holing up. There was no sign of pursuit. Hopefully we decided that, our tracks having been well covered by the first night's snow, the hunt had probably been organised eastward as being the shortest and most feasible escape route. Cautiously we congratulated ourselves on the choice of the flight to the south. We started to travel by day, advancing roughly abreast in a spread-out formation and making up to thirty miles a day. Watching the occasional watery sun, reading the sign of the moss growing on the sheltered side of the trees, we held to an approximate course south. Several more ice-bound streams were negotiated and I judged they were all flowing southwards to drain into the great Lena River. It was a time of hardship, of a constant battle against cold and fatigue, but our spirits were high. Most of all at this time we wanted to be able to light a fire and we spurred ourselves on with the promise that we should have one as soon as we sighted the Lena.

After about a week of travel we began to sort ourselves out. The two regular soldiers, Makowski and Paluchowicz, kept close together. Marchinkovas, reserved and serious, but with an occasional unexpected dry wit, was befriended by Kolemenos. Smith, now completely accepted as a kind of elder counsellor of the party, was my own particular companion. The buoyant, fun-loving Zaro, was impartially friendly with everyone and moved happily from group to group. A rare fellow, this Zaro. I saw him, at the end of a gruelling day when we had to flog our aching muscles for the energy to build the night's hide-out, mocking at his own and our weariness by squatting down in the snow, hands on hips, and giving us a lively version of a Russian dance until Kolemenos was bellowing with laughter, tears running down into his beard. Nothing could ever daunt Zaro. Of all the gallant jokers I had met, Zaro was undoubtedly the greatest. He taught us all that the grimmest twists of life were not entirely humourless.

On this race to the Lena we had our first and minor hunting success. We caught and killed a sable which was floundering in the snow. About the size and general appearance of a weasel, it made great efforts to get away as we ringed it, each of us armed with a birch club. It may have been injured. I don't know. But one thud of Makowski's club and it was dead. We skinned it but had not yet reached the stage of hunger when we could bring ourselves to eat it.

On the eighth or ninth day the going was unmistakably easier. The ground was falling away in a long, gradual slope southwards. The bare earth between the trees began to show tufts of the typical tough, rustling Siberian grass, there was more moss on the tree trunks. In the early afternoon the forest suddenly thinned out and we saw the Lena, ice-sheathed and well over half-a-mile wide, at this point already a mighty waterway with still some 1,500 miles to run to its many-mouthed outlet into the Arctic Ocean. We stood, partially under cover, in an extended line, listening and watching. The day was clear and sounds would have carried well, but all was silent, nothing moved. We were then about a mile from the nearest bank of the river on low-lying land which looked as if it might be marshy when the ice broke up.

The American walked quietly over to me. "We'd better stay this side tonight," he suggested, "and cross over at first light tomorrow." I agreed. "We'll turn back and get well under cover." I signalled the others, jerking my arm back in the direction from which we had come. We all turned and started back, retracing our steps for about twenty minutes of brisk walking. We built a shelter and, as darkness came on, we lit our first fire, setting it off with *gubka* moss and small dry twigs which we had carried for days inside our jackets against our fur waistcoats.

The distance already travelled was not, in relation to what lay ahead, very great, but it represented to us a considerable early success, with the Lena as our first objective. Quietly, as the wood smoke curled up into the upper branches of the trees and disappeared into the night, we celebrated with a hot dinner—a steaming *kasha*, or gruel, of water, pearl barley and flour, flavoured with salt. Our only cooking pot was an aluminium mug of about one-pint capacity. We had a couple of crudely-made wooden spoons and the mug was passed around the circle, each taking a couple of spoonsful at a time. When the first lot disappeared— and it went very quickly—we melted some more snow and made a fresh mugful. The Sergeant was allowed to soak his bread in the gruel and we all congratulated ourselves on a magnificent meal. All night long we kept the fire going, the man on watch acting as stoker.

And so, in the half-light of the day's beginning we silently crossed the Lena, mightiest river in this country of many great rivers, and came to the steep bank on the far side. There for some minutes we stood, looking back across the ice. Some of the tension of the past weeks was already falling away from us. In all our minds had been the idea we might never reach the Lena, but here we were, safe and unmolested. We could face the next stage with fresh confidence.

Inconsequentially someone started to talk about fish. It set me on a train of thought and memory. I told the others that in winter in Poland it was possible to catch fish by hammering a hole through the ice.

"And having made the hole," interjected Zaro, "what do we

do next—whistle them up?" No, I explained, the fish, stunned by the hammering, will be forced out through the change of air pressure when the ice is broken through. The others laughed and bantered, congratulating me on my ability as a teller of tall tales. "All right then," I said, "let's try it." Kolemenos went off and returned with a solid baulk of timber and we walked out about twenty yards on to the river ice. Kolemenos wrapped his arms around the timber, Zaro and I took hold near the bottom to direct the business end and we started thumping away with pile-driver blows. Eventually we broke through. The water gushed up like a geyser, swirling icily round our feet. And yes! There were fish—four of them, about the size of herrings. We swooped on them and picked them up. We were as excited as schoolboys. The others crowded round me, slapping my back, and Zaro made a little speech of apology for having doubted my word. Then Smith, looking anxiously around, said we had better not play our luck too hard and should get moving under cover again. We had a drink of the cold, clean Lena water and moved off.

We turned south again, climbed the river bank to the higher ground beyond and headed on the next leg of the journey with Lake Baikal as the immediate objective. The nature of the country ahead was familiar, much like that through which we had marched to the westward to the logging camp. Here there were no great forests such as the one in which we had worked to the north, although trees grew hardily at intervals and crowned the succession of rearing mounds and hill ridges. Stunted bushes and scrub defied the assault of winter and in most places the characteristic brown-green sighing grass flourished almost luxuriously, dancing to the moaning whistle of the Siberian wind.

That first night across the river we spent the night in a copse of trees on a low hillock and lightly grilled our fish spitted through the gills on a skewer-pointed twig, ate sumptuously of this our first fresh food, and finished up with more gruel.

In the morning Marchinkovas, who had gone off to relieve himself a little distance from the camp, came back and beckoned us to follow him. We trailed along at his heels wondering what it was all about. He led us to a small clearing. He said nothing, just pointed. In the shade of a tree stood a stout oaken cross, some four feet high. We crowded round. I rubbed at the mould and green moss and found my fingers following the outlines of an inscription. We scraped away and uncovered the Russian letters for V P, a customary abbreviation of the phrase *vechnaya pamyat* (in everlasting memory), three initials of a name, and the date 1846. We made sure that the wood of the cross was indeed oak and fell to speculating how it could have got here, because all the trees around us were coniferous.

"You know," said Marchinkovas, "we are probably the first men to see this cross since the day it was planted here." Sergeant Paluchowicz put his hand up to his fur helmet, slowly removed it and sank his bearded chin down on his chest. We looked at him and each other. All our caps came off. We bent our heads and stood silent. I said a little prayer to myself for the one who had died and for our own deliverance.

By now the Irkutsk issue of rubber boots had been discarded as worn out. Our feet were still wrapped in the only article of clothing handed out in the camp, the long strips of thick linen. All were now wearing moccasins with skin gaiters wound round with straps of hide. Movement south was at the steady rate of about thirty miles a day and we kept going for a full ten hours daily. Although there had been no sight or sign of other men we rigidly maintained the extended line of advance with the practical idea that if one or two ran into trouble the main party could still press forward. Relations between us were generally more relaxed, we talked more freely and during the nightly halts Smith was often plied with questions about America. From his answers we gathered he had travelled extensively through the States and I remember our being impressed with his description of Mexico and how he had bought there a magnificent, silver-ornamented saddle.

He told us, too, that when he worked in the Soviet mines in the Urals he had met another American he had known in Moscow and so gathered he had not been the only one of the American colony to have been under N.K.V.D. surveillance.

A lucky throw with a cudgel and a feverish scramble in a bank of powdery snow earned us a luxury meal of Siberian hare and added a fine white skin to our reserve store.

The party's hunting successes were accidents. Armed with only one knife, an axe and an assortment of clubs, we were ill-equipped for finding and killing our own meat. It would have been comparatively easy to set simple and efficient fall-down traps such as the camp guards had laid, but the necessity for constant movement left no time for watching and tending traps. There was the consolation that while our bread, flour and barley lasted, the extra good fortune of a few fresh fish and a squatting hare that left its bolt for freedom too late elevated our diet far above the bare existence level of the camp. On a number of occasions we saw the *suslik*, the little Siberian marmot, popping an inquisitive head from the opening to his burrow, but we never caught one. Zaro would make faces at them and whistle.

In matters of woodcraft and hunter's tricks, mine was the opinion always sought. The other six were all townsmen. My happy days as a youth in the Pripet Marshes were often now turned to practical account. I was confident that with an occasional glimpse of the sun and the signs of the trees I could maintain a fairly accurate course due south. I had in my mind, too, a quite clear picture in broad map form of south-east Siberia, dominated by the Lena and Lake Baikal. Let us but find the northern tip of the lake, I told the others, and its long eastern shore will lead us through Trans-Baikal and almost out of Siberia.

This thought of Baikal as a natural guide out of this country of bondage was the goad which kept us going fast and determinedly for the next few weeks.

XI

BAIKAL AND A FUGITIVE GIRL

I FIND IT difficult to remember in sequence the many changes in the face of the country through which we passed. In my mind there are thrown up images, clearly detailed, of stretches of Siberian landscape highlighted and fixed by the memory of some extraordinary incident, like the scenic background to a moment of drama in a play.

From a tree-topped knoll we looked south and rolling away from us stretched twenty or thirty miles of openish country, sliced through by a broad river and melting away in the farthest distance to forested hills. Through scrub, dwarf trees and tufted grass we plodded cautiously for a whole day to reach the cover of the forest. Our way lay through the trees for some days. On about the third day we were enveloped in an early morning ground mist as we started out. We abandoned for once our practice of advance in extended line and pushed on through the mist in a bunch. Somebody hissed urgently for silence. We stopped dead and listened.

Ahead of us and quite near came a shuddering, deep-throated cough, a violent thumping on the ground and a succession of crashing noises as though some heavy body were hurling itself towards us through the undergrowth. We stood as still as a collection of statues. Then I reached down for the knife, Kolemenos swung his axe up to his shoulder and the others purposefully swung their cudgels. The furious commotion stopped. We waited a full minute, straining our ears. Faintly came the sound of choked, laboured breathing. Another minute went by. The uproar exploded again and we felt the vibrations as the earth was pounded. Kolemenos came up beside me. "What is it?" he whispered. "Must be an animal," I said. "Well, it's not coming any nearer," said the big man. "Let's go and look." We spread out and went forward.

Through the mist a few yards away I saw an animal bulk thrashing convulsively from side to side, its head down and hidden from me. I made the remaining short distance at a crouched run. The others came up fast behind me. There, kicking, snorting and struggling, its muzzle flecked with spume and its breath pumping out steamily to join the morning's white mist, was a full-grown male deer. Its eyes as it took the fearful taint of our human scent, were wide with desperate fear, showing the whites. The flailing front legs had dug a small pit in the hard earth. But it was trapped and could not run. The fine spread of antlers was locked fast in the tangled roots of a fallen tree. From the chaos around, from the hard-beaten ground and the fact that the animal was almost spent with its efforts to break free, it seemed that it must have ensnared itself hours earlier. Flailing, kicking, grunting and slobbering, terror of our presence injected into its tiring muscles one last surge of strength. Then it quietened, nervously twitching the off front leg. We looked at Kolemenos and Kolemenos looked at the stricken beast, nodded and moved in.

Kolemenos walked softly round the deer. He stepped up on to the trunk of the fallen tree, balanced himself expertly and swung the shining axe blade down with a vicious swish. The edge struck home where the back joined the neck and the deer slumped, quite dead. Kolemenos jerked his axe free, wiped the blade on his leggings. We all ran forward and unitedly tried to get the head of the animal free. Kolemenos got his shoulders under the roots and heaved upwards, but even he could not release the antlers, and eventually he brought his axe out again and hacked the head from the body. We hauled the carcase into a clear space and I cut it open and carefully skinned it.

The thing had happened very quickly and in the flurry of killing and cutting up we had not spoken much, until Makowski, speaking to us in a general way, but with his eyes on Mr. Smith, said, "What are we going to do with this lot?" My arms bloodied almost to the elbows, I stopped the work of carving one of the hindquarters and stood up. "We had better have a conference," said the American.

Mr. Smith opened the meeting with the statement that we could not carry all this meat and we could not afford to leave any behind. In all our minds was the idea that we had our scheduled twenty or thirty miles to do that day. We tried to estimate the maximum amount of meat we could carry, but it still seemed we could not take it all. Marchinkovas propounded the obvious solution. "We must not waste food," said the Lithuanian. "Therefore there is only one answer to our problem. We must stay here for twenty-four hours and eat as much meat as we can hold. What's left we ought to be able to carry." Zaro, licking his lips, said he was quite sure he could help to lighten the load. "All agreed, gentlemen?" asked Mr. Smith. There was a chorus of approval.

Paluchowicz busied himself gathering wood, laying and lighting a fire while the rest of us built a shelter and completed the butchering. Within an hour we had choice cuts of venison grilling on a wooden spit over the flame and the melted ice and barley gruel was steaming fragrantly with the addition of titbits of liver and tender meat. We could not wait for the joints to cook through; I kept hacking slices off and handing them round. It took a bit of chewing, but it was excellent meat. Paluchowicz borrowed my knife and cut his share into small pieces because of his lack of teeth and we let him later have the first go at the mug of gruel. We ate and ate, the fat of the meat running down into our beards, and we belched loudly and laughed, congratulating ourselves on our miraculous good fortune. We smoked and dozed in the shelter for an hour or two afterwards and then decided we must get to work on the skin.

The preparation of the skin took some time. We armed ourselves with pieces of wood and painstakingly scraped off the adhering lumps of fat. We found that the sandy soil churned up by the stag was also a help in this part of the operation. Faced always with the necessity of travelling light, the big stretch of hide presented its own portage problem. The answer was on the same lines as that for the disposal of the carcase. We made moccasins, fourteen pairs of them. We put one pair on over those we were wearing and packed the spare pair in our sacks. And there was still a piece of skin each left. I carried mine rolled on the top of my sack. We broke off from our shoemaking to cook and eat another great meal, and again at night we fed off venison until our bellies were blown out with food. Not quite so heartily, but still willingly, we ate meat again just before dawn and distributed the best of what was left among our packs.

Somewhere about halfway between the Lena and Baikal we had been making heavy going of hours of climbing towards the upper slopes of a range of hills and towards mid-afternoon entered the cover of woods. The day had been arduous and the widely-spaced trees caused us to wander on tiredly for a couple of hours looking for suitable shelter. At this higher altitude the wind was blowing a gale and it was imperative we got as much protection as possible from it. We found more than we had been hopefully seeking—a long-disused trapper's hut of logs, the main roof timbers hanging down into the interior. We scouted carefully, but there was no need for caution. The place was derelict. Moss and fungus covered the earth floor. We set to work, roughly repaired the roof, got a fire going and slept, each man taking an hour's guard duty.

Zaro was first out in the morning after taking the last guard shift. He burst back into the hut. "Somebody's playing the violin out there," he shouted. We roared with laughter and asked Zaro what new trick he was up to. He was trying to be serious but suffering from his reputation as a humorist. "I tell you somebody out there is trying to play the violin," he insisted. We went on laughing. Mr. Smith suggested Zaro might do a Russian dance to the music. Zaro stood his ground. 'Come outside and listen," he invited. The Sergeant, eyeing him for a sign of a smile, got up to go out with him. We followed. About twenty yards back of the hut Zaro held up his hand for silence. We stood with our heads cocked.

Zaro *had* indeed heard something extraordinary. The description of someone trying to play a violin was setting it a little high musically. It was like the plucking of a string on a double-bass. The note was loud and sustained, dying gradually away. It was being struck about once a minute and throbbed through the trees. We looked at one another in wonderment and started a stealthy general move in the direction of the sound. Fortunately—and quite accidentally—we reached the source downwind of it, and froze. We were on the edge of a clearing, on the other side of which was a tree blasted by lightning. The main trunk had fallen outwards from the clearing without having torn itself completely free of its lower part. At the break about five or six feet above the ground, a long splinter stuck straight up. And as we watched, the splinter was drawn back until it was bent like a bow. Then it was released and the "music" vibrated on our ears. And the performer? A great, black Siberian bear, reared up on his hind legs to his full and impressive height.

Peering round trees we saw him pull at the splinter again and again, standing each time with head on one side listening in comical puzzlement to the sound he was producing. The performance lasted several minutes before he got tired of it and shambled off—away from us.

The incident was good for a laugh for a long time afterwards. Zaro's act, entitled "The Russian Fiddler", was well worth seeing. Incidentally, the bear had a considerable advantage over us on his chosen instrument. We found afterwards that not one of us could haul the splinter back far enough to set up any vibration. It took Kolemenos and two others to reproduce the note. This was the only bear we saw, although the older inmates of the camp had told us they were not uncommon and, especially in early spring, were dangerous to meet. Wolves, the other menace, we never saw, although we heard their howling and often came across their tracks. Our immunity from attack we probably owed to the size of our party.

The weeks slipped by into the middle of May and we noted gratefully the first signs of the short Siberian spring. The wind was milder, there were a few buds on the trees. Overhead we heard the beat of wings and looked up to see geese and ducks flying in to their summer feeding and breeding places. The streams we crossed were still frozen hard and the carpet of snow lay undisturbed, but conditions generally were easier and we felt the worst climatic hardships were behind us.

The last thing we wanted was to meet other men and in this our luck held. We crossed the very occasional roads only after thorough reconnaissance. There were nights when we saw afar the lights of a village or small township. There were days when we saw the faraway outlines of buildings and tall chimneys plumed with white smoke. In these areas we proceeded with extra caution.

At times there were minor outbursts of irritation and temper, almost always at the end of a particularly trying day's march and almost always concerned with the allocation of camp duties before settling down for the night. But they were short-lived. Happily, among the seven there was no clash of personality between any two men. It was not necessary for anyone to impose a one-man leadership. Helpful suggestions from whatever quarter were accepted and acted upon. If there was divided opinion on any issue, Elder Counsellor Smith, by general consent, gave the casting vote and a course once decided on in this fashion was never questioned thereafter. The few altercations about camp duties were usually ended by Kolemenos, who never argued with anybody, walking off and doing whatever had to be done. He always did more than his share without thinking about it, a tireless, generous and altogether admirable gentleman.

Oddly, we knew we were near Lake Baikal a couple of days before we actually saw it. We became aware of the peculiar smell of water, combined with the faint flat fragrance of water plants and indefinable other things that bring nostalgia to people who have dwelt beside great waters. We still had not reached the lake when we came upon a heap of the bones of big fish. There was no water near this spot and we speculated how they had got there. Coming down from the Baikal Range, we began to meet real roads, probably of secondary importance but far better than anything we had encountered since we broke from camp. Borne on the wind from the direction of the lake came the sound of a distant factory hooter.

We came to a high point from which we could look down into a valley and we decided excitedly this must be the beginning of Baikal. Miles away to the west groups of factory buildings caught the eye. The panorama included a view of massive ochre-coloured rocks wearing copses of firs like a savage's dark top-knot. Alongside the water at one point was a huddle of sturdy small wooden houses, beside them a few upturned boats and spaced-out wooden poles such as fishermen use for drying their nets. Visibility was excellent, the air was still and the smoke from the factory chimneys went pencil-straight into the sky. Nothing moved in the fishing hamlet and we wondered if the houses were used only during summer. Far below, between us and the water, there wound a road alongside which were telephone poles with their big white insulators carrying a weight of wires which indicated the presence of a fairly important highway. Our difficulty was to discover at what point we had struck the lake. We talked it over and finally made up our minds that we had swung too far west and were now somewhere near the north-east corner. This meant that we should have to follow the north shore westwards until it turned down to point our route through Southern Siberia.

For upwards of an hour the seven of us squatted there, absorbed in the widespread scene below. Once we thought we heard the hoot of a steamer siren. All of us were in good humour at the thought of having attained another objective on our long trek south. We exchanged opinions, we faced the fact that our food supplies were down to a few scraps, including some small pieces of high-smelling venison. We talked of Baikal and I told the others it was claimed as the world's deepest lake, a great, scooped-out basin nearly a mile deep in parts. I recalled the story told me by an uncle who had fought with the White Russians in Siberia of the disaster which overtook the remnants of an anti-Bolshevik army which had tried to cross the frozen lake. The Baikal was not frozen in the middle and the fleeing men had died in their hundreds. I vaguely remembered reading reports that this vast stretch of water, restless with the strong underwater currents of the many turbulent rivers which fed it, could never be completely frozen over.

Smith finally broke up the session. "Let's go down and take a look round," he suggested.

It took longer than we expected to reach the road. A weather-beaten signboard showed the direction and distance of a town, or village, named Chichevka, which must have been the place with the factories we had seen from the heights. We bolted smartly across the road into the undergrowth on the other side. Between us and the lakeside was a mile of flattish country in which junipers grew in profusion amid oak, ash, birch, lime and willow. Thriving in damper soil were tall, rustling bamboo-like plants. We broke through a fringe of small trees to find ourselves on the edge of a river. I held up my hand and the others closed in from left and right.

We had to decide whether or not to cross. It was only about 150 yards wide but the ice had broken up in the middle channel and the brown water swirled on a swift current. Here we found that all of us could swim. The general opinion was that as we should have to negotiate many rivers from now on, there was no point in delaying our first test. I volunteered to go first and we unwound our yards of rawhide strap from about our waists to make a safety line. Each man had up to seven turns of the stuff around him and the joined line was impressively long. The others kept watch as I trod carefully out on to the ice edge. It gave way suddenly with a crack and I was in and gasping to get my breath. I struck out the short distance to the ice across the channel, reached it and tried to climb up. The ice broke away and I tried again. It seemed a long time before I was able to haul myself out and then I crawled flat on my stomach a few yards before I risked standing. Chilled and miserably wet, I signalled the others to follow.

It was not so difficult for the rest but no less uncomfortable. They came across with the line to guide them, one by one, and Smith, the last over, was hauled over with the other end of the line around his waist. The next time I went over one of these half-frozen rivers I took the axe with me and chopped away at the ice until the blade bit in, using it to help me out of the water.

We ran under cover as quickly as we could and then took off our three garments—the padded trousers and jacket and the fur waistcoats—one by one and wrung as much water out as we could. We put them on again to dry on our bodies and went off briskly towards the lake to bring back circulation to our limbs. We sighted the lake, took our bearings and swung away eastward.

Late in the afternoon we huddled together to make plans for the next immediate stage of the journey. Common sense dictated that to hug the lake verge too closely was to invite discovery by inhabitants of the fishing villages or semi-industrial townships, well spaced here in the north but clustering thicker together on the southern side towards the sizable cities within reach of the Trans-Siberian Railway. The proposal we all approved, therefore, was to bear away north and make our way clear of roads and towns on a course parallel with but safely distant from the lake. We accordingly set off obliquely north-east, aiming to cross the road again farther along. Our clothes were still damp and we moved at a fast pace to dry ourselves off. We had covered about five miles when we saw ahead of us a line of trees marking the bank of another river.

Over to my right Zaro gave the halt and alert signal with upraised arm. I repeated the signal and the advancing line straggled to a stop. Zaro pointed urgently in the direction of the river. I saw something moving between the trees. It could have been an animal or it could have been a man—at this distance of several hundred yards in the fading light it was impossible to tell—but we had to investigate. I went over to Zaro and asked him what he thought he had seen. Zaro said, "It might be a man. Whatever it is, it acts as though it had seen us and is trying to hide." The others crept up to us. "If it's a man," said Makowski, "we shall have to hit him on the head and throw him in the river. We can't risk anyone giving us away." We spread out again, Smith and Zaro on my left, Paluchowicz, Makowski, Marchinkovas and Kolemenos on my right. Crouching low we moved forward from bush to bush until we were able to see that the line of trees was about fifty yards from the river, its waters now clearly visible. About ten yards from the first of the belt of trees I stopped and listened. The others pulled up, too, and everyone peered ahead. Suddenly a figure which had been motionless behind a tree trunk threw itself forward and downward into a clump of bushes. In that flash of movement I saw trousers and heavy boots. I broke cover and ran forward, the others at my heels.

The boots were rubber-soled, felt-topped and knee-length. They stuck ludicrously out from the bush as I threw myself on them and hauled outwards to bring the owner into view. The next instant I was asprawl with the boots in my hands. Kolemenos was breathing heavily down my neck, peering down at a ridiculously small pair of linen-swathed feet and slim ankles. And from beneath the bush came terrified, heart-broken sobbing. We looked at one another, still panting from our run, in sudden embarrassment. Someone whispered in awed tones, "It must be a woman."

Kolemenos bent down, shouldered aside the bush and gently lifted. We all crowded round. It was a girl—a slip of a girl, round-eyed with fright, her tears making clean rivulets through the grime of her face. A few moments ago we had been a bunch of desperate men who could contemplate killing to prevent discovery. Now we stood around, clumsily contrite, like a crowd of romping boys caught in mischief and seeking the words to repair some act of over-rough horseplay. Through her tears she stole a look at my face and cowered back. "Don't be afraid of us," I said in Russian. She looked at me again and her eyes went from me to the other six solemn and anxious bearded faces. She went on crying and I cannot blame her; we must have looked the worst gang of desperadoes she had ever had the ill-luck to meet.

"Please don't cry, little girl," said Sergeant Paluchowicz.

She was still very frightened. She was fighting hard to stop her sobbing. "We won't hurt you," I tried to console her. "We all have sisters and sweethearts of our own." The others nodded agreement.

Everything she wore seemed too big and bulky for her. Her thin shoulders were hunched in a long, wide, padded *fufaika* and her slim ankles emerged incongruously from a pair of heavy padded trousers. Like our own, both garments were of some sombre black heavy material. Beneath the jacket showed the upper half of a well-worn and dirty purple velvet dress, the skirt of which was tucked into the trousers. From two sleeves of a green woollen jumper or cardigan she had made herself a scarf which was wrapped about her neck. Her tear-brimming eyes were very blue. Wisps of chestnut hair strayed out from under a moth-eaten fur hood. She looked like a schoolgirl masquerading in the clothes of a grown man. And because she looked so helpless we stood around silently and waited for her to dry her tears and speak. We were tongue-tied.

She lifted her hands to draw the jacket sleeves across her face and I saw she was holding a little crucifix. She dropped her hands, looked down at her feet and turned her eyes on me. She was standing all but barefoot in the snow—and I was still holding her boots. I bent down and helped her slip her feet back into them.

She spoke then, in a quaint mixture of Polish and halting Russian. "I have lost my way to the *kolhoz* where I work. I am Polish and I was deported here to work." The look she gave us was apprehensive.

Paluchowicz and Makowski pushed forward. I talked and they talked in a rush at the same time. In the gabble of explanation she finally understood we were telling her that we were Poles, too, that we were escaping prisoners, and that she had nothing to fear. Impulsively she flung herself into my arms and cried her relief and sudden happiness. Over and over again she repeated, "God is good to me." The other two Poles awkwardly patted her head and shoulders.

113

It was an emotional scene. Too emotional and noisy for one cool head in the party. Smith had moved apart and had been keeping an anxious watch. In Russian he called out. "Break it up. Are you forgetting where we are? For God's sake let's get under cover."

The group quickly broke up. We moved off to find a hiding-place.

XII

KRISTINA JOINS THE PARTY

HER NAME was Kristina Polanska. She was just seventeen. She had not eaten for two days and she was very, very hungry. We rummaged in our bags and handed her our scraps of food. She ate like a half-starved animal with absorbed concentration, now and again sniffling and rubbing her padded sleeve across her nose. She fascinated us. We squatted on our haunches and never took our eyes off her. Only Mister Smith sat back a little, watching her, too, but with a more detached air of appraisal. Then she stopped eating and told us her name.

"I am not lost from the *kolhoz*," she volunteered. "I ran away. I have been running for many days." She paused. "And you are the first gentlemen I have met since I left my home." She put a lot of emphasis into the word gentlemen.

"Where was your home, Kristina?" I asked.

"My father had a farm near Luck, in the Polish Ukraine," she said. "I last saw it in 1939. I have no home now."

Quietly the American interposed with a question about our immediate plans. It was getting dark, he pointed out, and he thought we should make some distance along the river bank northwards to a point which looked favourable for a crossing early the next day. He suggested it would be senseless to give ourselves another soaking that night. At least we could sleep dry.

There was no argument. We walked for four or five miles along the tree-fringed river. I saw the girl several times looking at Smith. She did not speak to him. I think she sensed that in this calm and thoughtful man was the only likely opposition to her presence among us. We Poles talked to her. Smith said nothing.

It was quite dark when we found a place to rest. We built a hide against a fallen log. We laid down our food sacks for her and she curled up among us, completely trustful, and slept. Ours was a more fitful rest. Throughout the dark hours we took sentry duty in turn, according to our practice. She slept on like a tired child, oblivious of the chill of the night. She still had not awakened when, in the first hint of day, Mister Smith touched me on the shoulder and beckoned me away from the group.

He came to the point at once. "What are we going to do with this young woman, Slav?" I had known it was coming and I did not know what to say. It might be a good thing, I said, to find out from her what were her plans. It was evading the question and I was well aware of it. Out of the tail of my eye I saw Makowski talking to Paluchowicz. They strolled over to us. On their heels came Kolemenos. A minute later the other two left the hide and joined us. "Very well," said the American, "we'll make it a full conference." We talked, but we did not come to the point. Were we going to take the girl with us? That was the only question. The only result of our talk was that we would talk to Kristina and reach some decision afterwards.

We woke her gently. She yawned and stretched. She sat up and looked at us all. She smiled in real happiness to see us. We grinned back through our beards and basked in that rare smile. Busily we fussed around to rake out some food and we all quietly break-fasted together as day began to break. Paluchowicz, clearing his throat embarrassedly, asked her then how she came to be where we found her and where she was heading.

"I was trying to get to Irkutsk," she said, "because a man who gave me a lift on a farm lorry and was sorry for me told me that if I got to the big railway junction there I might steal a ride on a train going west. He dropped me on the road a few miles away and I was trying to find a way round the town."

Her glance rested on the American. He returned the look gravely. Her fingers fluttered to the strands of hair straying out-side her cap, tucked them away in a gesture pathetically and engagingly feminine. "I think I should tell you about myself," she said. We nodded.

It was a variation of a story we all knew. The prison camps were filled with men who could tell of similar experiences. The location and the details might differ, but the horror and the leaden misery were common ingredients and stemmed from the same authorship.

After the first World War Kristina Polanska's father had been rewarded for his war services by a grant of land in the Ukraine under the reorganisation of Central European territory. He had fought against the Bolsheviks, and General Pilsudski was thus able to give a practical expression of Polish gratitude. The girl was an only child. They were a hard-working couple, these parents, and they intended that Kristina should have every advantage their industry could provide. In 1939 she was attending high school in Luck and the Polanskas were well pleased with the progress she was making.

Came September 1939. The Russians started moving in. Ahead of the Red Army "Liberators" the news of their coming reached the Ukrainian farm workers. The well-organised Communist underground was ready. It needed only a few inflammatory speeches on the theme of the overthrow of foreign landowners and restoration of the land to the workers, and the Ukrainian peasants were transformed into killer mobs. The Polanskas knew their position was desperate. They knew the mob would come for them. They hid Kristina in a loft and waited. "Whatever happens, stay there until we come back for you," said her mother.

She heard the arrival of the mob, the shouts of men, the sounds of destruction as hammers and axes were swung in a wrecking orgy among the equipment in the surrounding farm buildings. She thought she recognised the voices of men from the nearest village. Outside in the yard Polanska called by name to some of the men he knew. The appeal came through clearly to the terrified child in the loft. "Take away what you want, but don't destroy our home and land." Silence for a minute or two after this. A growling murmur followed, increasing as the men bunched together and advanced towards the house and Polanska. Kristina heard nothing from her mother, but she was sure she was there beside her father. Someone began to harangue the men. The phrases were violent and venomous. She heard her father's voice once more, but it was drowned in a sudden uproar. Her mother screamed once and then Kristina pressed her hands over her ears and shivered and moaned to herself.

Kristina stayed in the loft for what seemed like hours but she thought perhaps it was not really very long. The men had gone. The house was very still. All the personal servants had fled the day before. Her mother and father never came for her. She thought the villagers might have taken them away. Kristina crept down

117

through the silent house and into the yard. Polanska and his wife lay dead in the yard, close against the side of the house. She crept to them and looked upon them for the last time. They had been beaten and then strangled with barbed wire.

I watched her white face closely as she told of the horror of that bright September morning. She spoke flatly, with little change of expression, as a person does who is still under the influence of profound shock.

"I went back into the house then," she said, "and I picked up some food and wrapped it in a cloth. I ran very hard for a long time."

She did not remember the next few days in detail. Some compassionate people in villages she passed through gave her a night's shelter and some food. She was obsessed with the idea of having to keep ahead of the Russians and out of their hands. Ironically they caught her in the act of crossing the border when she did not even know she was near it. The Red Army handed her over to a civilian court which swiftly sentenced her to be deported to Russia as a *kolhoz* worker in the Yenisei River area of Western Siberia.

More vividly she described her life on the Soviet farm. This was a sharper and more recent experience. Most of the workers were strapping, big-bosomed, tough Russian women, and Kristina was the only Pole among them. On the second day after her arrival she was set to threshing and moving huge sacks of corn. The other women taunted her for her refinement and her weakness. They laughed at her failure to do the heavy work they managed themselves with ease. Aching from head to foot, she would cry herself to sleep at night. Food was poor and the main item was one kilo of bread a day—for her as for the other workers.

But it was not the women who eventually caused Kristina to run. The farm was controlled by a foreman, whose attentions the other women were always inviting. Kristina was frightened of him and tried always to keep out of his way. He was a big fellow, she said, tall, swarthy and powerful. He would occasionally seek out the girl and try out some heavy pleasantries, tell her how different she was from the Russian women and that she needed someone to look after her. And after he had spoken to her the Russian women would joke coarsely, remark on the skinniness of her body, warn her she had better look out for herself.

There came the day when she was told she would not accompany the other workers in the horse-drawn farm cart but would report to the foreman's house "for interrogation". His intentions were obvious from the start. He promised there would be no more heavy work for her if she were kind to him, Kristina panicked, appealed to him to let her go after the others and join them. What followed was a plain attempt at rape. She screamed, clawed at his face and frenziedly kicked out with her heavy boots. Surprised at the fury of her resistance, he relaxed his hold just long enough for her to break away and bolt blindly out and back to the women's quarters. He called vile names after her and threatened that he had means to make her change her mind.

She waited until the light began to fade in the afternoon, expecting all the time that he would come for her, but he did not show up. When she felt that the return of the other women must be imminent, she slipped out, keeping the *kolhoz* buildings between her and the foreman's house, and ran. She slept that night in reeds by a river, and after following the river along for many miles the next day, finally reached a road, and was given the first of two long lifts eastwards by drivers of big farm lorries.

"All Russians are not bad," said Kristina. "These two were sorry for me and gave me some of their bread to eat. The second one told me to try to get to Irkutsk but he could not take me any further."

She looked round at us all and her eyes finally rested on Mister Smith. "So that is how I came to be here," she added.

The American dug his hands into his *fufaika* pockets. He spoke levelly. "We are not going anywhere near Irkutsk; we are heading south around the other side of the lake. What are you going to do now?"

Kristina looked surprised and taken aback. She turned an appealing gaze on the other six of us. We said nothing. We knew what we wanted but were content to let Mister Smith handle this his own way. Her lips trembled slightly. Then she jutted out her little chin. "I am coming with you. You can't leave me on my own."

The American looked over her head for some moments at the river beyond. "Can you swim?"

"I swim very well," she said, and there was no mistaking the note of pride. "In school I was a very good swimmer."

119

Through Mister Smith's grey-streaked beard came the flash of a smile. We relaxed as we heard him tell her, "Forgive me, child, if my questions have seemed to be abrupt. We just thought you might have plans of your own. All we can offer you is a lot of hardship. Our food has run very low and we have a great distance to travel. You must consider, too, that if you are caught with us you will not get off so lightly as you would if you remained on your own. If you want to join us, however, we accept you completely."

"Thank you," replied Kristina simply. "The only thing I wanted was to be with you."

The girl went away from us then into a screen of bushes and in her absence I called for a check on food. All seven sacks were opened up, the rolled-up skins set on one side and the food brought out. We were, as we feared, badly off. There remained perhaps a couple of pounds between the lot of us of barley, a little flour, some salt and a few pounds of almost black deer meat. We decided on strict rationing to one small meal a day until we could replenish our stocks. The only stores item still in plentiful supply was the *gubka* moss for fire-lighting. At least, we had the means of warmth.

Probably each one of us had, in addition to the communal food openly displayed, at least one piece of hard, dried bread, stuffed deep down in his long jacket pocket. I know I had one, and there was evidence later that the others also had this tiny personal cache. There was nothing dishonest or anti-social about it. To hide away bread was a prisoner reflex, a symptom of captivity. A prisoner holding one crust of bread felt that he still had a hold on life, as a man in civilised surroundings will carry round with him a lucky coin to insure that he will never be penniless. It was a measure of the great affection we developed for this waif Polish girl that later on one and another of us would dig out this last piece of bread to allay her hunger.

We ate hurriedly there that morning and decided to make an immediate river crossing. This first hour of daylight gave promise of a fine spring day and we had a common desire to make distance fast and to return as soon as possible to a straight course to the south.

For the girl this first river was a new ordeal. We persuaded her to take off her warm jacket, trousers and boots. I had a moment of great pity for her as she stood with us in the shelter of the trees in her faded purple dress. I went carefully out to the edge of the ice with the line paying out behind me, the axe stuck firmly in the back waistband of my trousers, and I made it fairly quickly across the open channel to the other side. Kolemenos crossed, holding her rolled-up clothes, with some difficulty, above water. Palucho-wicz and Makowski came over together, the girl behind them with the bight of a length of spare line about her, the ends held by the two Poles. The other three followed, one of them bringing the girl's boots. We ran for cover, winding in the line as we went.

Kristina was blue with cold and she could not stop her teeth chattering. Kolemenos handed her her clothes. "Don't stand still, child," the American told her. "Run off from us now and take that dress off. Wring it out quickly, wipe off the water as much as you can and jump into your dry trousers and *fufaika*." She nodded and ran. We stripped off, danced around, wringing out our garments as we did so. The operation did not take long and in our wet rags we waited a few minutes for the girl to rejoin us. She came running, with her dress and underwear under her arm in a soggy bundle.

"Did you see? I *can* swim, can't I?"

Mister Smith grinned. "Yes. I saw." And, aside to me, "The little lady is not going to be much trouble, after all."

We walked hard all through that day, halting for only the briefest rests, and Kristina kept up with us uncomplainingly. The midday May sun was pleasantly warm, helping, with the heat of our exertions, to dry out our clothes. We must have covered thirty miles north-east away from Lake Baikal by nightfall and we slept easier for being back among tall timber.

On the third day after leaving the lakeside, I judged we were in a position for turning south on a route which would take us down to the border, with Baikal lying some fifty miles to our right. It was guesswork, but I don't think the estimate was far out, although it would have been impossible to maintain a truly parallel course. The country was hilly and well wooded and our progress was a series of stiffish climbs, with scrambles down into steep-sided valleys carrying small rivers and streams down to the lake. The valleys ran almost uniformly south-west. Many of

121

the streams were fordable, although the current, swollen by the break-up of the ice, was strong. Kolemenos led the way across these, prodding ahead of him with a long sounding pole.

I marvelled at the way the girl stood it all. I fear we all still had misgivings about her frailty and I am sure she was aware of them. In these early days she never once held us up. She was even gay and happy when we were soured and foot-weary after a particularly trying march. She treated us like a crowd of big brothers—all except Mister Smith. Between those two there grew almost a father-and-daughter relationship. Often in the night shelter she would get him to tell her about America and on more than one occasion I heard him tell her that when this was all over she should come to the States with him. He would gently tease her about her big Russian boots and then say, "Never mind, Kristina, in America I will buy you some beautiful dresses and elegant high-heeled shoes." And Kristina would laugh with the wonder and promise of it.

She grew on us until there was not one of the bunch who would not cheerfully have died to protect her. She would wake in the morning, look at the unhandsome collection around her and say "It is wonderful to see you all. You make me feel so safe." On the march she loved to get Zaro up to his funny business. Even Zaro sometimes was glum, but Kristina never failed to chaff him back to his normal sparkling humour. Zaro, spurred on by her interest, would effervesce with fun. Sometimes as I watched them together, I found it hard to realise we were on a desperate mission, half-starved and with the worst of the journey yet to come. Most reserved of the party was the Lithuanian, Marchinkovas. He talked little and generally only gave his advice when he was asked for it. Kristina would walk alongside him for miles, talking softly and seriously, and then there would be the phenomenon of Marchinkovas smiling, even laughing out loud.

Now, too, the party had a nurse. Kolemenos began limping with sore toes. Kristina bathed his feet for him, tore strips off her petticoat and bound up the raw places between his toes. When my leg wound opened up, she dressed that. A cut or an abrasion was her immediate concern. When the bandages were finished with she washed them through in stream water, dried them and put them away for further use.

Approaching what was probably the Bargusin River, about halfway down the lake, Kristina was herself a casualty. She began to drop behind and I saw she was hobbling. I stopped the others and went back to her. "My boots are hurting me a little," she said. I took them off. The soles and backs of the heels were raw where blisters had formed and burst. She must have had hours of agony. The boots had been too heavy and big for her. All seven men fussed about her while she insisted that she was quite well enough to continue. I bandaged her feet with some of her own linen and then persuaded her to let us cut off the long felt tops of the boots to see if she could get on more easily with the reduced weight. Off came the felt and was stowed away to be used later inside moccasins. But an hour later she was hobbling as badly as ever and we decided to throw the boots away and make her some moccasins.

So I made Kristina a pair of moccasins. I lavished on them all the care and artistry of which I was capable with the materials at hand. The others sat round and watched every cut of the knife and every stitch of the leather thonging. I doubled the soles so that they would be stiff and long-wearing and I lined them with sable. Everybody congratulated me on my handiwork and Kristina planted an impulsive kiss right in the centre of my forehead.

We began to feel the girl was good luck to us. We suffered no real slow-down until we reached, at night, only five days after turning south at the lake tip, the Bargusin River. The trouble with all the bigger waterways was that we had to spend extra time reconnoitring for the best position to attempt a crossing. We discovered the next day there were three fair-sized rivers in our path. Having crossed the first we encountered the second after only an hour's march. The third, and biggest, held us up three hours later and we wasted hours surveying it and eventually negotiating it. We guessed that all three rivers must join to the westward to enter the Baikal Lake as the main Bargusin River. We climbed a hill on the far bank of the third river and lit a fire to dry ourselves out. We were all dog tired and very hungry.

About this hunger business, I found that the real pangs did not hit me for about eight days. All the others would in the meantime have been suffering badly. But when I was attacked by the pains of starvation I was worse affected than any. We made a little *kasha* with the barley that night, but the quantity was so small that it was almost worse than nothing at all. We could think of little else but food. There were suggestions that we should creep up on a farm or smallholding and steal something, but even in our extremity we had the great fear of jeopardising the whole escape by bringing ourselves to the notice of the people who lived in the country. If we were determinedly hunted some of us at least must be recaptured.

Kristina was fast asleep even while we were talking.

The Sergeant looked down on her. "Let us sleep. I think she will bring us luck tomorrow."

"Let us hope so," said his friend Makowski.

XIII

ACROSS THE TRANS-SIBERIAN RAILWAY

THE BARGUSIN crossing took place at the end of May and was the last of the major water hazards. On the south bank the Siberian summer seemed to be waiting for us. From the northern tip of Baikal we had been favoured by exceptionally mild spring weather, dry and quite rainless. Now the sun beat down on us, all was green, there were flowers and the birds were back from their distant migrations. In six weeks we had walked out of the bitter tail-end of Central Siberian winter into the warm embrace of the Southern summer, where village orchards in the distance were gay and beautiful with blossoming cherry and apricot trees. Sleeping out became less of an ordeal even when it was considered prudent not to risk lighting a fire. During the day we were forced to discard our fur waistcoats but we put them on again after sunset to protect us against the night's chill.

For a full two days after the Bargusin we ate nothing and the thought of food obsessed all minds. Then it was that we saw the horse through the trees betraying its presence with restless movement in the shafts of a crude sledge. It had scented our approach and obviously did not like what it smelt. Zaro and I went forward for a close look. The horse turned the whites of its eyes over its shoulder towards us. It had every reason to suspect our intentions. We were quite ready to eat horsemeat.

Zaro and I saw it at the same time—an old single-barrelled twelve-bore shotgun, stock and barrel held together by windings of copper wire. It lay across the sledge alongside a little leather pouch which we guessed to be for the ammunition. The thought struck me hard. We must get that gun before the owner can reach it. I ran forward with Zaro and whipped it quickly under my arm, barrel pointing down. I waved the others forward. Kristina, with Mister Smith's arm protectively about her shoulder, stood well back as the rest of the party came up to Zaro and I.

Kolemenos went towards the horse to talk to it and to try to quieten its restiveness, but the animal shied from him.

The man must have been quite near, near enough to hear the nervous movements of his horse. We faced him in a tense bunch. He was about sixty, a solid, broad-shouldered woodcutter, his big axe held on his right shoulder. He was heavily bearded but both his beard and long hair were neatly trimmed. His approach impressed me. He saw us but his slow, deliberate walk did not falter. His eyes looked steadily ahead and took in the fact that I held his gun under my arm. He gave no sign of fear or alarm. He went to the horse's head, ran his hand through the mane, turned aside and swung the blade of his axe into the bole of a tree, where he left it.

He looked at me and beyond me to where the girl stood with the American, "Who are you?"

Smith answered, moving forward as he did so. "We are prisoners escaping. We shall not harm you. We only want food."

"Times have changed," said the man. "At one time you would have found food waiting for you, and no questions asked."

There was a simple dignity about the man. He looked us all over with easy frankness. He turned his head towards Kristina again and I thought he was going to ask us about her. But he said nothing. Instead he walked around the horse's head and reached down to the sledge for a long, slim sack which he picked up. His fingers busied themselves with the leather thong around the neck. "You don't have to worry about me," he said. "I live alone and I am the only man for miles around here."

From the sack came treasure. A loaf of dark brown bread. Four smallish dried fish. A thick, mouth-watering hunk of salted fat pork. From his belt he took a long hunter's knife. These were the provisions of a man who was intending to be away from his home for a whole day and it was evident he had not yet eaten. We watched his performance with concentrated attention. Carefully he cut off one slice of bread and one slice of salt pork which he replaced in the sack. He motioned to Kolemenos, positioned nearest to him. Kolemenos took a couple of paces forward and the woodcutter put into his big hands the loaf of bread, the lump of pork and the dried fish.

Kolemenos stood for so long looking down at the food in his

hands that eventually I said to him, "Put it in your bag, Anastazi, and we'll share it out later."

The sound of my voice caused the Russian to turn towards me—and to the gun I was holding. There was an unspoken question in his eyes. I walked over to Smith and we talked about the gun. We agreed the thing would be useless to us. We could not hunt with it because the noise of it would attract attention to us, especially in the well-populated southern areas we were now approaching. Nevertheless, security demanded we should not leave it with the woodcutter. Paluchowicz and Makowski added their opinions and the final decision was that we could not afford to take the slightest risk of the gun being used against us or as a signal to summon assistance.

I faced the Russian. "We are sorry, old man, but we have to take your gun with us."

For the first time he appeared perturbed. He lifted his hands as though to appeal to us, dropped them again. "It will not be safe for you to use it," he said. "I understand the way you feel. Hang the gun on a tree somewhere and perhaps one day I shall find it."

We turned to go. Once more he looked at Kristina. "Good luck to you all," he called after us. "May you find what you seek."

We moved on for about an hour without much talk, all of us feeling a nagging sense of guilt at having taken that shotgun, a thing of inestimable value to a man like the woodcutter.

"Well," said Zaro eventually, "the old man still has his horse." We laughed at that, but felt no better for it.

About five miles from the scene of the encounter I hung the gun on the low branch of a tree overhanging a faint track, having first bound a piece of deerskin round the breech. It was the best I could do.

The food remained untouched until the day's march ended at nightfall. Kolemenos divided it into eight portions. So small was each lot that I could have bolted mine in a couple of minutes and still remained hungry. But the well-developed instinct of hoarding food against the possibility of even worse trouble prevailed with all of us. We decided to use what we had as an iron ration spread over three days—a little for this night and the two following nights. Kristina listened to our talk and ate as we did, one-third of her small store. She looked very white and tired that night, I remember.

In spite of the natural preoccupation with food, progress remained good as we pressed south over a succession of low ranges.
The farther we went the more the signs of human settlement
increased. Our method was to approach the top of each hill warily
and scout from there the country ahead. Frequently we saw
people moving about in the distance. We swung off course to
avoid roads along which went telephone poles—always the
mark of an important route—and which carried a fair amount of
lorry traffic. On other occasions we heard men calling to one
another and the clatter of tractors. There was often the sound of a
not-far-distant factory hooter.

Daylight travelling was getting hazardous. One day after the
last of the woodcutter's food had gone, we sat down to review
our situation. This was a day, I recall, when Kristina had been
unable to keep up with us. Several times she had slipped away and
held us up. There had been good-natured grousing. She was away
from us now as we discussed plans for covering the dangerous
terrain between us and the border.

"What is the matter with the little girl?" asked the Sergeant
suddenly.

I turned rather sharply on him. "There is nothing the matter
with her that a day's rest won't cure. Don't forget she is a woman.
All women become unwell. Have you forgotten?"

Paluchowicz's face was a study of consternation. "I hadn't
thought of that," he said slowly. Nor had the others, apparently.
"The poor child," murmured Makowski.

Mister Smith spoke up. "Obviously we shall have to revert to
night marches very soon. We might as well start the new scheme
now, and Kristina can have her rest. Slav, you are the youngest of
us. You have a quiet word with her and tell her we won't start
until she feels quite fit to go."

I moved away from them and met her as she came out from
among the trees. "Kristina, we are all going to rest for a day and
then start travelling at night."

"Is it because of me?" There was a bright pink spot in each
cheek.

"No, no. It will be safer at night."

"I have been holding you back today. I am very sorry. But I
could not help it, Slav. I am very tired today."

128

"I understand. Please don't worry."

She turned away. "You are very kind, Slav. You are all very kind. Thank you." And I led her back to the others. And everybody was immediately talkative in an elaborately casual way. Then she sat down beside Mister Smith and said, "Tell me some more about what the women wear in America." He smiled and talked. She listened without saying a word, her chin on her knees.

The new arrangement was pleasant. We slept warm during the heat of the day and had the light of the moon to guide us through the cool of night.

It was in bright moonlight that hunger forced us for the first and only time to raid a village. The scattered lights of houses about a mile and a half away stopped us on the crest of a rise. Clear to us came a single, thin squeal of a pig.

Zaro made a sucking noise through his lips. "My mother used to make beautiful pea soup with a pig's tail in it."

Kolemenos touched my shoulder. "Let's go and find that pig."

We weighed the risks. We had to eat. Smith offered the strongest opposition, then gave in. The pig-hunting party was selected—Kolemenos, with the axe, I with the knife, and the Lithuanian Marchinkovas. The others were to skirt the village off to the right from where we stood and make for a clump of trees showing up sharp on the skyline about a mile away, there to await us. It was understood that if they heard any commotion in the village which might indicate we were in trouble, they were to get away from the neighbourhood as quickly as possible.

The big Latvian and I set off, Marchinkovas following us a few yards behind. We made a beeline in the direction from which we thought the squeal had come and came to an orchard of young trees on the fringe of the village. Grass grew thickly among the trees.

At the edge of the orchard we left Marchinkovas on sentry duty and started a hands-and-knees crawl towards a small, barn-like wooden building at the other end. Kolemenos whispered close to my ear, "I smell pig." We came up off our knees in the shadow of a pile of cut logs. "Don't touch them," urged the big man, "or they'll all roll down with a hell of a clatter." We looked up to the roof of the building to make sure it was not after all a human dwelling place. We were reassured. There was no chimney.

I crept forward and flattened myself against the side of the building with my ear pressed against the wood. I could hear the pig moving around in rustling straw. He had scented me, too, and was snuffling at me inches away on the other side. Kolemenos ran from behind the wood-pile and joined me. We felt along for a door. There was none. "It must be around the other side," I hissed at him. The other side was the side of the village and its few lighted windows.

I found the door on the other side. It opened by a simple latch and creaked and groaned for lack of oil as I sweated to inch it open. Kolemenos squeezed in after me into the blackness. I moved over to the far side where I had heard from outside the pig moving about. By feel I discovered a small gate leading to a penned-off corner. I jumped as the pig grunted a foot away from me and brought its snout against my leg. Kolemenos came from behind me, slipped his powerful arms gently around the animal and gave a tentative heave to test the weight. "Too heavy to carry," he said.

There was only one alternative. We had to persuade the pig to come with us. "Make friends with it," I whispered. "Tickle its belly. Then get behind it and be ready to give it an occasional push." Kolemenos got to work and I got to work. The pig grunted with pleasure. I took it by the ear and started towards the door. Kolemenos encouraged it from behind. There were breath-taking seconds of indecision before it moved. We went out, shutting the door after us, got into and through the orchard, crouching low and murmuring endearments to keep the animal in the right frame of mind to stay willingly with us. A white-faced Marchinkovas met us at the top of the orchard and fell in behind us to cover our retreat.

With the luck of desperate men we made it. About a hundred yards from the rendezvous with the others, Kolemenos dispatched the pig with one swift axe blow. It died soundlessly. I felt a sharp pang of regret. It had been a very trustful pig. We worked fast, gutting the carcase in the moonlight and crudely cutting it up into pieces that could be carried by the seven men. The others had seen us and now came up. There were congratulations all round. It had been a nerve-racking hour or more for those who waited.

The killing had taken place only about three-quarters of a mile from the village and the signs could easily be found in the morning. There was an extreme urgency about putting as much distance as possible behind us before daylight. We were jogging along most of the hours before the sun began vaguely to show in the east. We climbed a rock-strewn hill and when we had almost despaired of finding a hide-out stumbled finally on a dank cave with a narrow opening well screened by dwarf trees.

As the sun came up we had a clear view across a plain to a long ridge a couple of miles away in the direction from which we had come. There were no signs of life, but we took great care not to expose ourselves. The meat-heavy sacks were dropped well inside the cave. Anxiously we deliberated what to do with the pork. In this June warmth it would not long remain eatable and we knew it must be cooked quickly. The solution again must be to gorge as much meat as we could while it was fresh-cooked. There was no alternative to the risk of lighting a fire.

The fire was set going with the driest wood we could find well back inside the cave. Kristina turned the long stake on which the joints of pork were spitted. The fire spluttered and hissed as the sizzling fat dropped on the burning wood. A delicious smell of roast pork and wood smoke filled the cave. Meanwhile Zaro and Marchinkovas were away with the metal mug searching for water. They were away for so long that we became worried. When they returned Zaro explained that they had walked about half-a-mile before they found a thin trickle of water among the rocks and then had had to sit patiently waiting while the mug filled.

Throughout that day we cooked and ate and slept, maintaining one man on sentry duty in approximately two-hour shifts. By mid-afternoon I was in the throes of the most racking stomach-ache. Smith, Paluchowicz and Makowski were also rocking in agony, holding their clasped hands across their stomachs. All of us suffered in greater or lesser degree from the effects of loading our digestions, idle for days, on the rich fattiness of half-cooked pig-meat. Towards evening the cramping pains eased and we drove ourselves to eat more.

Someone, I have forgotten who, put up the suggestion that we should try to smoke the meat we were to carry with us so as to preserve it. Dusk was falling as we piled on the bright flames green juniper boughs. The smoke billowed up causing an epidemic of

131

coughing and streaming eyes. For a couple of hours we smoked the lumps of meat until it turned a patchy brown. Then we packed it in our sacks and set off on the night march. As we left the cave I was doubled up by another spasm of pain and felt I should have to retch. The trouble persisted at intervals for many hours.

At this stage of the journey I knew we must be within a week's travel of the border. The knowledge made us edgy, silent and exaggeratedly watchful. We spent up to an hour scouting the position ahead before crossing a stretch of open ground or one of the many shallow streams across our route, despite the fact that the chance of discovery at night must have been remote. I had the feeling that we were moving among hostile people and that the odds were that we must at some time run into some of them. More imminently than the frontier I feared the crossing of the Trans-Siberian Railway. Already we were near enough to have heard in the far distance the passing of trains. Mister Smith shared my fears.

"The railway will be heavily patrolled," he said anxiously.

"We will cross at night," I replied.

It was difficult to sleep during the day. There was no need to post sentries. Everybody was alert. Only Kristina seemed to enjoy peace of mind. Her trust in us was absolute. She slept while we worried and, knowing that the trail must become progressively more arduous, I was glad to see it. She was vastly entertained one early morning to see in the distance a train of camels, loaded with cotton, moving slowly on their way less than two miles away from our hiding-place on a scrub-covered ridge. She had never seen camels before. Commented Zaro, "From reindeer to camels —now I have seen everything."

From high ground we saw the Trans-Siberian Railway through the clear air of a June morning five miles distant from us. Lying near the track and separated by four or five miles were two small villages; on the outskirts of each, hard against the side of the tracks, was a signalman's or maintenance man's stone house. On our side of the railway, the northern side, was a protective belt of trees, beyond which could be seen some kind of fence, both obviously having the common purpose of preventing snow from drifting and piling up on the line. All day long we watched. Several long trains passed in both directions. About midday a Red Cross train steamed west. An hour or so later a heavy freight train chugged from the east and we nudged each other at the sight of the heavy guns it was carrying on low-slung bogies. Some of the others dozed off from time to time during the day but the American, like me, was too restless and nervous to rest.

The advance towards the railway was made immediately after dark, with Paluchowicz and Makowski out on each flank as a special security patrol. The girl stayed close beside Smith while Kolemenos, Marchinkovas, Zaro and I fanned out a few yards ahead. It took us about an hour and a half to reach the screen of trees and we waited squatting on our haunches there for the two Poles on the flanks to edge their way into us. They had seen nothing suspicious, they reported.

"Right," I said. "Marchinkovas will come ahead with me to the railway. The rest of you will follow on to the edge of the trees where you can see us and wait until we signal you on."

The fence offered no difficulties. At the foot of the embankment there was a ditch. We climbed into and out of it. We crawled slowly up on to the tracks and lay there listening. I put my ear to the nearest metal rail. There was no sound. I stood up for a second, faced the trees and flapped my arms. I lay down again beside the Lithuanian and spent palpitating minutes awaiting the arrival of the rest of the party. Straining my ears for any warning sounds along the line, I heard every move of the approach of the others. I thought sickeningly they were making enough noise to be heard a mile away. It was the girl who came and crouched beside me. "All right?" I whispered. "Yes." I looked round. Everybody was there. I looked across the shining steel rails and listened for a few more seconds.

"Come on," I jerked my arm, jumped to my feet and leapt forward, taking Kristina with me by the elbow. There was an agitated scramble down the embankment on the far side and then we were running like crazy fools. We had covered about a hundred yards when someone shouted, his voice sharp with panic, "Down, down!" I glanced over my shoulder and saw the lights of a passenger train. I dropped, pulling the girl down with me. We all went down and hugged the ground as the train thundered by. It had been a near thing. If anyone on the train had seen us I am quite sure we should have been ruthlessly hunted down.

133

The morning found us after hours of hard travel basking in sunshine on the secluded bank of a clear-water river. It teemed with fish, but we might as well have been onlookers at an aquarium because we knew no way of catching them. We lay about for a while and then Smith said he thought it better if we got over the other side as soon as possible. Unlike the rivers of the Baikal Range, the waters of this one moved slowly and were warm. The swim across was pleasantly refreshing.

The country on the south side of the river was fairly flat and gave us good cover. It was criss-crossed by shallow streams and it was at one of these a couple of mornings later that Kristina suddenly said, "I would like to wash my clothes." We all agreed it was an excellent idea. Kristina walked away from us down the stream carrying her shoes and splashing her feet in the water until she disappeared from sight. We stripped off and started our laundering. All of us were infested with lice and I derived a savage pleasure from holding my clothes under the rippling stream in the hope I could reduce the army of parasites which had lived on me for all these months. We beat our clothes with stones and then trod some of the filth out of them. A couple of hours passed while the sun dried our clothes as we washed ourselves and stretched out naked in the long grass. With a shock we heard the girl call a warning of her approach and dived for our trousers and just managed to scramble into them as she appeared.

Kristina looked as though she had been scrubbing herself. Her face was shining. She had been doing something to her hair, too. The chestnut tints glinted in the sun. She had contrived to persuade it into some kind of order and had carefully plaited the long ends. Keeping a straight face and holding herself erect like a dowager at a tea-party she greeted us. "Good afternoon, gentlemen. Were you expecting me?" We all laughed at that and completed our dressing. And Mister Smith went away and picked a small posy of some pink flowers and gravely handed them to her. "You look beautiful, my child," he told her. Kristina smiled radiantly. It must have been one of her happiest days.

We were very near the border when we ran into the two Buryat Mongols. There was no avoiding the meeting. We saw one another at the same moment at a distance of not more than fifty yards and there was nothing to do but continue towards the

134

pair. One was middle-aged, if one can judge the ages of these people, the other was definitely a young man. They could have been father and son. They stopped and waited for us to come up to them and grinned widely and nodded their heads. They bowed together as we came to a halt.

The conversation was embroidered and ornamented with politenesses and I took the pattern from them. They spoke slowly in Russian. They inquired solicitously whether our feet carried us well in our travels. I assured them our feet had carried us well and returned the inquiry. The older man was naively curious to know about us.

"Where do you come from?"

"From the North—Yakutsk."

"And where do you travel to?"

"We travel very far to the South."

The old man looked shrewdly at me from beneath his wrinkled lids. "You go perhaps to Lhasa to pray."

I thought that an excellent idea. "Yes," I replied.

But the old man hadn't finished. He looked us over carefully. "Why do you have the woman with you?"

A bit of quick thinking here. "She has relatives who live on our way and we have promised to deliver her there."

The two Mongols exchanged smiling glances as though approving of our protection for the girl on her journey. Then both dug their hands in their deep pockets and brought them into view clutching fistfuls of peanuts which they cheerfully handed round.

Each in turn wished us that our feet carried us well and safely to our destination. They turned away together and walked from us. We waited to see them out of sight. They had gone only a few yards when the old man turned back alone. He walked straight up to Kristina, bowed and gave her a handful of peanuts for herself. He repeated his good wishes to her and to us all and left us beaming goodwill.

When they had gone we set off at a fast pace. We were too near the frontier to take chances now.

XIV

EIGHT ENTER MONGOLIA

PHASE ONE of the escape ended with the crossing of the Russo-Mongolian border at the end of the second week in June. It was notable for two circumstances—the ease of the crossing and the fact that we stepped out of the Buryat Mongolian Autonomous Republic of the Eastern Siberian Region of the U.S.S.R. with nearly a hundredweight of small early potatoes pulled out of a field only a few hours from the frontier. The timing of the potato field raid—at dawn on the day in which later we were to make our exit from Siberia—was particularly gratifying. I felt that, having gone into captivity with nothing, we were leaving with a valuable parting gift, even though the donors were unconscious of their generosity.

We reached the crossing point in late afternoon when dusk was deepened to premature darkness by massing black clouds heavy with rain. Far-off thunder rumbled like the uneasy mutterings of a troubled giant. The air was still, the atmosphere hot and oppressive. As far as the eye could see nothing moved. There was nothing to challenge our progress. The dividing line was marked by a nine-feet-tall red post surmounted by a round metal sign carrying the Soviet wheatsheaf, star, hammer and sickle emblems over a strip of Cyrillic initials. To east and west one more post was visible in each direction, so spaced in accordance with the contours of the country that an observer at any one post could always see two others.

I stepped round the post to see what might be inscribed on the other side of the plaque, but the reverse was blank. There was sudden laughter as Zaro called out, "What's it like in Mongolia, Slav?" He cavorted across to me with a hop, skip and a jump. The others followed with a rush. We pranced and danced, slapped one another on the back, pulled beards and shook hands. Kristina ran round, kissed each one of us in turn and cried with happiness and

136

excitement. Mister Smith put a stop to the noisy rejoicings by pointedly swinging his potato-filled food sack on to his back and moving off. We ran after him, still laughing.

"Let's get away from this place," he said, "as fast as we can go. We can't be sure how far below this border Russian influence extends. We don't know where we are and we don't know where we are going."

We walked fast after that, our sacks bumping against our backs. Behind us the frontier markers were swallowed into the distance and the darkness. The American had started a train of serious thought. I estimated we had covered 2,000 kilometres—about 1,200 miles—in not much more than sixty days. It was a feat of speed as well as endurance.

Paluchowicz broke in on my thoughts. "How far do we have to travel now?"

I thought about it. "About twice as far as we've travelled already," I guessed. Paluchowicz grunted his dismay.

Here it was that we first discussed seriously where we were going. Up to now we had thought ahead no further than the escape from Siberia. Back in the camp I had talked, without any great conviction, of making for Afghanistan. It sounded a safe, out-of-the-way small country where we might be received without too many questions asked. Now we began to turn our thoughts towards India. And the key to this, I think, lay in the talk we had a day earlier with the two Mongols. Lhasa. It was a word we could use in a country where few knew our language, a sound which could be understood and would always evoke the response of a flung-out hand to indicate direction. We talked mainly of Tibet in that first hour. India then seemed too far to contemplate.

The American spoke truly when he said we did not know where we were. We had no maps and there was no one to tell us. I have tried in recent years by reference to maps to plot our probable course, but the probable could err from the actual by as much as a hundred miles. Let me say, then, that I think we entered Outer Mongolia at a point which led us straight into the Kentei Shan mountains, that in traversing the range we must have borne west of due south to pass to the west of the only big city of the area, Urga, or, as it is now known, Ulan Bator. This theory fits in with the lie of the land as we found it, the hills, the cultivated plains, and the many rivers carrying loaded sampans. It would explain where the boatmen were going: Urga is at the confluence of three rivers, each of which has tributaries.

We were climbing steadily into the mountains two hours after leaving the border. Sweat oozed from us. The thunder spoke out nearer and nearer and a warm, sighing wind blew up from nowhere, rapidly increasing in strength as we plodded on.

Around midnight the gathering storm exploded. The first overhead thunderclap came like a near-at-hand battery of long-range artillery firing a simultaneous salvo. It was an assault on the ears. Lightning streaked and blazed across the black heavens while the thunder rolled, crashed and reverberated about us. A few large raindrops urged us to look for cover but the lightning revealed only a wilderness of rocky slopes. The torrent was upon us as we groped in the tumult. The rain dropped down by sheer weight, its vertical fall unaffected by the whining wind. My clothes were soaked in a matter of minutes. Streams of water trickled down the back of my neck inside my jacket. It was the worst electrical storm I have ever experienced.

We lasted that night out, the eight of us, in a shallow crevice between two smooth rocks. Only the innermost couple enjoyed any degree of comfort. The girl, in the most favoured position, huddled unspeaking in her wet clothes throughout the unending dark hours, shivering and bewildered at the unabating fury of the storm.

It was a relief to get moving at first light. The rain sheeted down all through the day as though it would never stop. It went on teeming throughout the next night and until evening of the second day. Then the downpour ceased as spectacularly as though someone had turned a tap off in the heavens. In the morning a hot sun transformed our dreary world and steam rose in clouds from the rocks. We dried our clothes and again began to take an interest in our position.

The continuing ascent was tiring but not difficult. The fifteen to twenty pounds of potatoes each of us carried did not make the effort any easier but no one grumbled on that account. From the heights on the fourth day there was a clear view of the range running roughly east and west and splaying out to the south like a series of great probing fingers. Our accidentally-chosen route crossed the middle of three ill-defined peaks, its summit a broad, uneven-surfaced plateau. Because it was too damp to light a fire we ate only a few peanuts and some partially-dried saucer-sized *rizhiki*, or agaric, which I knew from boyhood experience in Poland to be edible. I was the party's expert on edible fungi and after their first reluctant try at some succulent pink toadstools growing on a rotting log, which I recommended, the others always accepted my judgment on poisonous and non-poisonous growths.

From the southern rim of the plateau we could see to the eastward on the plain below a village of white, flat-roofed houses. Moving about in tree-shaded pasturage were animals I made out to be white goats. A group of camels, even at that range, were easily identified. The American strongly resisted the argument of Marchinkovas, Paluchowicz and Makowski that we should go off to the left and make friends with the villagers. He urged that we were still too near the border to take the slightest risk. Talking patiently and earnestly against gesturing arms and jabbing fingers, he won his point.

The negotiation of the Kentei mountains took about eight days. The last stages of the descent were notable because we were able to find wood to light a fire and there to cook the last of our stinking pigmeat. We laid a flat stone across one corner of the fire and roasted potatoes, which made a memorable meal. For dessert there were the last few peanuts.

Coming down on to the plain from the cool heights was like stepping into an oven. Off came the bulky *fufaikas* and we sweltered bare-armed in our camp-made fur waistcoats. Kolemenos carried Kristina's padded jacket and she walked along with her faded purple dress-top opened at the neck. The ground was hard as cement and coated with a powdery reddish dust. The mountains outcropped in an odd succession of low, oval mounds. Our exposed arms turned bright red, blistered, peeled and finally took on a deep tan. The twenty to thirty miles a day we imposed on ourselves were infinitely tiring. The nights brought with them a body-searching chill.

The treatment of sore feet became a preoccupation. Deep cracks developed between the toes and there were raw patches where the fine dust chafed inside our moccasins. We had occasion to bless the foresight of Paluchowicz, a chronic foot-sufferer, who had

139

collected the fat dripping from the cooking pork back in the cave in Siberia and carried it in a roughly-hollowed wooden cup shaped like half a coconut shell. This fat we sparingly applied to the cracks and sore patches.

This country, we discovered, was criss-crossed with rivers, but we marched a couple of days before we struck the first one. At noon on a sun-scorched day through a shimmering heat-haze, the promise of its cool waters sent our dragging feet lifting over the dry ground. It was a beautiful sight, about a hundred yards wide, its banks green-clothed with grass, its verges supporting flourishing growths of the long-stemmed, bamboo-jointed tall water plants we had met all through Siberia. We lay on our bellies and drank and then we sat in bliss soaking our aching feet. We washed ourselves, using fine sand as a scourer, and soaked the dust out of our clothes. We baked and ate some more of our potatoes, and lay down in the grass with a sense of relaxed well-being.

Along the river an hour after our arrival came a small sampan-type boat, high-built at bows and stern, broad-bottomed and with a flimsy canopy amidships. Athwartships, just forward of the canopy, ran a long stout pole extending beyond the boat a few feet on each side, to the ends of which were lashed two thick bundles of sticks riding an inch or two above the water. At first I thought they were fenders but afterwards I concluded they were stabilisers which, dipping into the water as the craft slewed, would keep it on an even keel. The boatman was Chinese. He was bare-footed, wore a coolie sun-hat, linen trousers ending below the knees and a loose flapping shirt with ragged sleeves torn off at the elbows. The sampan was poled along with a length of strong bamboo. The spectacle was new to all of us and we waved as the sampan glided by. The Chinaman waved back and grinned. Three or four more craft moved past in the couple of hours we rested there. Propulsion was the same for all—a long bamboo pole—although one had a stumpy mast which could have been used for a sail.

There were many other boats on many other rivers in Outer Mongolia, but the men who plied their trade in them were always Chinese. On the roads I never once met a Chinese. Road travellers seemed always to be Mongols.

Our first face-to-face meeting with natives of the country occurred after we had crossed the river and moved a few miles to the south. We were following no track but planning our progress according to the lie of the land to avoid small hills, seizing on a landmark ahead and then walking steadily towards it. Our path was cut eventually by a road lying east and west. Coming slowly from the west was a group of travellers, and it was obvious that if both they and we maintained our pace we must meet. We were less than fifty yards from the road when the Mongols drew abreast. They stopped and waited for us. They were talking busily among themselves as we came within earshot but became silent as we halted before them. They smiled and bowed, keeping their eyes on us the while.

There were a dozen or more men, one camel, two mules and two donkeys. The animals were lightly laden and were also saddled for riding. Only the camel was being ridden now. Perched comfortably on it was an old man with a wispy grey beard. The men might have been a family party, of which the old man was the patriarch. All wore the typical Mongolian conical caps with their long ear-flaps turned back alongside the crown, in material which ranged from leather to quilted homespun cloth. All wore calf-length boots of excellent soft leather and the old man's, in green leather simply embroidered on the outside of the leg in coloured silk or woollen threads, were of specially fine quality. The bottoms of their heavy loose coats reached the top of their boots. The coats opened to show broad belts, a few of leather, the rest of some strong woven stuff. I thought it strange they should wear so much warm clothing in that hot weather.

In their belts each had a knife and all seemed to be of different patterns. One had a horn-handled long clasp-knife hanging from a silver chain. The patriarch, as befitted his venerable position, carried stuck in his leather belt a knife which was about eighteen inches long overall. It was broad-bladed and slightly curved and the sheath was banded with brass into which some design had been etched or beaten.

When the bowing on both sides had been completed in silence, the greybeard got down from his camel. We bowed again and he returned the greeting. He spoke in his own language and we shook our heads. Mister Smith whispered to me, "Try him in

Russian, Slav." The old man heard and turned his attention to me.

"May your feet carry you well on your journey," I addressed him in Russian.

A long pause followed.

In Russian, haltingly and with an obvious searching for words in an unfamiliar tongue, came the answer: "Talk more, please. I understand you well but I speak little Russian. Once I speak this language but not for many years."

I talked slowly, he listened intently. I said we were going south (that was obvious anyway), that we had crossed a river some hours before. I didn't know what else to say. There was such a long silence when I finished that I thought the parley was over. But the old gentleman wanted to satisfy his curiosity and, as it turned out, was grappling with his rusty Russian in order to phrase his questions. The conversation, in the fullness of time, proceeded thus:

You have no camels?—We are too poor to have camels.

You have no mules?—We have no mules either.

You have no donkeys?—No donkeys.

Having established us on the lowest stratum of society, he went on to question me about our journey. The word Lhasa came up. He pointed to the south and mentioned the names of a number of places. The information was valueless because we had no maps and just did not understand what he was talking about.

"It is a very long way," he said, "and the sun will come round many times before you reach this place."

The question he had been itching to ask came at last. He looked at Kristina. Her hair, bleached several shades lighter in the sun, was in sharp contrast to the dark tan of her face, in which the blue eyes frankly returned the old man's gaze. He asked how old she was, if she were related to any of us, where were we taking her. I answered as I had done that other old man to the north.

This leisurely catechism had taken over half-an-hour and the patriarch had appeared to enjoy it immensely. I suspect he was proud of the opportunity of showing his younger kinsmen how he could converse in a foreign tongue. He turned from us and spoke in his own language to the others. They smiled among themselves and bustled about the packs on the animals.

From the packs they brought him food and smilingly he distributed it between us. He was meticulously fair in ensuring that each of us had exactly the same share. At one stage he saw that he had given big Kolemenos one fig more than the rest of us. Politely he took it back. He handed round nuts, dried fish, some partly-cooked swollen barley grains and biscuity, scone-sized oaten cakes. We all bowed and I, as the spokesman, thanked him in the finest phrases I could lay tongue to. I thought the meeting was over, but the Mongols made no move. They were waiting for a signal from their leader but he seemed to be in no hurry to part from us.

He volunteered the information that his party were bound for a "big market" not far away to the east to buy some goods. He went over to his camel, busied himself for a while and came back smoking a rolled tobacco leaf held in shape by a reed tied around the middle. He held out to me a flat-pressed wad of about fifteen whole tobacco leaves. I thanked him and made to put the leaves in the pocket of the jacket I was carrying over my arm. He put out a restraining hand. "Please smoke," he said.

I explained that I was unable to make his kind of smoke with the whole leaf and that we had no paper to roll cigarettes. He went over to the camel again and returned with the inside double sheet of a newspaper. "For you," he said. "Please smoke." I looked at the paper and saw it was the Russian *Red Star* printed the first week in May. The American, standing close beside me, saw it too. "Take care of that, Slav," he murmured. I needed no telling.

From the top of the paper I carefully tore off a strip so as not to cut into the reading matter. From one of the tobacco leaves I rubbed up some shreds in the palm of my hand, rolled my cigarette and fished out my piece of flint, my steel rod and a thumbnail-sized scrap of *gubka* tinder. I held the tinder tight against the flint in the thumb and forefinger of my left hand and struck with the steel in my right hand. The tinder took spark first go. I blew on it until it smouldered red and applied it to my cigarette. The Mongols watched in open admiration of my skill.

"What do you call that fire-maker?" asked the patriarch.

"The Russians give it the name *chakhalo-bakhalo* in some places," I told him.

The sound tickled him. He repeated it twice. I puffed happily at my cigarette, the Mongol leader at his cigar. As the glowing end crept towards the middle he moved the knotted reed band along

143

ahead of it. We finished our smokes standing in the group there beside the road. It was time to break up.

Our host thrust his right hand down to the level of his left hip, withdrew it and bent his ear down to the object he was holding. I craned forward. He was holding a watch, a big silver watch, attached by a short length of heavy silver chain to his belt. He was immediately aware of our interest. We all crowded round and he allowed me to hold it and examine it. It was an old key-winder, made in Russia, and might have been fifty years old. Certainly it was a pre-Revolution product. In flowing Russian script on the watch face was the name of its maker and by some odd quirk of memory the name has always remained with me. It was Pavel Bure—some Czarist craftsman probably long dead.

"When the Russians were fighting each other," the old gentleman explained, "some of them ran away to my country many years ago." It explained not only the possession of the watch—a gift, a payment for services or an article of exchange—but also his ability to speak Russian.

We parted with many expressions of felicitation for our respective journeys and many kind wishes for the continuing health of our feet. It was perhaps our most interesting encounter in Mongolia but we were to find that all these people, whatever their station in life, had those typical qualities of courtesy, complete trust, generosity and hospitality. The help we received was according to the means of the giver, but that help was always cheerfully given. Another delightful quality was their naive and frank curiosity. Unfortunately, the language barrier ruled out conversation with the people we subsequently met, although we became adept at putting over simple ideas by gesture, talking the while in our own languages because it was easier and less embarrassing than employing only silent mime.

When the caravan had disappeared from view we whipped out the *Red Star*. There was little news in it, but we read every line because it was the first newspaper we had seen since those sheets, six months and more old, which were issued back in the camp for cigarette making. It did not tell us what we were most anxious to discover, the eventuality confidently forecast from the beginning by every prisoner I ever met in Russian hands—whether Russia and Germany were at war. There were some dull internal

144

political items, the aftermath of May Day celebrations and the usual promises by industry and agriculture to exceed their production targets. One odd paragraph, which seemed to dispose of the idea of an immediate clash between the two great Continental powers, recorded the dispatch of a big consignment of wheat to the Germans.

Having read the paper we tore it up and shared it out, using each piece to wrap the apportioned tobacco cut in chunks with the knife. We travelled on over undulating country until we met a stream about seven o'clock in the evening, where we camped, set a fire going against the night cold, ate a meal and enjoyed luxury, smoking and yarning together.

By the end of our first fortnight in Mongolia our methods of advance had been modified from those employed in Siberia. No longer was it necessary to post night sentries. The urge to keep on the move persisted; it had become a habit of our existence. But we were not now bedevilled by fears of imminent recapture, we could make contact with the people of the country, we could ask for food or work for food. We did long day marches from the cool hour before dawn until the late evening setting of the sun, but we had adopted the hot country custom of resting in shelter for the two hours of fiercest heat at midday.

The country ahead presented a prospect of a series of round-topped low hills which we skirted when we could and surmounted when we had to. Some of the hills were clothed in heather, which always grew more profusely on the northern slopes. There were few trees except near the villages and the waterways but hardier bushy vegetation—among which I recognised a type of berberis with juicy, oval red fruit, and the wild rose—was fairly widespread. The population was sparse and the villages, sited near water, were widely separated. A very small part of the vast land through which we travelled was cultivated.

Our first thought on reaching the crest of a hill was always to look for the next river. This Outer Mongolian journey was in essence a succession of forced marches through great heat from water to water. Streams and rivers meant solace for the feet, water to slake thirst, water to bathe in. The navigable waterways, too, brought us food on a few occasions, and the incidents, not unnaturally, remain in my mind.

The first time we struck lucky was when we came across a laden sampan held fast on a mudbank. The boatman jabbed first one side and then the other with his bamboo pole, but though he heaved and grunted the craft only swung a little across the current and remained fixed. Kolemenos said "Let's give him a hand," so we waded out to the boat ten yards or so from the bank. Kristina watched from the grass as the Chinese handed us a spare bamboo. We rammed the pole under the bows and started levering, while the boatman thrust away above us with his own pole. After a few minutes of pleasantly hard work we got her off. The Chinese was delighted. His cargo was melons, nearly the size of footballs. As the sampan glided off he bombarded us with the fruit.

Between us and the bank on which Kristina waited as we splashed happily ashore was a belt of a few yards of thick mud marking the limit of the river in the rainy season. The top was patterned with deep cracks where the sun had formed a drying crust, but underneath was squelching grey-brown mud which came up to the calf. Zaro had just thrown Kristina a melon and was standing laughing in the mud when he suddenly let out a yell. We called out to ask him what was the matter, but before he answered I felt a wriggling movement under my own feet. I bent down and groped. Twice the thing eluded me after I thought I had a good grip and then I found the head and gills and hoisted it, lashing violently about my hand and wrist, into the sunlight. It was nearly a foot long, round and thick-bodied, superficially like an eel. I recognised it as a species of loach which the Russians call *viyuni*.

"Can you eat it?" the American asked. "Yes," I said.

That started a hilarious half-hour of mudlarking, at the end of which we were ready for a distinctly unusual evening meal. Like eels, they were tenacious of life and we had to cut off the heads before we could prepare them for cooking. We washed the slime off in the river and found them to be a velvety jet black. We roasted them on hot stones and while I cannot remember exactly their taste, I do remember that it could not be mistaken either for fish or eel. The word we used at the time to describe the taste was "sweet". The flesh was hard-packed and filling.

The rare meal was rounded off with succulent melon slices. Marchinkovas had the brainwave of taking two hollowed-out

146

halves of melon to use as gourds for drinking. The idea was good but in practice did not work out. As the skin dried it cracked. He threw the two halves away next day.

XV

MAINTAINING a schedule of around twenty miles a day hard slogging for days on end made us welcome an occasional break. These days when we eased off were never wasted. One reason for stopping a few hours was to repair and remake worn-out moccasins and tend cut and swollen feet. The other reason was the necessity of earning our food—we could not always expect to be handed food out of charity.

In the second month of our Mongolian journey we arrived at a village of straggling smallholdings. To European eyes a strange feature would be the absence of fences or indeed any boundary markings. Possibly the life of these villages was largely communal and no fences were needed. We approached a stone-built, flat-roofed shack of a house, in front of which, in a hard-beaten, cleared space, we could see a bullock gyrating slowly and patiently round an upright thick stake driven into the ground. It was mid-morning and we had already covered ten or fifteen miles. As we walked we swung our long cudgels. We were a little hungry, a little thirsty, but by no means in desperate straits.

We stopped quite near to watch the bullock and decide what work he was doing. Between the beast and the house were four people—the Mongol farmer squatting, lazily lifting his cap to scratch his bald pate, a lusty-looking boy of fourteen or fifteen armed with a stick with which he encouraged the bullock now and again as it trudged past him, and two women, one of whom might have been the boy's mother and the other his grandmother. The women took no notice of us, but the farmer got up off his haunches and with the boy came over to us and bowed. We returned the greeting. The farmer talked and we talked, but it got us nowhere, and we all, bobbing and smiling, sat down together on the hard earth. The bullock, freed of the boy's attentions, stopped work. By then I could see what was happening. The beast was threshing rye. It was tethered to the central stake by a rope of plaited rushes or osiers. At the outer limit of its tether were spread out in a circle sheaves of ripe rye with the ears outermost. As the bullock trampled the sheaves the grain dropped to the ground where it was gathered by the womenfolk.

I turned to Kolemenos. "That's a slow way of threshing. Let's give the old boy some help." Kolemenos nodded. "Show me how."

We went over and gave the sheaves a few tentative clouts with our sticks. The grain, bone-dry, showered down. I looked over to the farmer. He was grinning broadly and watching closely. I went over to the others. "Let's do the job. It won't take long." Everybody agreed quite willingly, and Kristina, armed with a light staff she used as a walking stick, came too. We stationed ourselves round the circle and set to. The boy, laughing, un-harnessed the bullock and led him away. When it was almost done, the farmer spoke to the two women and they went into the house. He stood near me and I ran grain from one hand to the other and then held out to him a thick bunch of cornstalks. He ran his hand along it and shook it and when he saw it had been beaten clean of seed, showed evident pleasure.

I made gestures to inquire of the man whether he had a sifter for separating the chaff from the grain. He called to the boy, who went to the house and came back with a sieve, the meshes of which were formed from the tail-hairs of a horse. We cleaned up thoroughly, sieved the grain into baskets and then poured it into sacks. The boy led the way to the house as I humped one of the first filled bags.

The interior of the house was interesting. Two-thirds of it was living space, the remainder storage space. There was no partition and little else that could be called civilised refinement. As I stepped inside one of the women was working a primitive flour-mill comprising a pair of well-fashioned circular stones set on a yard-high wooden bench. Pivoting from a hole in a roof-beam was a length of bamboo, the other end of which fitted loosely into a hole near the rim of the upper millstone. Grain was fed through a central hole in this top stone and the woman ground it by swinging the bamboo round and round. The other woman was busy over a stone fireplace in the middle of the floor, the fuel for which, judging by the smell, was dried animal dung. There was no chimney. The smoke curled out through a hole in the roof.

The boy had a sack, too, which he took over to a tall wooden bin, roughly the shape of a barrel, iron-hooped. As we tipped our sacks into the bin I looked round. On a wooden peg driven into the wall were three or four sheepskin coats for winter wear. Bunches of what looked like dried herbs hung from the roof. On the floor were a couple more bins and some tall unglazed brown earthenware jars narrowing at the necks. One of them had a small piece of cloth over the top. I later found the jars held water and milk.

When the operation was over the farmer disappeared. The boy stayed with us. I said to the others in Russian, "The women are cooking something in there." There were hopeful glances at the smoke spiralling up out of the hole in the roof. About half-an-hour passed and then we heard the characteristic creaking and groaning of wheel-hubs on ungreased axles. Round the corner of the house came the farmer leading his bullock yoked to a four-wheeled cart piled high with sheaves.

Mister Smith broke the dismayed silence which had fallen on us. "Gentlemen, the joke is on us. We have some more work to do before we dine."

Zaro jumped to his feet. "Come on, all of you. Let's see how quickly we can get through it." He pulled Kristina up by her wrists and led the way over to the cart.

We worked until well on in the afternoon and became more proficient as a team the longer we went on. I found it was easier on the back and no less efficient to beat out the grain against the tethering stake. As I was the only one of the crowd who had any previous experience of such agricultural pursuits, I was agreeably surprised at the results of our combined labours. So, understandably, was our Mongol friend trotting happily behind each sack as it was toted from the threshing ground to the bin.

The women came out to us then with our reward. One of them carried a shallow straw pannier piled with oaten cakes held with an outstretched arm against her right hip. The older woman brought one of the tall jars I had seen in the house. It was filled with whey. The boy ambled along behind with what looked like three glass tumblers, but when he came close enough for me to examine them I saw they were what was left of bottles from which necks and shoulders had been cleanly removed, probably by the application of heat followed by cold water. The cakes, still warm, were delicious and filling, but the first draught of whey was tainted by paraffin which had been in or near the drinking receptacles. We switched over to our communal metal mug.

This was a period when I had a great craving for salt. I used to dream of the taste of it. It occurred to me then that I would lose nothing by asking the farmer for some. In dumb show I made my request. I pointed to him and to myself. I held my left hand out and made the motion of taking a pinch of salt with my right. I conveyed the hand to my mouth, drew in my cheeks to demonstrate the sharpness of salt upon the tongue, smacked my lips and smiled. The man comprehended immediately. He turned towards the house and beckoned me to join him. Inside he spoke to the women and it was quite a long palaver. Finally the older woman took the tight-fitting lid off a small wooden bowl and produced the salt. It was brown and the crystals were large. She handled it with a care that indicated it was a rare and precious commodity as she spilled out a quantity which would barely have filled a matchbox on to a square of sacking stuff and wrapped it up. I bowed, smiled and thanked them all for the gift.

As we moved off down the track leading through the village I was intrigued with the primitive mechanics of the square-sunk well, from which open-topped sections of wooden conduit led away for irrigation. From two opposite sides heavy planks reared up six feet above ground level to hold the winding spindle. But there was no familiar winding handle. The rope took two turns around the spindle; one end disappeared into the well and the other led off to a point ten feet clear of the well where it was secured to a thick, well-rounded post socketed deeply into the ground and extending vertically above ground a height of eight or nine feet.

About four feet above ground and well below the point at which the well-rope was made fast, a stout wooden bar was slotted through the post, making of the whole contraption a capstan for which the motive power was, as usual, the patient bullock moving in a circle. Provision was made, too, for employing the other hard-labour force of the country—the women—by four arms thrust through the post at breast height, a kind of auxiliary four-women-power motor. It seemed rather an elaborate arrangement for raising water, but the well was deep and the bucket, twice the size of the Western household type, was of solid wood hooped with iron and difficult to lift even when empty.

Growing wild at the foot of the ridge against which the place nestled were clumps of blossoming azalea which attracted a variety of gaudy-hued butterflies. A couple of specimens among them were the largest and most beautiful butterflies I have ever seen and we stopped to look at them. Zaro made a half-hearted attempt to catch one, but little Kristina begged him not to. We made our camp in the shade of half-a-dozen small trees which from a few hundred yards away had looked like young oaks but which were, I think, camphor trees.

Thereafter vegetation became scarcer until only heather clung to the hillsides. We were heading into the desert, the extent and character of which we did not know. Had we been fully fore-warned of its formidable terrors, we might have made more prudent preparations. The word Gobi was just a word to us. We hardly discussed it. The sun rose on our left hand in the morning and we kept moving restlessly on until it sank on our right.

The last human activity I remember featured two Chinese fishermen between the willow-shaded banks of a river the water of which ran cool and clear over a pebbly bed. We had reached the river at midday, appropriately enough, and first saw the fisher-men an hour or so after our arrival. One walked on our side, the other near the far bank, sometimes up to their waists in the stream, at other times barely managing to keep their chins above water. Each carried a long bamboo stave in one hand while the other hand was occupied in hauling on two ropes slung over the shoulders. They went forward with the current. The performance was new to all of us, so we stepped into the shallows for a close look as they drew up to us.

The pair had a net stretched out between them across the river. It consisted of two wings each about twenty yards long joined in the middle to a trap, wide-mouthed and roughly five feet square tapering almost to a point as it trailed out behind. The whole length of net and bag was·buoyed along the top by oval floats of light wood. The device did not give the fish population much chance of survival. The Chinese vigorously beat at the water with their sticks, driving the fish out of the vegetation along the banks, and the only ones to escape were those which leapt over the top of the net. We were lucky that they chose to stop at the point where we stood. The fisherman on the far side crossed over to his partner, using his length of net to close the mouth of the bag. As they came together in the shallows I saw that the bottom of the net was weighted at intervals with stones and the tapering end of the bag was held down with a smooth rock. The ropes the men were holding were attached to top and bottom of the net and rove through the complete length.

One man now took over all four rope ends while the other waded out to take hold of a big floating cigar of a thing made of lengths of bamboo which had been twisting and turning lazily downstream well behind the net. This, we discovered, was the mobile storage tank for the catch. It had a square flap tied in position over the broadest part. Through the hole went the pick of the catch.

We made signs to indicate we would like to help. The Chinese seemed to be willing. Caught in the meshes of the net were dozens of small fish. One of the fishermen took hold of one and pulled it through by the head. He threw it wriggling on to the bank. He looked at us and pointed to the net. We followed his example, clearing the net of fish, bits of wood grass and leaves.

The Chinese hauled the net bag with its shining, wriggling harvest of fish, just clear of the water. Skilfully and rapidly they removed the bigger ones one by one and slipped them into the floating bamboo chamber. When they had finished there were two stone of fine, medium and small fish left which they indicated we could have. Normally, I hope, these would have gone back to re-stock the stream. Some escaped through our unpractised fingers, but most were landed flopping and gasping on the grass above the water line. The Chinese ran their net out again and went on to fish the next stretch.

Here was more food than we could eat in many days, so we decided to eat what we needed there and then and dry the rest in the sun on flat stones to take with us. While Kolemenos chopped the heads off, holding his axe near the blade, I gutted them and the others, in turn, took them to the water to wash them. Kristina and

Zaro got a fire going and a thin flat stone was cleaned to act as a hotplate. Soon there was the savoury smell of grilling fresh fish. There were about five varieties in the catch, among which I recognised perch by its characteristic spiny back.

Fish drying was a novel occupation for us, but we had often seen the finished product and now tried to achieve the same result. The gutted fish was opened flat and the spine removed. Then in relays we partially smoked and dried them round the fire. It took several hours and it was agreed we must stay the night and complete the job. Throughout the next morning the fish were laid out under the heat of the sun while we flapped with our *fufaikas* to keep the flies away. When we judged the process complete, we shared them out and stowed them away in our bags. Later we had reason to bless the success of the operation. We were to carry the last of this food into the Gobi Desert with us.

Not so pleasant was the experience of a day or two later. The time was afternoon when the hot sun in a vast blue sky was beginning its long decline to the west. Marchinkovas pointed out a couple of miles ahead a great brown moving cloud and asked what it could be. Not one of us could enlighten him. There was no doubt it was moving and I thought it might be a dust storm, except that the air was barely agitated by the lightest of breezes. This thing was covering ground rapidly, getting larger and larger as we looked.

"It's a locust swarm," Mister Smith called out suddenly. "It's no good walking into it. We'd better stop here."

We sat down on the hard-baked earth, slipping our jackets on and covering our heads with our food sacks. The glare of the sun was blotted out as the locust myriads reached us. We turned our backs to them and huddled down. The sound as they struck our clothes was audible. They were all over us, around us and above us. The air was alive with the throbbing hum of their beating wings.

"Thank God they can't eat us," said Zaro.

"I wouldn't be too sure about that," answered the American. "They'll eat almost anything."

Kristina turned a worried-looking face to him. "I am only joking, child," he reassured her.

It took at least two hours for the swarm to pass over us. The sun shone through again and the casualties of the great migration littered the ground about us. Some were moving, others appeared to be dead. We shook them in dozens from our clothes. They had found their way into our pockets, up our sleeves, inside our trouser legs. One consolation was that they had not got into our food sacks with their precious small store of dried fish.

To relate time and distance has been the greatest of my difficulties in recording the story of this bid for freedom. Particularly is this so concerning the passage through Mongolia, where we had no common speech with the inhabitants and where, even if we were given the names of rivers, villages or other landmarks, there was no means of setting the sounds down to help the memory in later years. But I believe our progress through inhabited Outer Mongolia to the wastes of Inner Mongolia occupied us from six to eight weeks.

This much I remember: The entry into the Gobi was not an abrupt transition. Twice we thought we were in it as we traversed long sandy stretches, but on each occasion a range of fairly tall hills intervened, and at the foot of the second range there was the boon of a shallow, sandy rivulet, beside which we camped for the night. That was our last drink of fresh water for a long, long time.

Towards nightfall of the next day we encountered a caravan trail at right-angles to our course, alongside which were seated four Mongolians watching over a steaming iron cauldron suspended from a metal tripod over a fire. They all appeared to be aged between thirty and forty, but the seniority of one was marked by the possession of a magnificent old rifle, long-barrelled, short-stocked, the almost black woodwork extending along the barrel and held to it by bands of gleaming brass. As he stood with the others to greet us the rifle showed as tall as the owner. The usual courtesies were exchanged but this time none of our guests knew Russian. They motioned us to one side of the fire where we sat in a wide semi-circle while they faced us across the flames.

These were poorer travellers than those we had first met. I noticed that their jackets had been neatly patched in places. They had one mule between them on which the bare necessities for their journey were carried, including two water bags made, I think, from the stomach of camels. More water was added to the pot while we grinned and gestured futilely at the man with the gun to show our pleasure at the unexpected meeting. In deference to Smith's grey-streaked beard, the Mongol directed his attention to the American, whom he obviously regarded as the senior and therefore the leader of our party.

Eventually Mister Smith used the magic word Lhasa and the Mongol, after a minute of deliberation, pointed our direction. From inside his coat he drew a contraption which I can best describe as a metal cylinder on a long rod. From within the cylinder he drew out a length of silk ribbon in the manner that a Westerner will produce a tape measure of the mechanically-retracting kind. The silk was covered with symbols in a series of frames like the separate pictures on a cine film. He spent some time tranquilly contemplating the ribbon and finally, with a spinning motion of the hand returned the roll within its case. This performance we took to mean a prayer for the happy completion of our pilgrimage. Mister Smith bowed his acknowledgment.

The man in charge of the cauldron produced a brick of compressed tea, black in colour, broke a piece off and fed it into the water. For several minutes he stirred the brew with a long-handled wooden spoon and the fragrance from the boiling pot assailed our noses most agreeably. Next was produced a wooden jar from which the lid was removed to reveal a substance that looked to me like honey but which later turned out to be butter. Spoonsful of the stuff were added to the brew and the stirring and simmering went on for some time.

Two mugs were produced and these were sufficiently unusual for me to ask to handle one before it was used for the tea. It was of burnished brass and had once been the lower part of the casing holding the explosive charge for a small shell. A strip of the same metal had been bent round and attached to the cup by bronze rivets to make a handle. I turned the cup upside down to see if there were the usual marks of origin on the base. There were a few faint imprints but they had been so worn away with use that I could make nothing of them. The Mongols seemed flattered by my interest and I was sorry that I could not have asked them where they picked up the mugs.

The procedure for passing around the tea was rather amusing, since it involved guessing our ages in order that the more senior on both sides should be first served. About Mister Smith they had no difficulty. The first two cups dipped into the brew went to him and the Mongol gun-owner. When we turned over our own mug to the cook, he filled it and passed it without hesitation to Paluchowicz. I saw the Sergeant make a face of great distaste at his first gulp, look at the American and then smack his lips as Smith was doing to show appreciation of what he was drinking. Smith sipped away with great composure.

Kristina and I were the last to be served. While we awaited our turn I teased her about the custom of a country that ruled "Ladies last". She replied that placing her last might mean only that they recognised her as the youngest of us. The Mongols watched the laughing exchanges between us and I am sure they would have loved to know what we talked about. When our turn did come I could sense the others looking at us surreptitiously. The tea was comfortingly hot but it tasted foul. We kept our faces straight and avoided each other's eyes. The savour of the fragrant leaves was overborne by the sickening tang of rancid butter which floated in glistening globules of fat on the surface. But we got through it and I had to exercise great self-control to stop laughing out loud as Kristina gave out a couple of decorous lip-smackings.

The Mongols' hospitality was rounded off with the gift of a little tobacco and a few nuts. We all stood and made our farewells. We walked away and when I looked back from fifty yards away they were squatting down again, their backs towards us. In that short distance we had passed out of their lives and they out of ours.

I was to remember later that they thought our trail to Lhasa merited a special prayer. We were striding into the burning wastes of the Gobi waterless and with little food. None of us then knew the hell we were to meet.

XVI

THE GOBI DESERT: HUNGER, DROUGHT AND DEATH

TWO DAYS without water in the hillocky, sand-covered, August furnace of the Gobi and I felt the first flutterings of fear. The early rays of the sun rising over the rim of the world dispersed the sharp chill of the desert night. The light hit the tops of the billowing dunes and threw sharp shadows across the deep-sanded floors of the intervening little valleys. Fear came with small fast-beating wings and was suppressed as we sucked pebbles and dragged our feet on to make maximum distance before the blinding heat of noon. From time to time one or other of us would climb one of the endless knolls and look south to see the same deadly landscape stretching to the horizon. Towards midday we stuck our long clubs in the sand and draped our jackets over them to make a shelter. Alarm about our position must have been general but no one voiced it. My own feeling was that we must not frighten the girl and I am sure the others kept silent for the same reason.

The heat enveloped us, sucking the moisture from our bodies, putting ankle-irons of lethargy about our legs. Each one of us walked with his and her own thoughts and none spoke, dully concentrating on placing one foot ahead of the other interminably. Most often I led the way, Kolemenos and the girl nearest to me and the others bunched together a few yards behind. I was driving them now, making them get to their feet in the mornings, forcing them to cut short the noon rest. As we still walked in the rays of the setting sun the fear hit me again. It was, of course, the fundamental, most oppressive fear of all—that we should die here in the burning wilderness. I struggled against a panicky impulse to urge a return the way we had come, back to water and green things and life. I fought it down.

We flopped out against a tall dune and the cold stars came out to look at us. Our bone-weariness should have ensured the sleep of exhaustion but, tortured with thirst, one after another twisted restlessly, rose, wandered around and came back. Some time after midnight I suggested we start off again to take advantage of the cool conditions. Everybody seemed to be awake. We hauled ourselves upright and began again the trudge south. It was much easier going. We rested a couple of hours after dawn—and still the southerly prospect remained unaltered.

After this one trial there were no more night marches. Makowski stopped it.

"Can you plot your course by the stars?" he asked me. The others turned haggard faces towards me.

I paused before answering. "Not with complete certainty," I confessed.

"Can any of us?" he persisted. No one spoke.

"Then we could have been walking in circles all through the night," he said heavily.

I sensed the awful dismay his words had caused. I protested that I was sure we had not veered off course, that the rising sun had proved us still to be facing south. But in my own mind, even as I argued, I had to admit the possibility that Makowski was right. In any case, the seed of doubt had been sown and we just could not afford to add anything to the already heavy burden of apprehension.

So we went on through the shimmering stillness. Not even a faint zephyr of air came up to disperse the fine dust hanging almost unseen above the desert, the dust that coated our faces and beards, entered into our cracked lips and reddened the rims of eyes already sore tried by the stark brightness of the sun.

The severely-rationed dried fish gave out on about the fifth day and still we faced a lifeless horizon. In all this arid world only eight struggling human specks and an occasional snake were alive. We could have ceased to move quite easily and lain there and died. The temptation to extend the noonday halt, to go on dozing through the hot afternoon until the sun dropped out of sight, invited our dry, aching bodies. Our feet were in a pitiable state as the burning sand struck through the thin soles of our worn moccasins. I found myself croaking at the others to get up and keep going. There is nothing here, I would say. There is nothing for days behind us. Ahead there must be something. There must be *something*. Kristina would stand up and join me, and Kolemenos. Then the others in a bunch. Like automatons we would be under way again, heads bent down, silent, thinking God knows what, but moving one foot ahead of the other hour after desperate hour.

On the sixth day the girl stumbled and, on her knees, looked up at me. "That was foolish of me, Slav. I tripped myself up." She did not wait for my assistance. She rose slowly from the sand and stepped out beside me. That afternoon I found to my faint surprise and irritation I was on my knees. I had not been conscious of the act of falling. One moment I was walking, the next I had stopped. On my knees, I thought . . . like a man at prayer. I got up. No one had slackened pace for me. They probably hardly noticed my stumble. It seemed to take me a very long time to regain my position at the head again. Others were falling, too, I noticed from time to time. The knees gave and they knelt there a few unbelieving seconds until realisation came that they had ceased to be mobile. They came on again. There was no dropping out. These were the signs of growing, strength-sapping weakness, but it would have been fatal to have acknowledged them for what they were. They were the probing fingers of death and we were not ready to die yet.

The sun rose on the seventh day in a symphony of suffused pinks and gold. Already we had been plodding forward for an hour in the pale light of the false dawn and dully I looked at Kristina and the other shambling figures behind me and was struck with the unconquerable spirit of them all. Progress now was a shuffle; the effort to pick up the feet was beyond our strength.

Without much hope we watched Kolemenos climb laboriously to the top of a high mound. One or other of us did this every morning as soon as the light was sufficient to give clear visibility southwards to the horizon. He stood there for quite a minute with his hand over his eyes, and we kept walking, expecting the usual hopeless shrug of the shoulders. But Kolemenos made no move to come down, and because he was staring intently in one direction, a few degrees to the east of our course, I dragged to a stop. I felt Kristina's hand lightly on my arm. She, too, was gazing up at Kolemenos. Everybody halted. We saw him rub his eyes, shake his head slowly and resume his intent peering in the same direction, eyes screwed up. I wanted to shout to him but stayed quiet. Instead I started to climb up to him. Zaro and the girl came with me. Behind came the American and Marchinkovas. The two Poles, Paluchowicz and Makowski, leaned on their clubs and watched us go.

As I reached Kolemenos I was telling myself, "It will be nothing. I must not get excited. It surely can't be anything." My heart was pounding with the exertion of the slight climb.

Kolemenos made no sound. He flung out his right arm and pointed. My sight blurred over. For some seconds I could not focus. I did what I had seen Kolemenos do. I rubbed my eyes and looked again. There was *something*, a dark patch against the light sand. It might have been five miles distant from us. Through the dancing early morning haze it was shapeless and defied recognition. Excitement grew as we looked. We began to talk, to speculate. Panting and blowing, the two Poles came up to us. They, too, located the thing.

"Could it be an animal?" asked the Sergeant.

"Whatever it is, it is not sand," Mister Smith replied. "Let's go and investigate."

It took us a good two hours to make the intervening distance. Many times we lost sight of the thing we sought as we plunged along in the sandy depressions. We climbed more often than we would otherwise have done because we could not bear the idea that somehow the smudge on the landscape might disappear while we were cut off from view of it. It began to take shape and definition and hope began to well up in us. And hope became certainty. There were *trees*—real, live, growing, healthy trees, in a clump, outlined against the sand like a blob of ink on a fresh-laundered tablecloth.

"Where there are trees there is water," said the American.

"An oasis," somebody shouted, and the word fluttered from mouth to mouth.

Kristina whispered, "It is a miracle. God has saved us."

If we could have run we would have done so. We toiled that last half-mile as fast as we could flog our legs along. I went sprawling a few times. My tongue was dry and swollen in my mouth. The trees loomed larger and I saw they were palms. In their shade was a sunken hollow, roughly oval-shaped, and I knew this must be water. A few hundred yards from the oasis we crossed an east-west caravan track. On the fringe of the trees we passed an incongruous pile of what looked like rusting biscuit tins like some fantastic mid-desert junk yard. In the last twenty yards we quickened our pace and I think we managed a lope that was very near a run.

The trees, a dozen or more of them, were arranged in a crescent on the south side of the pool, and threw their shadow over it for most part of the day. The wonderful cool water lay still and inviting in an elliptical depression hemmed round with big, rough-worked stones. At this time, probably the hottest season, the limits of the water had receded inwards from the stone ring, and we had to climb over to reach it. The whole, green, life-giving spot could have been contained inside half-an-acre.

Zaro had the mug but we could not wait for him to fill it and hand it round. We lay over the water lapping at it and sucking it in like animals. We allowed it to caress our fevered faces. We dabbed it around our necks. We drank until someone uttered the warning about filling our empty bellies with too much liquid. Then we soaked our food sacks and, sitting on the big stones, gently laved our cracked and lacerated feet. For blissful minutes we sat with the wet sacking draped about our feet. With a mugful of water at a time we rinsed from our heads and upper bodies some of the accumulated sand and dust of the six-and-a-half days of travail. The very feel and presence of water was an ecstasy. Our spirits zoomed. We had walked out of an abyss of fear into life and new hope. We chatted and laughed as though the liquid we had drunk was heady champagne. We wondered what hands had brought these stones and planted these palms to make of this miraculous pool a sign that could be seen from afar by thirst-tortured men.

The full extent of our good fortune was yet to be discovered. Some twenty yards east of the pool, on the opposite side from which we had approached, there were the remains of a still-warm fire and the fresh tracks of camels and many hoof-marks, telling of the recent halt of a big caravan. It had probably departed at sunrise. These men, whoever they were, had cooked and eaten meat, and the bones, as yet quite fresh and untainted, were scattered around the wood ashes. They were the bones of one large and one small animal and the meat had been sliced from

162

them with knives, leaving small, succulent pieces still adhering. We shared out the bones and tore at them with our teeth, lauding our luck. Poor toothless Paluchowicz borrowed the knife from me and did as well as anybody. When there was no more meat we cracked each bone with the axe and sucked out the marrow.

For two or three hours during the heat of the afternoon we lay stretched out near the water under the blessed shade of the palms. Kolemenos, who had that rare gift of complete relaxation in any situation, snored with his arms behind his head and his cap pulled down over one eye. The sun's rays began to slant and I came out of a sleep haunted by blazing light and never-ending desert. I picked up the mug, climbed over the stones, scooped up water and drank again. The American stood up, stretched and joined me. Soon we were all up and about.

Zaro moved away. "I'm going to have a look at that pile of tins," he called back. "Maybe we'll find one we can carry water in."

The puzzle of that dump of civilised junk in the heart of the South Gobi must remain unsolved. There were about a hundred of the box-like metal containers and they had been there so long that, even in the dry air of that place, they had rusted beyond use. We turned them over one by one but could find nothing to indicate what they had contained or from where they had come. As we examined them we stacked them on one side. Beneath the pile, half-buried in the sand, Zaro pulled out a complete coil of rust-covered quarter-inch wire held together by circlets of thinner wire which broke away at a touch. I held a handful of sand in a fold of my sack and rubbed away at the heavy wire until I cleared the rust. The coating was thin; the wire was strong and sound.

That night we made a low-walled shelter from the tins, searched around for small pieces of wood and lit a fire. I lay awake for a long time trying to decide how long we should remain in this place, but the answer would not come. Sleep when it did come was dreamless and complete. I opened my eyes, according to the habit of the desert, about an hour before dawn, and Zaro was already pottering around, tugging tentatively at the free end of the coil of wire.

A conference of suggestion and counter-suggestion developed about that length of wire. We lugged it over to the pool and began pulling it out and rubbing it down with sand. No one had any clear notion what to do with it but there was unanimity on its probable usefulness to us some time in the future. Any metal object was precious. We just could not bring ourselves to leave treasure behind. Since we had to take it with us, the discussion finally boiled down to shaping it into an easily-portable form. That was how we came to spend hours of that day cutting off about four-feet lengths, turning the ends into hooks and making loops which could be slung around the neck. The metal was tough and bending it caused hard work with the back of the axe-head while the wire ends were jammed and firmly held in interstices between the close-set stones. When each of us had been supplied with a loop, Zaro and a couple of others made a few metal spikes about two feet long, one end beaten out to a point and the other looped to hang on the belt. Plenty of wire still remained when we had finished, but we thought we had all we could conveniently carry. The operation gave us a sense of achievement. To use our hands and our skill again was stimulating, and there was, too, the prisoner's fierce pride of possession, be the object only a loop of discarded wire.

Inevitably came the question of when to depart. Two of our problems were insoluble. The oasis had water but no food. We had nothing in which to carry water, except our metal mug. Makowski argued that if we waited here a few days we stood a chance of meeting a caravan and securing ourselves a stock of food for the next stage. But I wanted to go. I said that, as we had just missed one caravan, there might not be another for weeks. We would wait on for days until we were too weak from lack of food to move at all and the next travellers might find us dead from starvation. In the light of what was to come, I hope I may be forgiven for my insistence. Yet I think I may have been right. But there is no way of judging the issue now, nor was there then. There was no acrimony about the debate. We were in desperate straits and we had to decide immediately one way or the other. The thing was decided late that evening. We would set out before dawn.

We were on our way when the sun came up and for half a day we could look back and see the trees of the oasis. I was glad when I could no longer see their shape against the skyline. For hours

164

Zaro carried the mug, one hand underneath, the other over the top. He had filled it with water after we had all taken our final drinks and as he walked it slopped warm against his palm and little trickles escaped down the sides. When we halted at midday he had lost nearly half the quantity through spillage and evaporation and was complaining about the cramping of his arms in holding so tightly to the can. So, very carefully, sitting up under the small shade of our jackets slung over our clubs, we handed the water round and disposed of it a sip at a time.

This was the pre-oasis journey all over again, but this time we were deprived of even the scant sustenance of a few dried fish. For the first three days I thought we moved surprisingly well. On the fourth day the inescapable, strength-draining heat began quite suddenly to take its toll. Stumbles and falls became increasingly frequent, the pace slowed, speech dried up into short grunted phrases. I remember Makowski saying, "Hell can't be hotter than this bloody desert."

On the fifth day Kristina went to her knees. I turned slowly round to look at her, expecting her to get to her feet as she had done before. She remained kneeling, her fair head bowed down on her chest. She was very still. I moved towards her and Kolemenos stepped back at the same time. Before we could reach her she swayed from the hips and slumped forward, her face in the sand. We reached her at the same time and turned her on her back. She was unconscious. I opened the neck of her dress and started talking to her, gently shaking her, while Mister Smith set to with sticks and *fufaikas* to make shade for her.

She came to quickly. She looked at our anxious ring of faces, sat up, smiled through split lips and said, "I feel better now. I must have fallen over—I don't know how it happened."

"Don't worry," I consoled her. "We'll rest here a while and then you'll be all right again."

She leaned forward and lightly patted the back of my hand. "I won't fall down again."

We sat there a while. Kristina reached down to scratch her ankle and my eyes idly followed the hand. The ankle was swollen so that the skin pressed outward against the narrow-fitting ends of her padded trousers.

"Has anything bitten you, Kristina?"

"No, Slav. Why?"

"Your leg looks swollen."

She pulled up the trouser leg and looked, turning her foot about as she did so. "I hadn't noticed it before," she said.

We struggled on for a couple more hours. She seemed to be refreshed. Then she fell again and this time her knees buckled and her face hit the sand in almost one movement without even the action of putting her arms out to break the fall.

We turned her over again and wiped away the sand which had been forced into her nose and mouth. We put up the shelter. She lay with eyes closed, breathing in harsh gasps through her mouth. I looked at her ankles and they were a pitiful sight. Both were badly discoloured and so swollen that it seemed they would burst the restricting bottoms of the trousers. I took out my knife and slit the cloth upwards. The skin appeared to be distended by water right up to the knees. I touched the swelling and the mark of my fingers remained for some seconds.

Kristina was unconscious for an hour while we tried to stifle our gnawing anxiety with banalities like, "It must be just a touch of sunstroke." I had a feeling like lead in the pit of my stomach. I was frightened.

She was quite cheerful when she came round. "I am becoming a nuisance," she said. "What can be the matter with me?" We fussed around her.

Kristina got to her feet. "Come on. We are wasting time."

I walked alongside her. She stopped suddenly and glanced down at her legs, her attention attracted by the flapping of slit trousers about her legs.

"My legs are getting quite thick, Slav."

"Do they hurt you, Kristina?"

"No, not at all. They must be swelling because I have walked so far."

The time was afternoon on the fifth day. She walked on for hours without more than an occasional small stumble and was still keeping up with Kolemenos and I when the sun had gone and we stopped for the night. Sitting there among us she stole frequent looks at her legs. She said nothing and we affected not to notice.

It was a disturbed night. All except Kolemenos seemed too weary and worried for sleep, Kristina lay still but I sensed she remained awake. I chewed on the pebble in my mouth. My teeth ached, my gums were enlarged and tender. Thoughts of flowing water constantly invaded my mind. I had clear pictures of the sampans I had seen on those northern rivers. I had little fits of shivering that made me stand up and walk around. My head felt constricted. I ached from head to foot.

For the first two hours of the sixth day the air was cool and walking was as pleasant as ever it can be in the desert. But soon the sun began to blaze at us out of a sky empty of clouds.

I took Kristina's elbow. "Can you keep going in this?"

"Yes, I think so."

Five minutes later she had folded up and was out, face down in the sand. Again we ministered to her and waited for her to open her eyes. She appeared to be breathing quite normally, like a tired child.

I stood a few steps away from her and the others came over to me. "She is very swollen," I said. "Do any of you know what that means?" Nobody knew the symptoms. We went back to her and waited. I flapped my cap over her face to make some air.

She smiled at us. "I am being a trouble again." We shook our heads. "I am afraid you had better leave me this time."

We all broke into protest at once. Kolemenos dropped down on his knees beside her. "Don't say that. Don't be a silly little girl. We shall never leave you." She lay there for another half-an-hour and when she tried to force herself up on her elbows she fell back again.

I spoke to Kolemenos. "We must give her a hand." We lifted her to her feet. "I can walk if you stay near me," she said.

Amazingly she walked, Kolemenos and I lightly holding her elbows. After a quarter of a mile we felt her start to fall forward. We steadied her and she went on again. She pulled herself erect and there was not a sound of distress, not a whimper. The next time she slumped forward we could not hold her. She had played herself utterly out and even the gallant will in that frail body could not produce another torturing effort. We were all in a bunch around her as the sun climbed up over our heads. Kolemenos and I each put an arm about her and, half-carrying, half-dragging her, set off again. A mile or so of that and I had no reserve of strength to give her. We stopped and I bent double fighting for breath.

167

"Stick beside me, Slav," said Kolemenos. "I am going to carry her." And he lifted her into his arms, swayed for a moment as he adjusted himself to the weight, and staggered off. He carried her for fully two hundred yards and I was there to ease her down when he paused for a rest.

"Please leave me, Anastazi," she begged. "You are wasting your strength." He looked at her but could not bring himself to speak.

We made a shelter there and stayed for perhaps three hours through the worst heat of the day. She lay still—I do not think she could move. The ugly swelling was past the knees and heavy with water. Kolemenos was flat on his back, restoring his strength. He knew what he was going to do.

The sun began to decline. Kolemenos bent down and swung her into his arms and trudged off. I stayed with him and the rest were all about us. He covered fully a quarter of a mile before he put her down that first time. He picked her up again and walked, her head pillowed on his great shoulder. I can never in my life see anything so magnificent as the blond-bearded giant Kolemenos carrying Kristina, hour after hour, towards darkness of that awful sixth day. His ordeal lasted some four hours. Then she touched his cheek.

"Put me on the ground, Anastazi. Just lay me down on the ground."

I took her weight from him and together we eased her down. We gathered round her. A wisp of a smile hovered about the corners of her mouth. She looked very steadily at each one of us in turn and I thought she was going to speak. Her eyes were clear and very blue. There was a great tranquillity about her. She closed her eyes.

"She must be very tired," said Sergeant Paluchowicz. "The poor, tired little girl."

We stood around for several minutes, dispirited and at a loss to know what to do next. The shoulders of Kolemenos were sagging with exhaustion. We exchanged glances but could think of nothing to say. I looked down at Kristina. I looked at the open neck of her dress, and in a second I was down at her side with my ear over her heart. There was no beat. I did not believe it. I turned my head and applied the other ear. I lifted my head and

168

picked up her thin wrist. There was no pulse. They were all looking at me intently. I dropped her hand and it thumped softly into the sand.

The American spoke, hardly above a whisper. I tried to answer but the words would not come. Instead the tears came, the bitter salt tears. And the sobs were torn from me. In that God-forsaken place seven men cried openly because the thing most precious to us in all the world had been taken from us. Kristina was dead.

I think we were half crazy there beside her body in the desert. We accused ourselves of having brought her here to her death. More personally, Makowski, speaking in Polish, blamed me for having insisted on leaving the shelter of the oasis.

The American intervened, his voice cold and flat. "Gentlemen, it is no use blaming ourselves. I think she was happy with us." The talk ceased. He went on, "Let us now give her a decent burial."

We scraped a hole in the sand at the base of a dune. Little pieces of stone that we sifted from the grains as we dug deeper we laid apart. I slit open a food sack and laid the double end gently under her chin. We lowered the body. On her breast lay her little crucifix. We stood around with our caps in our hands. There was no service, but each man spoke a prayer in his own language. Mister Smith spoke in English, the first time I had heard him use it. I opened out the sacking and lifted it over her face and I could not see for tears. We covered her with sand and we dotted the mound round with the little stones.

And Kolemenos took her tall stick and chopped a piece off it with his axe and bound the one piece to the other with a leather thong to make a cross.

So we said goodbye to her and went our empty way.

XVII

SNAKE MEAT AND MUD

THE AWFUL thing was that there was so little but the girl to think about. Walking was sheer painful habit—it required no thought to perform. The sun beating down hour after hour would addle my brains and check the orderly sequence of thinking. I found I could imagine she was still there, just behind my shoulders and I could scuff along for miles seeing her. But there always came a time when the idea of her presence was so strong that I must turn my head, and bitter grief would knife at me all over again. I came slowly out of a troubled, thirst-ridden sleep that night and I was sure once more that she remained with us. And each fresh realisation of her death renewed dumb agony.

It took another tragedy to dull the sharp edges of our memory of her. Oddly, too, it relieved some of the load of guilt I felt about her death.

On the eighth day out from the oasis Sigmund Makowski pitched over into the sand. His arms were still at his sides when his face thumped down and he had made no effort to use his stick to prevent the fall. He lay there a minute or two and was barely conscious. We looked down at him and saw the tell-tale sign. Over the top of his moccasins the flesh was soft and puffy. We exchanged glances and said nothing. We turned him round and flapped our sacks in his face and he recovered quickly. He got to his feet, shook his head from side to side, grabbed his stick and plunged off. He keeled over again and again, but he kept going. And all the time the sickening flabby swelling grew upwards and weighed upon his legs.

Makowski lasted longer after the first onset than Kristina had done. On the ninth day he must have slumped down half-a-dozen times in a couple of hours. Then, lying flat and heaving desperately with his arms to get himself to his knees, he called out the name of Kolemenos. Both Kolemenos and I knelt down beside him.

170

"If you give me a hand to get to my feet, I can keep going."

Kolemenos took one arm, I took the other. We got Makowski upright. Feebly he shook our hands off and stood swaying. I felt myself choking as he staggered off like a drunken man, still going forward, but weaving from side to side, stabbing his stick into the yielding sand as he went. The six of us stood there hopelessly and watched him go.

"Mustn't let him fall again," Kolemenos said to me.

It was not difficult to catch up with him. Kolemenos took his stick from him and we took an arm each. We put his arms about our shoulders and stepped out. He swung his head round to each of us in turn and gave a bit of a smile. He kept his legs moving, but progressively more weakly so that towards the end of the day he was an intolerable, sagging burden about our necks.

That night he seemed to sleep peacefully and in the morning of the tenth day he was not only still alive but appeared to have regained some strength. He set off with the rest of us dragging his feet but unaided. He moved for half-an-hour before his first fall, but thereafter he pitched over repeatedly until Kolemenos and I again went to his rescue. When the time came to make our noon-day halt he was draped about our shoulders like a sack and his legs had all but ceased to move. Mister Smith and Paluchowicz eased his weight away from us and gently laid him down on his back. Then we put up the shelter and squatted down around him. He lay quite still and only his eyes seemed to be alive.

After a while he closed his eyes and I had thought he had gone, but he was still breathing quietly. He opened his eyes again. The lids came down and this time he was dead. There was no spasm, no tremor, no outward sign to show that life had departed the body. Like Kristina, he had no words for us at the end.

The dossier for Sigmund Makowski, aged 37, ex-captain of the Polish frontier forces, *Korpus Ochrony Pogranicza*, was closed. Somewhere in Poland he had a wife. I would like her some day to know he was a brave man. We buried him there in the Gobi. The first grave we scratched out was too small and we had to lift out the body and enlarge the hole. We laid his sack, empty of food for so long, that he had carried with him for two thousand or more miles, over his face, and scooped the sand over him.

Kolemenos made another small wooden cross, we said our prayers and we left him.

I tried hard to keep count of the days. I tried, too, to remember if I had ever read how long a man can keep alive without food and water. My head ached with the heat. Often the blackest pall of despair settled on me and I felt we were six doomed men toiling inevitably to destruction. With each hopeless dawn the thought recurred: Who will be next? We were six dried-out travesties of men shuffling, shuffling. The sand seemed to get deeper, more and more reluctant to let our ill-used feet go. When a man stumbled he made a show of getting quickly on his legs again. Quite openly now we examined our ankles for the first sign of swelling, for the warning of death.

In the shadow of death we grew closer together than ever before. No man would admit to despair. No man spoke of fear. The only thought spoken out again and again was that there must be water soon. All our hope was in this. Over every arid ridge of hot sand I imagined a tiny stream and after each waterless vista there was always another ridge to keep the hope alive.

Two days after Makowski's death we were reaching the limits of endurance. I think it was about the twelfth day out from the oasis. We walked only for about six hours on that day. We moved along in pairs now. There was no effort to choose partners. The man next to you was your friend and you took each other's arms and held each other up and kept moving. The only life we saw in the desert about us were snakes which lay still, heads showing and the length of their bodies hidden in deep holes in the sand. I wondered how they lived. They showed no fear of us and we had no desire to molest them. Once we did see a rat, but generally the snakes seemed to have the desert to themselves.

At the end of that twelfth day I was arm-in-arm with Zaro. Mister Smith and Paluchowicz were helping each other along and Kolemenos walked with Marchinkovas. In the middle of the night I felt a fever of desire to get moving again. I think I knew that if the miracle did not happen within the next twenty-four hours we could not expect to survive. I stuck it out until a couple of hours before dawn. Marchinkovas, Zaro and the American were awake, so I shook Kolemenos and Paluchowicz. I rasped at them through my dry and aching throat. I stood up. No one argued.

As I started away they were with me. Paluchowicz stumbled a little at first because he was still not quite awake and his legs were stiff, but soon we were paired off again and making distance south.

It was easy to imagine in those pre-dawn hours that we were re-covering ground we had trudged over before, but the first light of the rising sun showed we were on course. We tacked from side to side as we walked, two by two, but it seemed to me we had made a remarkable number of tortured miles by the time the heat forced us to stop and rest. It was almost too much trouble to erect our flimsy canopy, but we did it because it was by now one of the habits of survival.

We sweated it out for about three hours in throbbing discomfort, mouths open, gasping in the warm desert air over enlarged, dust-covered tongues. I eased the sticky pebble round my sore gums to create a trickle of saliva so that I could swallow. I was at my lowest ebb, working on the very dregs of stamina and resolution. It was the devil's own job to haul ourselves upright again. We were all perilously weak and dangerously near death.

All my visions of water had been of exquisite cool ponds and murmuring streams. The water that saved our lives was an almost dried-out creek, the moisture compounded with the mud at the bottom of a channel not more than a couple of yards wide. We came over the last ridge and failed to see it. We were looking for water and this was no more than a slimy ooze which the killing desert was reluctant to reveal to us. We were almost on it before we saw it. We fell on our faces and sucked at the mud and dabbled our hands in it. For a few minutes we acted like demented men. We chewed mud for the moisture it contained and spat out the gritty residue.

It was the American who got the right idea. He swung his sack off his back and thrust a corner of it down into the mud. He waited some minutes, pulled out the sack and sucked at the damp corner. We followed his example. The amount of water we obtained in this way was infinitesimal compared with our raging, thirteen-day-old thirst, but it was something and it gave us hope. We began to talk again for the first time for days, to exchange suggestions. We decided to walk along the watercourse with the idea that if at this point there was dampness, somewhere there must be real water.

The creek narrowed until it was a mere crack in the ground and here we found water collected in tiny pools in the mud. By pressing down our cupped hands, palms uppermost, we were able to drink, really to drink again, to feel water trickling down our parched throats. We drank it, sand, mud and all, in ecstasy. It was probably as well that we were prevented from gulping it down in large quantities. After each drink there was a waiting period of several minutes before the little hollows filled again with up-seeping water. My split, puffed and bleeding lips burned as the water touched them. I held the water in my mouth before swallowing and washed it about my tongue, my tender gums and aching teeth.

For a couple of hours we lay sprawled out exhausted close against the creek. Then we drank some more. Late in the afternoon Zaro pulled off his moccasins and sat with his feet deep in the cool mud. He smiled through his broken lips at the bliss of it and called out to us to join him. We sat round in a rough circle. After those never-ending hot days with blistered and cracked feet being pushed on and on through the burning sand, this was an experience of wonderful relief. After a while I felt the water slowly trickling through into the depressions made by my feet. The balm of it seemed even to ease the aching bones. Now and again I pulled out my feet just for the joy of dropping them back again into the squelching mud.

Sitting there in the only comfort we had known since the far distant oasis, we began to talk, to face up to our still bleak future and to plan. The first fact was that we were starving and near the end of our strength. The second was that, in spite of this God-sent ribbon of moisture, we were still in the desert and the prospect was unchanged for as many miles ahead as we could see. The first decision reached was that we would stay here for a night and a day. This night we would sleep and in the morning we would make an extended exploration along the creek, hoping to find at some point flowing water. Where there was water, we reasoned, there might be life, something we could eat.

Early next morning we piled our *fufaikas* in a mound, split into two trios and set off in opposite directions along the creek.

Kolemenos, the American and I in one party walked a mile or more eastward and found nothing. At times the watercourse disappeared entirely, as though it had gone underground. When we found it again it was still only a damp trail. Reluctantly we concluded that if there were flowing water it must be in some spring below ground and inaccessible to us. Two remarkably healthy-looking snakes were the only sign of life we encountered. We turned back and arrived at the meeting point. We had some time to wait for Zaro, Marchinkovas and Paluchowicz, and had begun to entertain some hopes that their delayed return might mean good tidings when we saw them approaching. Zaro stretched out his hands palms downwards to indicate that the investigation had produced nothing.

"No luck," said Marchinkovas as they came up to us.

"We found nothing, either," I told them.

We drank more of the brown, turgid water. We bathed our feet again and watched the sun mounting in the sky.

Kolemenos spoke. "All this bloody desert and only us and a few snakes to enjoy it. They can't eat us and we can't eat them."

"Only half-true, that statement." It was Mister Smith. "It is not unknown for men to eat snakes."

There was an immediate ripple of interest.

Mister Smith stroked his greying beard thoughtfully. "American Indians eat them. I have seen tourists in America tempted into trying them. I never tried to eat snake myself. I suppose it's a natural human revulsion against reptiles."

We sat in silence a while thinking over what he had said.

He broke in on our thoughts. "You know, gentlemen, I think snakes are our only chance. There's hardly anything a starving man can't eat."

The idea fascinated and repelled at the same time. We talked for a while about it but I think we all knew we were going to make the experiment. There was no choice.

"We need a forked stick to catch them," said Marchinkovas, "and we haven't got one."

"No difficulty about that," I told him. "We'll split the bottoms of a couple of our sticks and jam a small pebble into the cleft."

Kolemenos got up off his haunches. "Let's make a start with the sticks straightaway."

We decided to use Zaro's and Paluchowicz's. The splitting was done by Kolemenos with the axe. The wood was bound with thongs above the split and the small stones rammed home. The result was two efficient-looking instruments.

"How shall we know if the snakes are poisonous? Shall we be able to eat the poisonous kind?" This was Paluchowicz, and he was echoing a doubt that existed in most of our minds.

"There is nothing to worry about," said the American. "The poison is contained in a sac at the back of the head. When you cut off the head you will have removed the poison."

Apart from catching our meal, there remained one problem—fuel for a fire to do the cooking. We turned out our bags for the bits of tinder we always carried. Heaped together the pile was bigger than we had expected. From the bottom of his sack Zaro brought out three or four pats of dried animal dung and solemnly placed them on the collection of hoarded fuel. On another occasion we might have laughed, but smiling through split lips was painful.

"I picked it up at the oasis," said Zaro. "I thought it might be needed for fires some time."

I was sorry that we all had not done as Zaro had done back there. This dried animal waste was excellent fuel which burned slowly and produced fair heat. There had been occasions, too, since the oasis when we had come across little heaps of sun-dried debris deposited by the swirling, dancing whirlwinds which we had seen spiralling across the desert. But we had been too intent on our plodding progress to stop and gather these tiny harvests of the wind. From now on the search for tinder was to be a pre-occupation ranking almost in importance with the hunt for snakes.

Smith and I got down to the job of preparing a fire while the others went off with the two forked sticks. We scratched down through the powdery top sand to the layer of bigger grains below and through that to the bed of small stones beneath. We were looking for a thin flat stone on which to cook our snake. It was fully an hour before we found one. Among the surrounding dunes we had glimpses of the others creeping quietly around in their quest for some unsuspecting reptile. In the way of things in this life, they spent a couple of hours without seeing a sign of one.

When we cared nothing for them we seemed always to be finding them.

The fire was laid. In the blazing sun the flat stone seemed already hot enough for cooking (certainly I think it would have fried an egg easily). Marchinkovas came back to us droop-shouldered. "The snakes must have heard we had changed our minds about them," he said wryly. The three of us sat around the unlighted fire in silence for about another half-an-hour. There came suddenly a great yell from Zaro. We could not see him but we saw Kolemenos and Paluchowicz running in the direction of the sound. We got up and ran, too.

About fifty yards away Zaro had his snake. His stick was firmly about the writhing body a couple of inches behind the head and Zaro was sweating with the exertion of holding it there. We could not judge the size of the creature because all but about six inches of it was hidden in a hole in the sand and the wriggling power of the concealed length was slowly inching the stick back towards the hole. We were tired, weak, slow and clumsy and we ran around and got in one another's way in an effort to help Zaro. Then Paluchowicz jabbed his stick a couple of inches behind Zaro's. I pulled a thong from about my waist, slipped a loop about the snake against the hole and heaved. But there was too much snake inside and too little outside. It was stalemate.

Kolemenos settled the issue. The bright blade of his axe swished down and separated the snake's head from its body. The still wriggling length was hauled into the sunlight. The thing was nearly four feet long. It was as thick as a man's wrist, black above, with a creamy-brown belly lightening to a dull cream-white at the throat.

Zaro struck a pose. "There's your dinner, boys."

The thing still twitched as we carried it back to the fire. We laid it on my sack and, under the direction of the American, I started to skin it. The beginning of the operation was tricky. Smith said the skin could be peeled off entire but I could get no grip at the neck. Eventually I slit the skin a few inches down and with difficulty started to part the snake from its tight sheath. I had never seen an unclothed snake before. The flesh was whitish at first, but in the sun it turned a little darker while we waited

177

for the fire to bring the flat stone to the right heat. We cut the body lengthwise and cleaned it out.

There was still a little reflex of life left as we curled the meat up on the stone over the fire. It sizzled pleasantly. Fat trickled down off the stone and made the fire spit. We streamed sweat as we sat around the fire. We could not take our eyes off the snake. With our sticks we lifted the stone off, turned the meat and put it back for the final stage of grilling, When we thought it was ready to eat we lifted it, stone and all, on to the sand to cool a little.

It lay eventually on my sack a yard or two away from the dying fire. We squatted round it but nobody seemed in a hurry to start carving it up. We looked at one another. Kolemenos spoke. "I am bloody hungry." He reached forward. We all went for it at the same time. Paluchowicz, the man without teeth, stretched his hand out to me for the knife. We ate. It was not long before the snake was reduced to a skeleton. The flesh was close-packed and filling. I had thought the taste might be powerful, even noxious. It was in fact mild, almost tasteless. It had no odour. I was faintly reminded of boiled, unseasoned fish.

"I wish I had thought of snakes earlier," said Mister Smith.

We drank some more of the muddy water. We watched the sun drop from its zenith. We knew that soon we must move again, and we were reluctant to go, to leave this precious ribbon of moisture and launch out again into the unknown, heat-baked country ahead. Sprawled out there, my stomach rumbling as it contended with its barbaric new meal, I longed for a smoke. We still had newspaper but the tobacco had long gone.

No one wanted to bring up the subject of when we should leave, so we talked about other things. For the first time we exchanged ideas freely about Kristina and Makowski. Why should death have overtaken them and left the rest of us still with the strength to carry on? There was no answer to this question, but we mulled it over. We talked of them with sadness and affection. It was, I suppose, an act of remembrance for two absent friends. And it took some of the heavy load of their great loss from us.

I found myself looking at the five of them, taking stock of them, trying to assess our chances. We were all sick men. Kolemenos had his moccasins off and I could see the inflamed raw patches where blisters had formed on punctured blisters, and I knew he was no worse off in this respect than any other of us. All our faces were so disfigured that our nearest relatives would have had difficulty in recognising us. Lips were grotesquely swollen and deeply fissured. Cheeks were sunk in. Brows overhung red-rimmed eyes which seemed to have fallen back in their sockets. We were in an advanced state of scurvy. Only the toothless Paluchowicz escaped the discomfort of teeth rocking loose in sore gums. Already Kolemenos had pulled two aching teeth out between finger and thumb for Marchinkovas and he was to practise his primitive dentistry several times more in the future for others of the party.

Lice, scurvy and the sun had played havoc with our skin. The lice had multiplied with the filthy prolificacy of their kind and swarmed about us. They fed and grew to an obscenely large size. We scratched and scratched at our intolerably irritated bodies until we broke the skin and then our sweat-soaked clothes and untended dirty finger-nails caused the tiny cuts to become septic. This unclean affliction, superficial though it was, was a constant source of depression and misery. I killed the lice when I caught them with savage joy. They were pre-eminently the symbol of our fugitive degradation.

In the end no one took the initiative over our departure. There came a time when Kolemenos and Zaro stood up together. We all rose. We adjusted the wire loops about our necks, picked up our sacks. Into my sack went the flat cooking stone. The American carefully stowed away the little pile of fuel. Grimacing, Kolemenos pulled on his moccasins. We drank a little more water. And in the late afternoon we started off.

Many miles we walked that day, until the light of day faded out and until the stars came out in a purple-black sky. We slept huddled close together and were awake before dawn to start again.

Half-an-hour later Paluchowicz stopped with a groan, clutching his belly, doubled up. In the next hour we were all seized with the most violent, griping pains. All of us were assailed with diarrhoea of an intensity that left us weak and groaning. With the frequent stops we could not have covered more than five miles by late afternoon, when the attacks began to subside.

What had caused it—the snake-meat or the water? We asked one another this question.

Said Mister Smith, "It might well have been the dirty water. But most probably it arises simply from the fact that our empty stomachs are reacting against the sudden load of food and water."

"There's one good way to find out," Kolemenos said. "We'll eat some more snake. I am still hungry."

Marchinkovas shrugged his shoulders. "It will be snakes or nothing."

Paluchowicz gasped with another spasm of stomach ache.

"May God help us," he said, fervently.

XVIII

THE LAST OF THE GOBI

UNQUESTIONABLY the snakes of the Gobi saved us from
death. We caught two within minutes of each other the
next day. One was like the common European grass snake,
the other arrayed in the brilliance of a silver-grey skin marked
down the back with a dull red broad stripe flanked closely parallel
with two thin lines of the same colour. Profiting by the experience
of my difficulty in skinning the first specimen, we clubbed these
two to death and held the heads in Zaro's forked stick while I
stripped off the skins.

We did not like these two coloured snakes as much as we had
the first capture. They were thinner-bodied and we imagined they
tasted less pleasantly. I think the colours affected our judgment.
The big black was not unlike a conger eel in appearance and in the
texture of the flesh. Thereafter we sought specially for this species
and counted ourselves lucky when we found one.

The clear fat which oozed out over the heat of the fire we used
as a balm for our lips, our sore eyes and our feet and the soothing
effect lasted for hours.

Two days after leaving the creek we had visitors. First there
wheeled lazily over us half-a-dozen ravens. They stayed with us
throughout the morning and then made a leisurely departure as
we erected our shelter at midday. We were wondering what had
prompted their departure when two great shadows skimmed
along the sand. We looked up and saw not twenty feet above a
pair of magnificent, long-necked eagles, their plumage looking
black against the sun. They passed over us several times and then
alighted on the top of a sandy hillock twenty yards away and
looked down on us. The spread of wings as they came into land
was enormous.

"What do you think *they* want?" someone asked.

The American considered. "It's fairly obvious, I think, that they saw the ravens and came to investigate the prospects of food."

Zaro said, "Well, they're not having *me*."

"Don't worry," I assured him. "They won't attack us."

Zaro stood up and shouted at the great birds. He made motions of throwing. The pair disdained to notice his antics. He scratched away at the sand and produced a couple of pebbles. He aimed carefully and threw. The stone sent up a puff of sand a yard short of them. One held its ground and the other did an ungainly single hop. Zaro hurled the second stone wide of its mark and the two eagles sat unmoved. They took off in their own good time as we dismantled the shelter and followed us for about an hour, high in the sky, before swinging away to the south and disappearing.

"Eagles live in mountains," said the American. "Perhaps we haven't far to go to get out of the desert."

We could see a long way ahead and there were no distant mountains. "They can also fly great distances," I said.

For three or four days we were tormented with stomach pain and its attendant diarrhoea; then, as we began to long for water again, the stomach trouble passed away. As we trudged on there were days when we caught not a glimpse of a snake. Another day and we would pick up a couple basking in the sun in a morning's search. We ate them as soon as we found them. There was a red-letter day when we caught two of the kind we called Big Blacks within half-an-hour. The days dragged by. We were inspected again by both the ravens and the eagles. We were able now to make a fix on a couple of bright stars and sometimes walked long after dark. We began again to dream longing dreams of water.

I lost count of the days again. My fitful sleep was invaded by visions of reptiles so tenacious of life that though I beat at them with my club in a frenzy they still hissed at me and crawled. All my fears came bursting through in dreams. Worst of all was the picture of myself staggering on alone, shouting for the others and knowing that I should never see them again. I would wake shivering in the morning cold and be happily reassured to see Smith, Kolemenos, Zaro, Marchinkovas and Paluchowicz close about me.

Almost imperceptibly the terrain was changing. The yellow sand was deepening in colour, the grains were coarser, the smooth topped dunes taller. The sun still burned its shrivelling way across

182

the blue, unclouded heavens but now there were days when a gentle breeze sighed out from the south and there was a hint of coolness in its caress. The nights were really cold and I had the impression that we were day by day gradually climbing out of the great heat-bowl.

It might have been a week or eight days after leaving the creek that we awoke to discover in a quickening of excitement and hope a new horizon. The day was sharply clear. Far over to the east, perhaps fifty miles away, shrouded in a blue haze like lingering tobacco smoke, a mountain range towered. Directly ahead there were also heights but they were mere foothills compared with the eastward eminences. So uninformed were we of Central Asian geography that we speculated on the possibility that the tall eastern barrier could be the Himalayas, that somehow we had by-passed them to the west, that we might now even be on the threshold of India. We were to learn that the whole considerable north-to-south expanse of Tibet, ruggedly harsh and mountainous, lay between us and the Himalayas.

We plodded on for two more exhausting, heart-breaking days before we reached firm ground, a waste of lightly-sanded rocks. We lay there in the extremity of our weakness and looked back at our tracks through the sand. There were no defined footmarks, only a dragging trail such as skis make in snow. Lifeless and naked the rocky ridge sloped easily into the distance above us. In my mind was the one thought that over the hump there might be water. We rested a couple of hours before we tackled the drag upwards. We took off our moccasins and emptied them of sand. We brushed the fine dust from between our toes. Then we went up and out of the Gobi.

Over the ridge there was more desolation. By nightfall we had dropped down into a stone-strewn valley. We might have struggled on longer but Marchinkovas fell and banged his knee. In the morning he showed us a big bruise and complained of a little stiffness but was able to walk. The pain passed off as he exercised it and he experienced no more trouble from the injury. We climbed again. There was no talking because none of us could spare the breath and movement of the lips was agony. We hauled ourselves along through a faint dawn mist and did not reach this next summit for several hours. From the top there was the view again of the great range to the east, looking even more formidable than at our first sight of it. Ahead there seemed to be an unbroken succession of low ridges corrugating the country as far as we could see. Below us the floor of the valley appeared to be covered with sand and we decided to get down before dark to search for snakes.

It was the merest accident that we did not miss the water on our way down. We had all passed it when Zaro turned round and yelled the one wonderful word. It was no more than a trickle from a crack in a rock but it glinted like silver. It crept down over the curve of a big round boulder and spread thinly over a flat rock below. Kolemenos and I had been picking our way down the slope some twenty yards ahead of Zaro when his shout arrested us. We turned quickly and scrambled back. We found that the source of the little spring was a crack just wide enough to take the fingers of one hand. The water was sparkling, clean and ice-cold. We channeled the tiny stream to a point where we could lead it into our battered and much travelled metal mug and sat down impatiently to watch it fill. The operation took fully ten minutes.

I said to Zaro, "You had passed this point. What made you turn round and find it?"

Zaro spoke quite seriously. "I think I must have smelt it. It was quite a strong impulse that made me turn my head."

The water tinkled musically into the mug until it was brimming. Carefully Zaro lifted it away and I noticed his hand was trembling a little so that some of the water spilled over. He faced Smith and with a bow, and, in imitation of the Mongolian etiquette of serving the senior first, handed him the water. The mug was passed round and each man took a gulp. No nectar of the gods could have tasted so wonderful. Again and again we filled the mug and drank. And then we left it, full and running over, under the life-giving spring so that any of us could drink whenever he felt like it.

The time was around the middle of the day. We agreed readily that we should stay close to the spring for another twenty-four hours, but up here on the hillside nothing lived—and we were very hungry. I volunteered to go down into the sandy valley to search for a snake and Zaro said he would come with me. We took the two forked sticks and set off, turning at intervals to look back and fix the position of the squatting group about the spring.

The descent took us over an hour and the heat shimmered off the sandy, boulder-strewn floor of the valley. Our hopes were immediately raised by seeing a snake about a yard long slither away at our approach and disappear under a rock but we foraged around well into the afternoon after that without seeing another living thing. Then we parted and went opposite ways and I had almost decided it was time to give up the quest when I heard Zaro let out a whoop of triumph. I ran to him and found him pinning down a Big Black which was thrashing about desperately in an effort to break free. I reversed my stick and battered it to death. I put my arm about Zaro's shoulders and congratulated him. He was always our Number One snake-catcher.

Zaro wore his capture like a trophy about his neck as we toiled back up the hillside. We were soaked with sweat and exhausted by the time we reached the spring and Kolemenos took over my usual job of skinning and preparing the snake for the fire. Paluchowicz had laid a fire from our few remaining sticks on which was placed the last piece of camel dung which Zaro had gathered at the oasis. There was not enough heat to cook the meat thoroughly but we were too hungry to be squeamish. We ate and we drank as the sun went down. Only Kolemenos slept well that night; for the rest of us it was too cold for comfort.

The next morning we were on our way again. This time there were no stomach cramps, which led us to believe that we owed at least some of the previous trouble to the muddy creek. We travelled down the long slope, across the hot valley and up the hillside facing us—a total of at least fifteen miles. From the top of the ridge we took fresh bearings. Directly ahead were some formidable heights, so we set our course over easier ground about ten degrees east of the line due south. Towards evening we were heartened by the discovery of the first vegetation we had seen since the oasis. It was a rough, spiky grass clinging hardily to dry rootholds in fissures between the rocks. We pulled up a clump, handed it round and closely examined it like men who had never seen grass before.

The wearing trek went on day after day. Our diet was still confined to an occasional snake—we lived on them altogether for upwards of three weeks from the time of our first sampling back in the desert. The nights set in with a chill which produced a frosty white rime on the stones of the upper hillsides. In vain we looked for signs of animal life, but there were birds: from time to time a pair of hovering hawks, some gossiping magpies and our old acquaintances the ravens. The wiry mountain grass grew more abundant with each passing day and its colour was greener. Then the country presented us with struggling low bushes and lone-growing dwarf trees, ideal fuel for the fires which we now started to light every night. The spectre of thirst receded as we found clear-running rivulets. It was rare now that we had to go waterless for longer than a day.

There came a day when we breasted the top of a long rise and looked unbelievingly down into a wide-spreading valley which showed far below the lush green of grazing grass. Still more exciting, there were, crawling like specks five miles or more distant from and below us, a flock of about a hundred sheep. We made the descent fast, slipping and sliding in our eagerness to get down. As we got nearer we heard the bleating and calling of the sheep. We had about a quarter of a mile to go to reach the flock when we saw the two dogs, long-coated liver-and-white collie types. They came racing round the flock to take up station between us and their charges.

Zaro called out to them, "Don't worry, we won't hurt them. Where's your master?" The dogs eyed him warily.

Kolemenos growled, "I only need to get near enough to a sheep for one swing of my old axe. . . ."

"Don't get impatient, Anastazi," I told him. "It is fairly obvious the shepherd has sent his dogs over here to intercept us. Let us swing away from the flock and see if they will lead us to their master."

We turned pointedly away. The dogs watched us closely for a couple of minutes. Then, apparently satisfied, they had headed us away from the sheep, ran off at great speed together towards the opposite slope of the valley. My eyes followed the line of their run ahead of them and then I shouted and pointed. A mile or more away rose a thin wisp of smoke.

"A fire at midday can only mean cooking," said Marchinkovas hopefully.

The fire was burning in the lee of a rocky outcrop against which had been built a one-man shelter of stones laid one above the other as in an old cairn. Seated there was an old man, his two dogs, tongues lolling, beside him. He spoke to his dogs as we neared him and they got up and raced off back across the valley to the flock. Steaming over the fire was a black iron cauldron. The American went to the front and approached bowing. The old man rose smiling and returned the bow and then went on to bow to each of us in turn.

He was white-bearded. The high cheek-bones in his broad, square face showed a skin which had been weathered to the colour of old rosewood. He wore a warm goatskin cap with ear-flaps turned up over the crown in the fashion of the Mongols we had met in the north. His felt boots were well made and had stout leather soles. His unfastened three-quarter-length sheepskin coat was held to the body by a woven wool girdle and his trousers were bulkily padded, probably with lamb's-wool. He leaned his weight on a five-feet-tall wooden staff, the lower end of which was iron-spiked and the upper part terminating in a flattened "V" crutch formed by the bifurcation of the original branch. In a leather-bound wooden sheath he carried a bone-handled knife which I later observed was double-edged and of good workmanship. To greet us he got up from a rug of untreated sheepskin. There was no doubt of his friendliness and his pleasure at the arrival of unexpected visitors.

He talked eagerly and it was a minute or two before he realised we did not understand a word. I spoke in Russian and he regarded me blankly. It was a great pity because he must have been looking forward to conversation and the exchange of news. I think he was trying to tell us he had seen us a long way off and had prepared food against our arrival. He motioned us to sit near the fire and resumed the stirring of the pot which our coming had interrupted. I looked into the stone shelter and saw there was just room for one man to sleep. On the floor was a sleeping mat fashioned from bast.

As he wielded his big wooden spoon he made another attempt at conversation. He spoke slowly. It was no use. For a while there was silence. Mister Smith cleared his throat. He gestured with his arm around the group of us. "We," he said slowly in Russian, "go to Lhasa." The shepherd's eyes grew intelligent. "Lhasa, Lhasa," Smith repeated, and pointed south. From inside his jacket the old fellow pulled out a prayer-wheel which looked as if it had been with him for many years. The religious signs were painted on parchment, the edges of which were worn with use. He pointed to the sun and made circles, many of them, with his outstretched arm.

"He is trying to tell us how many days it will take us to reach Lhasa," I said.

"His arm's going round like a windmill," observed Zaro. "It must be a hell of a long way from here."

We bowed our acknowledgment of the information. From his pocket he produced a bag of salt—good quality stuff and almost white—and invited us to look into the cauldron as he sprinkled some in. We crowded round and saw a bubbling, greyish, thick gruel. He stirred again, brought out a spoonful, blew on it, smacked his lips, tasted and finally thrust out his tongue and ran it round his lips. He chuckled at us like a delighted schoolboy and his good humour was so infectious that we found ourselves laughing aloud in real enjoyment for the first time for months.

The next move by the old man had almost a ritualistic air. From his shack he produced an object wrapped in a linen bag. He looked at us, eyes twinkling, and I could not help thinking of a conjuror building up suspense for the trick which was to astound his audience. I think we all looked suitably impressed as he opened the bag and reached into it. Into the sunlight emerged a wooden bowl about five inches in diameter and three inches deep, beautifully turned, shining with care and use, of a rich walnut brown colour. He blew on it, brushed it with his sleeve and handed it round. It was indeed a thing of which a man could be proud, the work of a craftsman. We handed it back with murmurs of appreciation.

Into the bowl he ladled a quantity of gruel and laid it on the skin rug. He disappeared into the shack and came out holding an unglazed earthenware jar, dark-brown and long-necked. It held about a gallon of ewe's milk, a little of which he added to the gruel in the bowl. He made no attempt at working out our seniority but handed the bowl and spoon to Zaro, who was seated nearest to him. Zaro ate a spoonful, smacked his lips and made to pass the bowl around, but the shepherd gently held his arm and indicated he was to finish the portion.

Zaro made short but evidently highly enjoyable work of it. "By God, that tastes wonderful," he exclaimed.

It was my turn next. The main ingredient seemed to be barley, but some kind of fat had been added. The sweet, fresh milk had cooled the mixture down a little and I fairly wolfed it down. I could feel the soothing warmth of it reaching my ill-treated stomach. I belched loudly, smacked my lips and handed back the bowl.

He saw to the needs of each of us in turn before he ate himself. To what was left in the cauldron he added several pints of milk and started stirring again, making enough extra to give us each another bowlful.

He took the cauldron off the fire to cool off, moving it with some difficulty because it had no handle, although I noticed there were the usual two holes in the rim. To our unspeakable joy he then produced tobacco from a skin pouch and handed us each enough for two or three cigarettes. Out came the pieces of hoarded newspaper. We lit up with glowing brands from the fire. We were happy in that moment and brimming over with gratitude towards a supremely generous host. And he, bless him, sat there cross-legged and basked in our smiles.

Away he went after about half-an-hour, refusing offers of help, to wash the cauldron and the precious bowl at a nearby spring. He came back, stoked up the fire and made us tea, Tibetan style, and this time we even faintly approved the taste of the rancid butter floating in globules on the surface.

I felt I wanted to do something for the old man. I said to Kolemenos, "Let's make him a handle for his cauldron out of one of the spare wire loops." Everybody thought it an excellent idea. It took us only about thirty minutes to break off a suitable length, shape it and fasten it. Our host was delighted.

We tried to think of some other service we could render. Someone suggested we forage for wood for the fire. We were away about an hour and came back with a pile of stuff, including a complete small tree which Kolemenos had hacked down with his axe. The shepherd had been waiting for our return. As we came in he was finishing sharpening his knife on a smooth piece of stone. He had his two dogs with him again. He made us sit down and, with his dogs at his heels, strode off.

189

He returned shortly dragging by the wool between its horns a young ram, the dogs circling him in quiet excitement as he came. In something like five minutes the ram was dead, butchered with practised skill. He wanted no help from us on this job. He skinned and gutted the carcase with a speed which made my own abilities in this direction seem clumsy. The carcase finally was quartered. Salt was rubbed in one fore and one hind quarter, which were hung inside the stone hut. He threw the head and some other oddments to the dogs.

Half the sheep was roasted on wooden spits over the blazing fire that night and we ate again to repletion. We made signs that we would like to stay overnight and he seemed only too willing that we should. The six of us slept warm around the fire, while the shepherd lay the night inside his hut.

From somewhere he produced the next morning a batch of rough barley cakes—three each was our share. There was more tea and, to our astonishment, because we thought the limit of hospitality must already have been reached, the rest of the ram was roasted and shared out, and a little more tobacco distributed.

We left him in the early afternoon, after first restocking his fuel store. We did not know how to thank him for his inestimable kindness. Gently we patted his back and smiled at him. I think we managed to convey to him that he had made half-a-dozen most grateful friends.

At last we stood off a few feet from him and bowed low, keeping our eyes, according to custom, on his face. Gravely he returned the salute. We turned and walked away. When I turned he was sitting with his back to us, his dogs beside him. He did not look round.

XIX

I THINK IT probable that at the time we encountered the old man and his sheep we had not even entered Tibet but had come out from the desert into the highlands in the narrow neck of the Chinese province of Kansu lying along the north-eastern border of Tibet. The time then was about the beginning of October 1941 and it was to take us over three months to cover about fifteen hundred miles of difficult country to the Himalayas. We tried always to do at least twenty miles a day. Often we did more. There were occasional days, too, when we did no travelling, glad of the rest and refreshment provided by friendly Tibetan villagers. The tradition of hospitality to travellers was an innate and wonderful part of the life of these people, their generosity was open-handed and without thought of reward. Without their help we could not have kept going.

It seemed to me that our resistance to the increasingly sharp cold of the nights was markedly weaker than it had been when we first made our break at the end of the Siberian winter. The ordeal of the Gobi had left its imprint on us all. We found ourselves plodding on after the reasonable limit of a day's march had been reached in order to find a spot offering fair shelter for the night. On the other hand we sometimes cut short the scheduled distance on discovering a small cave or some other well-protected place. The gathering of fuel became almost an obsession and it became unthinkable that we should spend a night without a fire burning throughout.

In the mornings the ground was thick with white frost and it stayed for a long time after the sun had risen. The skyline to the east was indented with the silhouettes of peaks white-tipped with snow. As always, we wondered just where we were.

We came across our first village some five days after leaving the shepherd. We had been on the move for about an hour after dawn when I saw, over to the left of our course and up to ten miles distant, a smear of smoke. We were hungry, stiff and not very warm. We decided to investigate. We came down a hill scrub-covered on its upper reaches, giving way to grass of good sheep-grazing quality. As we got nearer we saw the smoke came from several fires and knew we were approaching some kind of settlement, hidden from us by the rounded shoulder of the opposite hill.

It was well past noon when we reached the village. The hill threw out a green-clothed buttress like a long arm and ten small box-like houses nestled there like a child in the crook of its mother's arm. Each house was about twenty feet by twelve feet, flat-roofed with overlapping wide boards weighted down with stones. The roofs sloped slightly forward in the direction of the overlap. A few of the dwellings were backed by a fenced-in enclosure containing an outhouse a couple of yards square. The slopes around were dotted with dozens of long-haired sheep, some brown and some grey. We came in slowly on an almost due west-east track, frequently pausing to look round so that the villagers would have ample warning of our visit. We did not know then what reception to expect.

A closer view of the village revealed the presence of a number of children, some chickens, goats and the first yaks any of us had ever seen outside a zoo. At a leisurely shuffle, strung out in couples, we came near to the first house and stopped, interested in the novel spectacle of a man harnessing a yak to a high two-wheeled cart. He had seen us but had his hands too full with the task in hand to do anything about it. Half-a-dozen shy but frankly inquisitive children, the eldest about ten years, positioned themselves about the cart and eyed us. The yak, its long silken hair riffling in the breeze blowing through the valley, was being difficult and was doing its best not to be attached to the cart. Possibly it had got wind of us and did not care for the evidence of its nose. (I couldn't have blamed it for any adverse opinion based on the smell of us!)

The villager decided suddenly to give up the struggle. He dropped the harness and let the beast go free. We stood our distance as he turned towards us. We bowed, our eyes on his young, flat, glistening face. Meticulously he returned the saluta-tion. The children watched silently. Kolemenos and I stepped forward a few paces, smiling. The children broke out into a chatter at the impressive stature of the big man, his long blond beard and hair. We stood in front of the man and bowed again. He talked and I talked but all the pair of us learned was that we could not understand each other. The children grouped themselves behind the man and listened to the exchange. All the time they kept darting glances at the blond giant. The villager turned round, walked a few paces, turned and motioned us to follow. The children ran past and ahead of him to spread the news through the village of our coming.

As we trod close on the heels of our guide I looked about me. I saw a few cultivated patches but nothing was now growing on them. I saw a woman leave a goat she was milking and hasten indoors. More children came out of houses and shyly scrutinised the strangers. Beyond the last house, some twenty or thirty yards from it, I saw the village was bounded on the eastern side by a stream. I thought how well the place was sited. I noted how quickly the children lost their shyness: soon there were a dozen pattering along beside us. At about the middle of the uneven row of houses the guide stopped. This dwelling followed the same unassuming pattern as the others, but it was distinguished from them by being slightly larger and having a porch formed of two sturdy timbers at its door.

"This looks interesting," Mister Smith whispered to me as the man disappeared through the door.

"I think he's gone inside to fetch the Mayor," said Zaro.

There was not much time for further speculation. Almost as though he had been waiting behind the door, a new figure emerged through the porch. I judged him to be about fifty and he wore the normal dress of the country topped with a loose sheepskin jacket. He was a little taller than the average Mongolian and, though as dark as any of them, his features were not of so pronounced a Mongolian cast. We exchanged the usual greetings before he spoke in the language of the country. I shook my head and replied in slow, precise Russian. His face lit up, he beamed at me.

"Welcome," he said in Russian. "Now we shall be able to talk."

We were rather taken aback. He spoke Russian easily and without hesitation. I had to remind myself that there could be no danger so far south of the Soviet in a chance encounter with a Russian.

He waited a moment for me to reply and when I did not he went on eagerly, "I am a Circassian and it is a long time since I met anyone who could speak Russian."

"A Circassian?" I repeated. "That is most interesting." I could not think of anything less banal to say.

His questions tumbled over themselves. "Are you pilgrims? It is not many Russians who are Buddhists. You came through the Gobi on foot?"

"Yes, on foot."

"It must have been a terrible experience for you. Once I nearly died myself on that journey."

He was going to ask more questions, but suddenly recollected his duty as a host. He apologised and invited us into his home. We trooped inside. A stone partition divided the one big room and I caught a glimpse of a woman I took to be his wife hustling three or four children out of the front half to presumably the kitchen at the rear. Little details leapt into notice—a few shining tin mugs, a row of wooden spoons on a shelf, a bunch of hanging dried herbs and, most oddly, in one corner a framed six-inch-square lithograph of Saint Nicholas in the Russian Orthodox style, much faded behind its glass pane. Underneath the lower edge of the frame was a metal stand on which stood a miniature oil lamp of simple construction with a red glass. There were wooden benches, solidly made, a stone cooking range, a heavy wooden bucket with a boat-shaped dipper, a flour mill, a primitive wool-spinning machine. The small amount of space available was well utilised. Around the walls were wooden bunks covered with home-woven rough wool blankets.

We sat, rather awkwardly in such unusual surroundings, on the benches. The Circassian—either designedly or perhaps forgetfully, he never gave us his name and we never volunteered ours—addressed himself to me again. The first question startled us.

"Are you armed?"

"No, none of us is armed," I answered.

"Have you nothing even to chop wood with, for instance?"

"Oh, yes. We have an axe and a knife between the six of us, unless you count the sticks we carry."

"Is that all? It isn't very safe to travel in this part, you know."

I was puzzled. "I don't understand you. We have met with no trouble up to now."

He paused a moment, looking us over. "Have you seen any Chinese? I mean armed Chinese, Chinese soldiers."

"No, not a sign of one."

Then he got up and went from the room. Smith leaned over to me and urged me to find out some more about the mysterious Chinese.

He came back in about five minutes. I think he had been out to give instructions about the preparation of a meal. He listened gravely to my question.

"I thought it right to warn you," he said, "that Chinese troops occasionally pass through this village. Sometimes they buy fowls from us. They seem to be exploring the area, although this is Tibet. I have seen them go off to the south in the direction of Lhasa. Since you speak only Russian they would be suspicious of you. If you see them it would be best to stay out of their way."

It was well-meant advice and I thanked him for it, but we never did run across any Chinese soldiers.

Within half-an-hour of our arrival we were being regaled with tea and oaten cakes. Nobody spoke much until the food had gone. We were too busy filling our empty stomachs. Then our host produced a pipe and a bowl of tobacco and handed round the bowl. Soon the place was a haze of blue smoke which drifted out through the open door.

"So you are going to Lhasa," he said between puffs of his pipe. He said it politely as a conversational gambit. I do not think he necessarily believed it.

"Don't forget," he warned us, "that the nights are fiercely cold, especially on the heights. You must never be tempted to seek sleep without adequate shelter. You must never be too tired to build yourselves a fire. If you go to sleep unprotected on the mountains you will be dead in the morning. It is a swift death and you will never know it is happening to you.

"You are going in the right direction for Lhasa. There is a track from here for the next stage of your journey which you will find easy to follow. Tonight you must all stay here and in the morning I will show you how to go. These tracks can be confusing and in following them you must keep your sense of direction. Some of them lead only from village to village in a small area and you would waste a lot of time on them. They are almost family affairs, trails beaten out over centuries.

"If you come across any village towards nightfall, stay there until the morning. You will always have a roof over your heads and be given a meal. No one will ask you for payment."

"Our trouble," Mister Smith broke in, "is that we do not know the language."

Our host smiled. "That is not such a handicap. If you bow to a Tibetan and he bows back, no other introduction is needed. You are accepted as a friend."

In the early evening we were treated to a meal of roasted mutton which one of the Circassian's elder sons had killed soon after our arrival. While we ate, the father cut off strips of meat for the younger children and they ran out through the door with the meat in their hands. Salt was produced in a bowl to help our eating and I fear I ate a lot more of it than a thoughtful guest should have done. It was a delight to savour its sharp piquancy again.

After the evening meal half-a-dozen men neighbours joined the party, packing the room to its limits. The hard-working Tibetan wife produced more tea. Each of the visitors produced proudly a fine wooden bowl of the kind which the lone shepherd had shown us five days before. Here again it was evident that these were precious possessions.

"What is so precious about these bowls?" I asked our host.

"Do you know," he replied, "that a man will sometimes trade two yaks for one of those?"

"But why are they so precious?"

"Because they just cannot be made in these mountain districts. They are fashioned with great skill from a special kind of hard-wood which does not crack. Age increases their polish and their value. One of the reasons they are kept in linen bags is that the cloth improves the shine by constant rubbing against the wood."

The men drank tea from their bowls and when they had finished the bowls were taken away and washed. Although they all looked alike to me, each man knew his own, and they were affectionately stowed away in their linen bags before the pipes were brought out and the tobacco handed round. Smoke was puffed out in great clouds and the Circassian was kept busy translating the busy talk between us and the neighbours. In this community he was obviously of great eminence, much respected for his gift of tongues and knowledge of matters of the big world outside the valley. He was human enough to enjoy his rôle, but carried it off with dignity and modesty.

As the place warmed up, the lice began to stir from their hideouts in our clothes. My body began to itch and so did my conscience. Out of the corner of my eye I saw the others reaching inside their *fufaikas* for a furtive scratch. I sidled over to the Circassian and spoke quietly.

"I think my friends and I should sleep outside tonight. We have picked up a lot of lice on our travels and can't get rid of them.

He laid a hand lightly on my shoulder. "Please set your mind at rest. Lice are no strangers to us. Tonight you all sleep under my roof."

The others asked me what the talk had been about. I retailed it to them. They smiled their relief. It seemed I had not been the only one to have worried about our uninvited camp-followers.

The neighbours bade us goodnight and went their way. They went like men who have had a rare and enjoyable evening. I could imagine that we had provided them with material for many a reminiscent talk to brighten their uneventful lives. We had told them only a fraction of what they must have wanted to know, but they would have fun filling in the blanks. Many of their questions had been about Kolemenos. This fair-haired big man from another world intrigued them mightily. We told them he came from a Western country near the sea. Kolemenos added the word Latvia, but it meant nothing to them.

We slept in bunks—our first night under a roof since our escape. How the family disposed themselves for the night I do not know. There was some makeshift arrangement behind the stone partition for the Circassian and his wife but I think the children must have been taken in by other villagers. For the first time I felt able to relax. I had a glorious, warm feeling of complete safety. I slept a deep, refreshing, untensed sleep and only half-woke at the urging of the rising sun. They let us lie on until the day was a few hours old. The household had long been astir and two of the younger children were peering in at us as we sat up in our beds. They ran out and I heard them chattering to their father.

Our benefactor came in with some squares of thick home-spun linen over his arm. "Perhaps you gentlemen would like to wash?" he inquired with a smile.

"This is real hotel service," Zaro joked. "Just lead us to the bathroom."

The Circassian joined in the laugh. "It is at the end of the village—nice, clean, flowing water."

We went down to the stream. The morning air was sharp but we stripped to the waist, immersed our heads in the water, gasped, splashed and rubbed vigorously. We were tempted to wash our jackets and fur waistcoats but decided that we should have to wait too long for them to dry. We felt fine and chuckled at some spontaneous clowning by Zaro on the way back. The inevitable following of curious children enjoyed his antics even more.

We were given more meat, more oaten cakes, more tea. Then it was time to go.

"When you come back this way," said the Circassian earnestly, "do not forget this house. It will always be a home to you."

The American answered, "Thank you. You have been very kind and generous to us."

I said, "Will you please thank your wife for all she has done for us."

He turned to me. "I won't do that. She would not understand your thanks. But I will think of something to say to her that will please her."

He spoke to her and her face broke into a great smile. She went away and returned with a wooden platter piled with flat oaten cakes, handed them to her husband and spoke to him.

"She wants you to take them with you," he told us. We shared them out gratefully.

There was one other parting gift—a fine fleece from the man, handed over with the wish that it might be used to make new footwear or repair our worn moccasins. We never did use it for that purpose, but later it made us half-a-dozen pairs of excellent mittens to shield our hands from the mountain cold.

He walked with us out of the village, pointed out our way.

For the only time in our travels we received specific and detailed instructions of our route.

"Some of the tracks you will follow will not be easy to find," he warned. "Don't look for them at your feet; look ahead into the distance—they show up quite clearly then."

He described landmarks we were to seek. The first was to be a crown-shaped mountain about four days distant and we were to take a path which would lead us over the saddle between the two north-facing points of the "crown". From the heights we were to set course for a peak shaped like a sugar-loaf, which we would find to be deceptively far away. It might take us two weeks to reach it, he thought. More than that he could not from here tell us accurately, but eventually we should reach a road leading to Lhasa which at some point forked east to the city and south-west to the villages of the Himalayan foothills.

We left him there, a little knot of children at his heels. When we turned round he made a most un-Mongolian gesture—he waved his arm to us. The last we saw of him was a figure still waving a farewell.

Marchinkovas spoke for us all when he said, "These people make me feel very humble. They do a lot to wipe out bitter memories of other people who have lost their respect for humanity."

For a few days we were on the look-out for Chinese troops, but we met no one and saw no one. We disciplined ourselves not to touch our oatcakes until the third day—we had three each—and then we spread out the eating of them as an iron ration. Our track was clearly marked and the way was not too hard. There were plenty of small bushy trees something like the dwarf junipers of Siberia which burned brightly and gave out good heat. At the end of the fourth day we camped at the foot of the crown-shaped mountain and started our climb at first light the next day. The ascent was long but not difficult and the crossing occupied us two days.

It had been fully a week since our last real meal when we came across a mixed herd of sheep and goats and found the two houses of the Tibetans who owned them. The day was warm and brightly sunny after the freezing temperatures of the heights. There were scattered bushes of a species of wild rose, attracting the eye with gay blooms of yellow and red and white.

199

The house into which we were taken by the Tibetan herdsman was in the same style as that of the Circassian but smaller and not so well equipped. But the courtesy and the hospitality was of the same impeccable standard. The family consisted of the man and his wife in their middle thirties, a woman of about 25 who could have been the wife's sister, and four children whose ages ranged from about 5 to 16. We were given milk to drink on arrival and later two massive meals of goatmeat. By signs we were urged to spend the night and willingly accepted the offer. The whole family turned out to bow their farewells in the morning.

After about an hour's walking Marchinkovas stopped to examine his moccasins and found the rocky going had worn a hole through one of the soles. We all sat down with him and had a mending session. All our shoes were in a bad state. Some of the repairs involved almost complete remaking.

The explicit directions of the Circassian led us unerringly to the looming bulk of the sugar-loaf mountain and over it. The crossing would have been easier for me had not my old leg wound just above the ankle started to break open. I made a bandage by cutting a length of the rough material from the top of my sack, but the wound remained sore and painful to touch.

For a well-accoutred tourist or explorer the country would have presented a picture of inspiring grandeur, range after range thrown up in some primeval convulsion of the earth's crust. To us it was a country besetting our escape route with obstacles. Our suffering feet were the arbiters of judgment and Tibet was cruel to them. There were nights when in the dancing lights of a blazing fire I could have slept soundly, but my feet, punished on a rocky climb, kept me awake, throbbing, aching and protesting at the burden put upon them. Pulses of pain reminded me, too, of the spite of a German grenade fragment which I had not felt at the time it thudded home.

On the other side of the sugar-loaf we found a stretch of country which presented comparatively easy travel. In the distance, throwing back the sun's rays we saw a lake about four miles in circumference. With visions of bathing and refreshing ourselves in its inviting waters, we hastened towards it. I tore my moccasins off and dipped both feet in. The cool water stung. Zaro cupped some of it in his two hands and took it to his lips. A second later he was spluttering and spitting it back. The water was salt, more strongly impregnated with salt than the sea, stiff with the stuff. I let my feet soak but I did not attempt to drink. We moved on to look for fresh water but after a few hours my ankle became so sore that I stopped to examine it. The wound was festering and I became racked with worry that it might halt me altogether.

Before the day was out we reached a fast-flowing river, chuckling over its stony bed. Here we drank and washed ourselves. The water raised goose pimples on our skins but the sun dried us and we felt better. Paluchowicz advised me to soak and rub my hessian bandage before replacing it about my ankle. I did as he said and hoped for the best.

We had deviated a couple of miles off our course to reach this river, which flowed, as far as we could judge, directly from north to south. For several days we followed it along. It made for easier travelling along fairly flat ground and we avoided the probing cold of the higher altitudes. In the end it turned on a sharp bend to the west and we swam it so as not to be diverted off our southerly course. My ankle was less troublesome, the skin showed signs of healing and the discharge from the wound had almost stopped.

We were in great need of food again and made detours if we thought a greener valley might support flocks and people. Marchinkovas had trod on a sharp spur of rock and was limping. We knew that we had to find somewhere to eat and to rest for a day.

XX

FIVE BY-PASS LHASA

THE WEEKS dragged on, October made way for November, the days were cool and the nights were freezing. Over long stretches of country too barren to support even sheep and goats we sometimes went for four and five days without food. There were bleak, mist-enveloped mornings when I felt leadenly dispirited, drained of energy and reluctant to flog my weary body into movement. We all had our bad days in turn. The meals we were so generously given were massive but we lacked fresh green-stuff. The result was that we continued to be ravaged by scurvy. But we counted ourselves fortunate that no member of the party suffered a major breakdown in health and the march went on. We swam turbulent rivers when we had to. We negotiated formidable-looking peaks which turned out on closer acquaintance to offer surprisingly little difficulty; we struggled over innocent-looking hills which perversely offered precipitous resistance to our advance.

Marchinkovas one night started a discussion on the advisability of pressing on right through to the Himalayas. He thought we should consider going to Lhasa or some other city where we could live for a time and build up strength for the last stage. He was mildly supported by Paluchowicz. The rest of us were against wasting time. I was afraid such temporising might soften the hard core of our resolution. The months had built up a compulsive migrant force in us, a rigid, driving habit of movement, and I wanted no interference with it until we had reached the final and complete safety of India.

The American put up the practical consideration that we might not find ourselves so warmly welcomed by the officialdom of a big city as we had been by the country people. There might be awkward questions, demands that we should produce papers.

Marchinkovas was not insistent on his idea. He had thrown it in to sound out opinion and was quite content with the outcome. It had not been a suggestion born of any sense of defeatism. Marchinkovas was as convinced of eventual success as the rest of us. We could not afford to think of failure.

It was about this time that we found a use for the strong wire loops we had brought with us out of the desert. We found our way blocked where the track over a hill had been broken away by a fall of rock. To get round we had to face the climber's hazard of an overhang surmounted by a sharp spur. We made a ten-foot length of plaited thongs, tied it firmly to Kolemenos's loop and had him from his superior height try to lasso the tip of the rock spur. It took a dozen throws before the wire settled over. Then, gradually, Kolemenos put the strain of his still considerable weight on the rope. It held firm. Zaro, as one of the lighter members, volunteered to go up first. He climbed with great care, not trusting absolutely to the rope but making use of what slight hand- and foot-holds there were. With Zaro tending the anchored end, we all made it quite easily, Kolemenos climbing last.

There was a well-spaced-out succession of unremarkable villages and hamlets, alike in their simple architecture and in the full measure of hospitality they accorded us. They presented no feature by which I can remember them individually. But there was one we found at this time that stands out sharp in the memory because of a most unlikely encounter.

The place was so small and so well tucked away, just six close-grouped houses, that we might easily have passed it by had not our route brought us just within sight of a corner of it. We were escorted in by a smiling young Tibetan who seemed to be unduly excited at the discovery that we spoke an unintelligible tongue. He led us with an unusual show of urgency to a group of men standing outside one of the houses. One of them was so much taller than the Tibetans with whom he was speaking that he immediately drew our attention. He turned with the others as we came up and we saw with surprise he was a European. Our escort performed the introductions and we saluted the villagers with bows, which were returned. The European inclined his head slightly. He scrutinised us so long that I began to feel a little uncomfortable.

This was a man of about seventy whose grey hair still retained traces of the sandy colouring of his youth. He was fully six feet tall and stooped slightly. He looked, despite his age, powerfully framed and well muscled. About him was the air of the man who has lived out of doors for many years; his strong hands and long, intelligent face were deeply tanned. His Tibetan-style clothes were topped by a thick, knee-length sheepskin surcoat, around which was a narrow black leather belt. It was difficult to see the colour of his eyes because the sun glinted off a pair of steel-rimmed spectacles, in themselves oddities in these surroundings. The Tibetans were standing round, looking expectantly from him to us and then back to him again. I thought it time someone broke the ice. I addressed him in Russian. I could almost feel the quickening interest of the local audience.

The tall man shook his head, paused and spoke—in German. Now Marchinkovas, Kolemenos and Zaro were as well versed in German as I was in Russian and delighted at the chance to exercise their skill. Paluchowicz and I knew enough to follow the conversation but I do not know whether the American could understand. I was struck by the stranger's reserve. He spoke shortly and crisply, answering questions precisely and volunteering nothing. He told us he was a missionary, a nonconformist, who had come here with a handful of Europeans of the same persuasion. He had been travelling in China and Tibet for nearly fifty years. I think he was either German or Austrian.

For no apparent reason he switched to French. Zaro spoke the language extremely well and carried on some talk with him before they reverted to German. The Tibetans were listening in openmouthed fascination at the flow of strange sounds. I had the strong impression that our new-found acquaintance did not like us. I think probably the cause of it was our appearance—the dirty matted hair, our torn clothes, our complete poverty. It seemed to me that in this and other villages he enjoyed a prestige as a Westerner built up and consolidated over long years. He might well have thought that the advent of six battered European tramps might weaken his reputation with the natives.

Zaro, who was doing most of the talking on our side, soon sensed that our arrival here was not entirely a pleasure to the stranger. It brought out the imp in Zaro. He answered the missionary's questions with jaunty insouciance. He described us as "a group of cosmopolitan tourists" and airily evaded an answer to the inquiry of where we had come from.

He looked frankly unbelieving when Zaro said we were travelling to Lhasa as pilgrims and in a few minutes there had developed an unmistakable atmosphere of mutual distrust. Only the Tibetans were enjoying the exchanges—and they did not understand a word.

"You carry nothing with you. How do you live?"

Zaro replied, "Through the hospitality of the country. The people are very kind, as you must have discovered."

"But you are not able to eat every day in that manner?"

"We take less than we need," said Zaro. "There are many days when we pull in our belts. We are used to it."

Marchinkovas broke in to ask the missionary where he lived. The man pointed to a mule cropping grass a few yards away. "That is my mule. Wherever it stops, that is my home."

Our entry into the village was about ten o'clock in the morning. The missionary sat with us while we ate—I remember particularly about this place that we were given rice and I wondered where it had been grown. He talked a little but it was a strained meal. He was puzzled by us and did not know how to tackle us. About three o'clock in the afternoon he announced that he would be moving on. We walked outside with him and he went off on a round of calls at the houses. He saddled his mule and looked round at us as he prepared to depart.

In German he said, "I wish you luck wherever you are going." We thanked him. He did not offer to shake hands. He said his farewells to the Tibetans and walked away, leading the mule.

The Tibetan who had made himself our host watched him go and then made signs to us, drawing himself up, thumping his thrust-out chest and flexing his muscles. He was trying to tell us, I think, that the parting guest was, or had been, a man of great physical prowess. I felt a spasm of regret that the meeting could not have been more friendly. With the barriers down between us, he could have told us so much we wanted to know.

The inevitable bunch of sharp-eyed, inquisitive children surrounded us as we made to follow our host back to the little house. One little fellow of about eight plucked at Zaro's trousers. Zaro made monkey faces at him. The children, about a dozen of them, crowded laughing about him. Zaro did some more clowning and the children loved it.

"Give them your Cossack dance, Eugene," I called out.

And down he went on his haunches, kicking up the dust as we stamped out the rhythm. The children screeched with joy and the grown-ups came out to laugh and wonder at his cavorting.

Zaro's uninhibited performance was like a derisive gesture towards the aloofness and dignity of the man who had just gone. And I think Zaro was not unaware of it.

In the fulness of time we came to a fork in the rough trail which we confidently accepted as that mentioned to us by the Circassian —the eastward branch leading to Lhasa and the other south-west to India. A few hours later we saw far off a big caravan of possibly fifty men and animals creeping slowly away from us in the direction we imagined to be Lhasa. It was the only large travelling group we ever saw in the country.

We found this to be a country not only of rugged ranges but also of great lakes. Near the end of November our way led us to a vast sheet of water like an inland sea. From the high ground as we came down to it we tried to guess its size. We thought we must be looking across the breadth of it and because we could not be sure that the thin line on the horizon really was the far shore, estimates of the distance varied from sixteen to forty kilometres. There was no way of even roughly calculating the length—we could not see either limit. We bathed in the fresh cold water and camped the night around a fire which did not throw out quite enough heat to keep out the damp night air from the lake.

Then followed a period of comparatively easy progress. The lake margin was our guide for many miles. A couple of days later we were in broken country again. There was a cluster of a few houses where we stayed for only one meal and on our refusal to stay overnight were given food to carry with us. We were moving well and morale was excellent. My leg wound had closed cleanly and I had discarded the bandage.

Three or four days after leaving the great lake we camped in a valley strewn with gaunt rocks where the thin vegetation struggled to exist. It had been raining and the ground was wet. Even with the tinder we carried it took a long time to get a fire going. In a shallow cave we settled down to eat what remained of our flat cakes of coarse-milled flour. The night breeze eddied the smoke from the fire about us and we sat close together for warmth. There was little to distinguish this night from dozens of others that now lay behind us. Certainly there was nothing to warn us that this was to be the setting for tragedy.

We slept, as always with the exception of Kolemenos, fitfully. One and another would awake mumbling from half-dreams to get up and tend the fire. Zaro it was who rose and went out as another day began palely to light the still desolation of the valley. I lay propped on one elbow as he came back.

"There's some mist about and it's cold," he said to me. "Let's get moving." He stepped over the others, rousing them one by one. Paluchowicz lay next to me, Marchinkovas was huddled between Smith and Kolemenos. I stood up and stretched, rubbed my stiff legs, flapped my arms about. There was a general stirring. Kolemenos pushed me with elephantine playfulness as I limbered up.

Zaro's voice cut in on us. "Come on, Zacharius. Get up!" He was bending over Marchinkovas, gently shaking his shoulder. I heard the note of panic as he shouted again, "Wake up, wake up!"

Zaro looked up at us, his face tight with alarm. "I think he's ill. I can't wake him."

I dropped on my knees beside Marchinkovas. He lay in an attitude of complete relaxation, one arm thrown up above his head. I took the outstretched arm and shook it. He lay unmoving, eyes closed. I felt for the pulse, I laid my ear to his chest, lifted the eyelids. I went through all the tests again, fearful of believing their shocking message. The body was still warm.

I straightened up. I was surprised at how small and calm my voice was. "Marchinkovas is dead," I said. The statement sounded odd and flat to me, so I said it again. "Marchinkovas is dead."

Somebody burst out, "But he can't be. There was nothing wrong with him. I talked to him only a few hours ago. He was well. He made no complaint. . . ."

"He is dead," I said.

Mister Smith got down beside the body. He was there only a minute or two. Then he crossed the hands of Marchinkovas on his chest, stood up and said, "Yes, gentlemen, Slav is right." Paluchowicz took off his old fur cap and crossed himself.

Zacharius Marchinkovas, aged 28 or 29, who might have been a successful architect in his native Lithuania if the Russians had not come and taken him away, had given up the struggle. We were stunned, we could not understand it, we did not know how death had come to him. Perhaps he was more exhausted than we knew and his willing heart could take the strain no more. I don't know. None of us knew. Marchinkovas the silent one with the occasional shaft of cynical wit, Marchinkovas who lived much with his own thoughts, the man with a load of bitterness whom Kristina had befriended and made to laugh—Marchinkovas had gone.

In the rocky ground we could find no place to dig a grave for him. His resting place was a deep cleft between rocks and we filled up the space above him with pebbles and small stones. Kolemenos carried out his last duty of making a small cross which he wedged into the rubble. We said our farewells, each in his own fashion. Silently, I commended his soul to God. The five of us went heavy-footed on our way. With us went Marchinkovas's *fufaika* and sable waistcoat. We thought they would be useful to us.

The country changed again, challenging our spirit and endurance with the uncompromising steepness of craggy hills. We learned to use our wire loops as climbing aids on difficult patches. We tried always to find a village to spend the night under cover but all too often the end of the day overtook us in the open with no human settlement in sight.

Once from the heights we saw, many miles off, the flashing reflection of the sun from the shining roofs of a distant, high-sited city, and it pleased us to believe that at least we had seen the holy city of Lhasa. What we saw may have been one of the greater monasteries of Tibet, but the direction was right for Lhasa and the idea of having seen it after using its name like a talisman all the way from the borders of Siberia appealed to us.

Towards the end of December we came across the biggest village of our Tibetan journey, almost a small township of some forty houses arranged with an unusual regularity on each side of the road. It had, too, the unusual refinement of a larger building which in Europe would certainly have been the village hall. We were taken along to this building by a villager who was well padded and clothed against the cold and we remarked on the way on the absence of children. The reason emerged when our escort fetched out from the building a slim, lean-faced, sharp-eyed Asiatic who may have been between thirty and forty. He looked us over, bowed, smiled and went back inside. A minute later a couple of dozen children exploded out and scampered down the street, throwing us glances as they went. The place was a school and the thin man apparently their teacher.

I am sure he was not a Tibetan. Chinese? I could not be sure. Three or four Tibetan villagers stood beside us as he came out a second time and there was an exchange of conversation between them and him the gist of which was that we were foreigners who did not understand their language. That much seemed obvious. He spoke to us in a couple of languages, which may have been Tibetan and Chinese, enunciating slowly and carefully. I said a few words in Russian and Zaro spoke in German. We were getting nowhere.

We stood there awkwardly for a minute. the Tibetans looking anxiously on. The teacher spoke again, very slowly. His language this time was *French*. Zaro fairly threw himself into the fray. The words tumbled from his lips. The teacher smiled and put up his hand, motioning Zaro to speak more slowly. Zaro complied. They talked together with evident enjoyment. It was a talk with a wealth of gesticulation on Zaro's side and many re-shapings and simplifications. The Tibetans were delighted with the way things were turning out and beamed on us all.

Then the man, in his slow and gentle voice, said to Zaro, "Go with the man who brought you to me. He will take you to his house and look after you. Later I will join you and you shall talk again to me." He turned and spoke briefly to the Tibetan. We were led off, taken into a house and regaled with tea while a meal was in preparation.

The teacher walked in quietly. He entered without knocking— nobody seems to knock on doors in Tibet—and bowed all round. He sat with us and when the meal came ate with us. He produced a clasp knife attached to a plaited leather thong about his waist and, noting my interest, handed it to me. It was single-bladed, bone handled and the inscription on the steel showed it had been made in Germany. He did not tell me where he had obtained it.

Zaro tried to get from him where he had been educated and

particularly where he had learned his little French but he cleverly allowed his attention to be distracted by his host, leaving the question hanging in the air. Zaro's inquiries on this point were, in fact, never answered. The man interested me tremendously and I felt sure he had not lived the whole of his life in Tibet. The thought has since occurred to me that he might have spent some part of his time in French Indo-China.

With our habitual caution we did not tell him the origin of our journey but Zaro satisfied his curiosity on the manner of our entry into Tibet. He was genuinely impressed to learn that we had crossed the Gobi. He said he had not heard of anyone making the crossing without animals and without food supplies.

"And where are you going now?" he asked.

"We are trying to reach India," said Zaro. It was pointless now to talk of a pilgrimage to Lhasa. We were off course.

The Tibetan householder interrupted politely to ask for a translation. The teacher answered and both men showed concern.

"You should change your route," he advised us. "The weather will be bad in the mountains and you will suffer greatly. The best thing you can do is to go to Lhasa and join up with a caravan. You may have to wait a long time but you will find it worthwhile."

Zaro said we would think over his counsel, but we all knew we were going on and that we should never enter Lhasa.

We asked the teacher to thank the Tibetan for the meal and for his kindness to us. The message was passed over. The Tibetan talked and the teacher said to us, "The man is pleased. He wishes your feet will preserve you and that you will not meet with any misfortune on your way. He says you will stay with him tonight and he will give you food for your journey tomorrow."

We sat there talking until long after darkness. Through Zaro I asked a question on a subject that had been bothering me ever since I entered the house—that was the peculiar, acrid, faintly farmhouse smell in the place.

The teacher smiled and pointed to the stone floor, which appeared to have been given a hard, thick coat of brick-red paint. The smell, he explained, came from the floor. The smooth painted effect was achieved by house-proud Tibetans in this part with the use of a fine red dust mixed with animal urine.

Zaro had him work out the date for us. It was 23 December 1941.

We slept soundly on sheepskins spread on the coloured stone floor and the next morning were given food as we had been promised and sent on our way with good wishes for the success of our journey.

On Christmas Eve we sat up around a bright fire. The night was freezing and no one wanted to settle down to a chilled half-sleep. We talked about Christmases we had known, of the awful Christmas a year ago when we were slogging north to the timber camp. Paluchowicz, that tough, devout old Roman Catholic, surprised us all by suddenly starting to sing in his rusty, off-tune voice a Polish carol. He got through two verses; then, finding we were not going to join in, became silent.

After a little while he said, "Every Christmas since I was old enough to remember I have sung carols on Christmas Eve. So tonight I have sung a carol. It will be good for us, I know."

The days were cold now, the nights colder. Snow-charged clouds hung menacingly over the distant, gaunt foothills of the Himalayas. In a poor hamlet of four stone-built shacks we stayed one night and the next morning spent several hours making warm mittens from the Circassian's gift fleece.

There came one clear day when we saw the snow-capped, cloud-topped soaring hump of the Himalayas, deceptively near. We were, in fact, a long way off and were to find the intervening distance fraught with trial and hazard.

We tried desperately not to be caught on the heights after darkness, but there was nothing we could do about it when early one afternoon we were enveloped in a howling snowstorm. It would have been folly to push on through it. The snow was whipping into our eyes and it was difficult to see more than a few yards ahead. As we crept along looking for shelter the snow packed hard on our moccasins. We were on a normally steep descent and the slippery soles threatened us at every downward step with disaster.

Luck or Providence gave us a natural, cave-like windbreak between two great rocks lying at an acute angle. With us we carried one sack of wood and some dried animal droppings which we took turns in carrying and we set about lighting a fire. We almost gave up the job as time and again the glowing *gubka* failed to get the small dry twigs alight in this high, snow-laden wind.

Zaro and I worked on the job for what must have been over an hour before we met success. Over the narrow opening at the junction of the two rocks we spread our sacks, pinning them down with the heaviest stones we could find and they were soon sagging with the weight of the snow. Then we jammed our sticks, rafter-fashion, under the sacks to take the strain.

By morning we were snowed in, but surprisingly cosy in our smoky little retreat. The worst of the storm was over and only small snow flurries under a watery sun greeted us when we dug our way out. The descent was perilous but we made it unscathed. It took us all day to get down from our high perch.

XXI

HIMALAYAN FOOT-HILLS

I ESTIMATE the time to have been late January when we came to the great river, iced over from bank to bank. This must have been the broad Tibetan waterway flowing west to east across the southern part of the country to find its way through the mountain barrier into India as the mighty Brahmaputra. Winter had overtaken us and the night temperatures were well below zero. There were occasional heavy snowfalls, sleety rain, winds which whipped down off the tops of the hills with the chill of the heights in them. Bitter though the conditions, they had not the severity of the Siberian winter. But they were grim enough for us, underfed and weakened by nine long months of continuous foot travel.

We crossed the river warily, Zaro, the lightest of us, leading to test the strength of the ice in the middle, where we feared it might not take our weight. There was no difficulty, however, until we reached the south bank, which was tall, steep and ice-coated. Kolemenos chipped steps out with the axe and we climbed up. We followed the river along westwards for a mile or so until we came to a point where the bank fell away, offering easy access to the water. Grouped here were three low stone huts and in front of them on a small sloping beach well back from the river edge half-a-dozen small boats lay keels upwards. Because of their high bows and sterns the boats were canted over, leaving space enough between the gunwales and the ground for a man to crawl under. I poked my head under and sniffed at the smell of long-dead fish. In the boat's planks I could see fish scales.

In a bunch we moved over to the huts. Inside they were so low that Kolemenos had to bend his head to avoid touching the roof. The construction of the roof was interesting: bamboo lengths supported a covering of tightly-interlaced wattles, into which were woven twisted cords of animal hair, probably yak's. The

213

floors were dry enough to suggest that the roofs were reasonably watertight. The construction was of the crudest—three stone boxes with mats thrown over the top, with doorless slits for entrances. They contained some old nets, some odd lengths of bamboo poles and a few short, big-diameter cylinders of wood, heavily rubbed and scored, which were obviously used as rollers upon which the boats were pushed to the water and launched.

We picked out the best of the huts and decided to sleep there the night. On the earthen floor was a blackened, hard-baked circle with a few charred pieces of wood, and overhead there was a small hole in the roof. Here we built our fire, splitting up some bamboo for fuel and banking it up for the night with animal dung which Zaro carried with him.

In February we encountered our last village, just eight or nine houses snuggled in a hollow a couple of hundred feet above a narrow valley. Behind the village reared the forbidding rampart of tall hills over which we had struggled for two days. Across the valley, hazy in the light of a wintry afternoon sun, another range heaved itself up towards the clouds. The houses had, for Tibet, a rare distinction. They were the only two-storey buildings we saw in the whole country, or, indeed, since we had left Siberia. We had descended to a point west of and below the little settlement and had to climb up to it along a rough track. We were profoundly tired, miserable and hungry. Paluchowicz was limping on his right foot, the arch of which had been bruised when he trod on a sharp stone.

The Tibetans, when they understood by signs whence we had come and where we intended to go, showed amazement at our hardihood, or foolhardiness. We were gently ushered into one of the houses, made to sit down on low benches polished with years of use, fussed over, given steaming hot tea and fed with mutton and the usual filling oaten cakes. Paluchowicz was given some grease, possibly sheep fat, to rub into his sore foot. From all the houses men and children came to look at us. There was much smiling and bowing and slow nodding of heads. Undoubtedly our arrival was an extraordinary event and would long be a topic for wondering talk.

In this house was an excellent example of a building custom

we had noted throughout Tibet—a flat-faced stone on which three or four lines of an inscription had been cut. This one had been built in near the door and about two feet above floor level. The Circassian had told us that these tablets could only be made by certain lamas and that the Tibetans set great store by them, for the words upon them were a holy injunction to the spirits of evil and misfortune to keep their distance. Our host, rather taller than the average Tibetan and aged, I guessed, about thirty, seemed pleased at my interest in his lucky stone. He came over, pointed to it and then to his left wrist, on which I saw a broad brass bracelet to which was attached a small metal box. This was, to me, a new variation of the prayer-wheel, and I think it is obvious the man was trying to show a religious connection between it and the inscription on the stone.

These people were skilled weavers. In the main downstairs room was a spinning wheel and a small loom, and the woollen material they produced was thick, warm and of good quality. The best examples of their work I saw were in blankets and bed coverings in gay and bold colours of red and yellow. The sheep which provided the wool were at this time in their winter quarters, a big dry-stone pound along one side of which were long, low stone sheds to protect them from the worst of the weather.

The link between upper and lower floors was a short, steep flight of rough-shaped stone steps leading out of a corner of the big lower room. There was no handrail and one entered the room above through a square aperture as though emerging from a hatch in a ship. Upstairs were the family sleeping quarters and a store for tightly-packed bales of wool. Here, in the warm, stuffy smell of sheep, we slept the night in cosy comfort while the wind moaned and whined around the thick walls outside. Daylight woke us gradually as it struggled through the tiny single window of thick mica stuff.

While we ate a substantial morning meal we were amused to watch the Tibetan householder going around our worn old sacks lifting them and feeling at the contents.

Said Zaro, "Perhaps he's making sure we haven't packed up the family silver."

The Tibetan could not have known what was said, but he was

pleased to see us laughing and joined in, completing his round of our belongings as he did so, finding out in the process that all we were carrying was an assortment of pieces of fur and fleece, and sticks and animal stuff for fire-making. When the investigation was over, he looked at us with some concern, pointed to the sacks and indicated the food we were stuffing into ourselves.

The American said, "He is worried because we are travelling without a supply of food."

He went off into the little back room and we heard him talking to the womenfolk. Then he passed through and out of the front door, followed by a youth of fifteen or sixteen. They were absent about half-an-hour and when they returned they carried a young sheep freshly killed and skinned. The carcase was split down the back and for some hours the two women of the house busied themselves with the task of roasting the meat on spits over the open fire.

Meanwhile the man walked round us all and examined our cut and bruised feet. He took himself off up the stone stairs and brought down a bundle of raw wool. Demonstrating with one of Paluchowicz's moccasins, he showed how the stuff could be used to insulate the feet against cold. He pulled out fistfuls of the wool and handed them round. The idea was excellent and I think we managed to convey our thanks to him.

When we left the little mountain hamlet we were loaded down with food, which included a complete side of the roasted sheep. Up to now we had kept whatever eatables we had been given in one sack, which was carried in turns. We decided at this stage to share the meat and flat cakes equally between us because of the danger of losing the lot if the precious single sack disappeared with its owner on one of the increasingly difficult climbs we were now encountering.

The Tibetan escorted us about half-a-mile on our way along a narrow track above the valley. Left to ourselves we should have dropped down to the lowest point and started on the stiff ascent on the other side in order to maintain our direction due south. He, however, gestured insistently south-west along the track and to each of us in turn indicated in the far distance the landmark of twin peaks which we understood we were to cross. He bowed us off on our journey, then turned and went back the way he had come.

"God be with you," said Paluchowicz fervently, in Polish.

It was early afternoon and with what remained of the day we covered possibly ten miles of fairly easy terrain. That night, around a small fire, we sat talking for hours trying to assess our position and how much further we had to go. When the conversation flagged, the extraordinary stillness and silence of the brooding mountains engulfed us. I had a feeling of great pity for myself and for us all. I wrestled with a desperate fear that now, with thousands of heart-breaking miles behind us, the odds might be too much for us. Often at night I had these bouts of despair and doubt. The others, too, I am sure, fought the same battles, but we never voiced our waverings. With the coming of morning the outlook was always more hopeful. Fear remained, a lurking thing, but movement and action and the exercise of the mind on the daily problems of existence pushed it into the background. We were now, more strongly than ever, in the grip of the compulsive urge to keep moving. It had become an obsession, a form of mania. Like automatons we set out each morning, triggered off by a quiet "Let's go" from one or another of us. No one ever pleaded for half-an-hour's respite. We just went, walking the stiffness out of our joints and the chill of the dark hours from our bodies.

We rationed the food out thinly and it lasted, one meal a day, for over a fortnight. It was insufficient for the heavy climbing and the perilous descents in which we were now involved but at least we had the comfort of knowing we could not starve while it lasted. Several times we were caught out on the heights and had to resort to the lessons of our Siberian experience in making a snow dugout and holing up sleepless until the dawn of another day.

Of the art of mountaineering we learned much as the weeks crept by. I had done some climbing in Poland before the war, but it bore little resemblance to this grim Himalayan business. Then I had stout spiked boots and all the civilised paraphernalia, plus the services of an expert guide. And we had climbed in summer, for sport. Here we would claw our way upwards for hours, sacks lashed on our backs, only to find our way blocked by a sheer, smooth, outward-thrusting rock face. We would cling to our holds and rest our toes, cramped and sore with their prehensile curling inside the soft moccasins for footholds. Then we would turn about and go down and down until we found a place from which to attempt a different approach to the summit. In these conditions the going was very slow. Our total equipment was one strong rawhide rope limited in use by its short length, the axe—by far the greatest single asset—the broad-bladed knife and the loops and spikes we had made back in the heat of the Gobi.

We climbed as individuals but in set order. Zaro, the lightest man, led the way upwards, testing the holds with the axe, breaking through the ice-crust on the snow, blazing a trail for the rest of us. I came next, sometimes changing over leadership with Zaro to give him a rest, then Kolemenos, Mister Smith and Paluchowicz. We tried to make things as easy as possible for the two older men, but they always insisted on taking the lead on the descents. We still carried our trusty sticks and on gentler slopes used them for probing through the snow for hidden crevices. At other times we carried them stuck through our belts at our backs.

Zaro would have made a skilled and intrepid climber in any company. A clumsy device we thought up and made for getting us past bulging overhangs of rock was a weighty piece of smooth, hard, black stone, waisted in the middle like a figure 8, to which we tied our rope. This we would throw up and over, again and again and again, until eventually, unseen somewhere above, it would jam itself and take hold. Kolemenos would haul gently at first at the rope until it took his full weight. Then Zaro heroically would start to climb while we watched with our hearts in our throats, knowing that the penalty for a slip was death. When I saw on one or two occasions by what flimsy chance the stone had taken hold on the original throw my stomach turned over.

Occasional bright days brought the additional trial of sun-glare off the white snow. We were harrowed, too, by a new experience of intense physical discomfort: the manner in which the cold struck at our foreheads until they seemed to be held in frigid bands of ice. This trouble we overcame by making sheepskin masks with slits for the eyes, the upper parts held under the rim of our caps and the lower parts hanging loosely at nose level.

The masks were effective for the purpose for which they were designed, and they also seemed to help with the trouble of snow-glare, but we found that moisture gathered beneath them, trickled and froze round the nose and mouth. There were times when I had to stop and thaw out the gathering ice by holding the lower part of my face in my mittened hands. We kept our hands covered as much as possible, but when climbing demanded the use of the fingers our mittens hung from our wrists by thongs. With the masks around our heads and tied at the back of the head and the ear-flaps of our Russian-style caps in position, we found it difficult to hear one another. Irritation piled on irritation. We were deadly tired, morose, always hungry. My nerves were strung up like piano strings. It was too cold to sleep.

About the beginning of March the five of us walked out of a snow-flurry along a sweeping downward east-to-west traverse into the sudden sunshine of a deep, white-clothed depression between the mountains. It was mid-morning and the sun invited us to take off our masks and caps. We sat down and rested, wrapped in silence. We had been foodless for a couple of days and our spirits were low. We sat hunched up without talking. Then I heard a sound and strained my ears to hear it again and identify it.

"I heard a dog bark," said Paluchowicz.

"I heard something, too," I put in.

Paluchowicz pointed excitedly. "It came from that direction. We must go and investigate."

We walked along for about a quarter of a mile with our ears pricked. The sound of the dog barking was so loud and so close when it came again that we stopped in our tracks. We looked around and could see nothing. We were expecting to see a house or a shack but there was no building of any sort in sight. The dog must have scented us, because it set up a prolonged yapping until we tracked down the source as the mouth of a cave, black against the surrounding whiteness. It was only about a hundred yards away, and as we went towards it we saw the figure of a man come out into the light and look in our direction. He spoke to the dog, now joined by another one, and it stopped its noise.

He was an elderly man, with wispy white hair around his chin and a seamed and wrinkled, weather-beaten brown face. His smile showed gaps where age had robbed him of some of his front teeth. He was well clothed against the cold with the usual Tibetan sheepskin surcoat over padded jacket and trousers. He wore a fine pair of boots of leather, the upper part around the lower calf fretted with an openwork pattern which showed an inner lining of green felt. I don't know which side was the more delighted at the meeting. The old man wagged his head and bowed and talked and flashed his great gap-toothed smile. We bowed and laughed and were happy enough to have danced in a ring about him. Even the dogs, gingery brown and looking like smaller editions of Samoyeds, were infected with enthusiasm and ran round us furiously swinging their bushy tails and yelping with excitement.

Outside the cave was a low wall about four feet high made of loosely heaped stones which acted as a windbreak. He led us round the wall and into half-gloom and immediately, before our eyes became adjusted to the change of light, our noses were assailed by the strong, clinging, fuggy odour of sheep.

The small size of the opening left me unprepared for the lofty spaciousness of the interior. The cave bent round so that its floor plan was like a boomerang. The man and his dogs lived in the space of about fifteen feet from the opening to a point where the cave was partitioned off with a rubble wall. Behind, into the farthest recesses, were sheep, about a hundred of them, I judged. This then was the winter quarters of a shepherd awaiting the coming of spring and the melting of the snows so that the sheep could be allowed out to graze on the fresh green grass of the valley. On pegs hung four or five packs of hay in big-meshed nets. A pile of empty nets showed that the sheep had been penned inside for many weeks.

A fire burned in the middle of the floor and nearby was a heap of brushwood and dung fuel. One large and one small iron cauldron stood against the stones of the fireplace. The large one, I discovered, was used for melting snow to provide water for the sheep. The other was the shepherd's general utility cooking pot, in which he straightaway started brewing tea and for the only time in Mongolia or Tibet I saw tea made with loose dried leaf. It came from a polished wooden box and was olive green in colour. This must have been a welcoming special treat because subsequent brews were made with the usual black brick tea.

From his waist the old man took out a clasp knife and opened it. He knelt down and began with slow deliberation to sharpen the blade on a flat stone. The dogs got up and danced around him as he worked. They knew there would soon be fresh meat. He tried the edge of the steel on the ball of his thumb, grinned at us, and went off among the sheep, the dogs frisking at his heels. He went outside the cave with a kicking, bleating young sheep under his arm and in a remarkably short time was back with the fresh-skinned carcase. The dogs were fed at the cave entrance with the head and tit-bits of offal and then he cut off joints for roasting. While the meat hung spitting and sizzling on a wooden bar over the fire, the old man amused us by putting his fine boots under the roast and allowing the fat to trickle over them, afterwards rubbing it into the leather, presumably to soften and preserve it. With coarse flour and a little water from the bottom of the big cauldron he kneaded up cakes and baked them on a flat stone over the side of the fire. We ate like starving men and there was no difficulty about the performance of belching our appreciation at the end of the meal.

When the old man went to lug the heavy water cauldron out of the cave, Kolemenos and I took it from him and carried it out. We all helped in the chore of filling it with snow. We made a move to carry it back when it was piled high, but he stopped us. With surprising agility he jumped up on top of the cauldron and began treading down the snow. He stepped down and we topped the cauldron up again. This time Zaro climbed up and danced with whoops of joy to press down the snow, while the old man chuckled with glee at the fun. The hard-packed mass of snow was melted over the fire and later the shepherd fed his flock with hay and watered them.

The presence of the sheep rather more than the smouldering fire made the cave very warm that night and I slept exhaustedly. A couple of times during the night the appalling stink of long-confined animals woke me and I wondered where I was, but I soon dropped off again, feeling warm and safe. Our Tibetan cave-man was astir before us in the morning and by the time we were fully awake had prepared a thick gruel which he was slowly stirring over the built-up fire. His parting gift to us was the last quarter of the sheep he had killed the day before.

Outside the cave he was obviously asking us where we were

going. We looked at the sun and pointed south. He took Zaro's outstretched arm and nudged it round until it pointed a few degrees west of south. And that was the way we went.

Events of the next few days showed that the shepherd knew this part of the country well. We were making distance south on a long tack which steered us clear of any very exhausting climbing. It must have been in distance a longer course but throwing ourselves against the mountains dead ahead might have been longer in time.

One incident at this stage sticks in my mind. Coming down a long, snow-covered gradient, Paluchowicz accidentally kicked off one of his shoes. We watched it go spinning off down the slope and come to rest. Paluchowicz stood awkwardly on one leg to keep his naked foot out of contact with the freezing snow and swore, in round sergeant's barrack-room oaths.

"I'll get it for you," shouted Zaro, and hared off after it. We saw him stoop to pick up the moccasin before he had checked his forward impetus. Where the slope ended, as far as our view from above showed, Zaro slapped his behind down to try to brake himself. The next instant, sliding on his seat, he had disappeared from our sight.

Running more carefully than Zaro had done, I was first at the spot where he had vanished. The ground fell away in a long sweeping curve and at the upcurling end of it was Zaro, roaring with laughter and beating the snow off his trousers. Paluchowicz came down last to join us, hopping on one foot, to wave and call across to Zaro three hundred or more yards away.

"Try it," bawled Zaro. "It's the easiest way down."

I sat myself down in Zaro's track and let go. It was an exhilarating slide down with the wind whistling past my ears. I finished up like Zaro, bellowing with laughter. One after another, Kolemenos, Mister Smith and Paluchowicz came whizzing down.

The incident remains with me because it was the only part of the whole long journey we covered other than on our feet.

XXII

STRANGE CREATURES

TOWARDS the end of March 1942 we were convinced that at last we were very near the sanctuary of India. Barring our way ahead reared the tallest and most forbidding peaks we had yet seen. We told one another that one final effort must bring us to the country where we were sure ultimate freedom, civilisation, rest and ease of mind awaited us. Individually we needed all the assurances and encouragement we could get. I was tortured with the fear that the exertion of one more great climb would finish me. I feared the onset of the insidious sleep on the heights from which there was no awakening. All my fears were sharpened by that shared conviction that after four thousand miles we were near success. I could not now banish the spectre of bitter failure. With all of us the resources of body and mind were drawn out thin. One shining, incalculable asset remained—the tight, warm friendship of men together in misfortune. While we remained together hope could not be quenched. The whole, in terms of spirit and resolution, was greater than the sum of its parts.

We sat around a fire made of the last of our hoarded scraps of fuel and ate the last crumbs of our rations. We got out the raw-hide rope, the axe, the knife, the wire loops, the slim spikes, examined them and tested them. We gave ourselves a couple of hours before dark for repairing footwear. When we had finished we were as well prepared for the last assault as we could be. The fire burned down and became ashes before midnight and we spent a pacing restless night until the first glimmer of dawn. Zaro wound the rope about him, took the axe from Kolemenos and started off. I was relieved to be on the move.

We were blessed with fair weather. The wind was cold, but the sun shone strongly enough to attack the top layer of snow so that it melted sufficiently to re-form in the freezing night temperatures into a skin of crisp, treacherous ice. We climbed more surely, more cautiously, than ever before, Zaro double testing every foothold and hand-hold as he led the way upwards, chipping away with the axe, steam issuing in little clouds from his nose and mouth beneath the mask.

At the beginning of the third day we were over the top, only to find ourselves confronted with another peak. It was the stuff of which nightmares are made. Always it seemed there was another mountain to block our way. Two days were spent scrambling down the south face from our exposed high perch and I found it more wearing on the nerves than the ascent. Down in the valley we made ourselves a snow shelter out of the whip of the wind and managed to get ourselves an uncomfortable few hours sleep in preparation for the next ordeal.

This next mountain was the worst in all our experience. From valley to valley its crossing occupied us six days and taxed our endurance to such a degree that for the first time we talked openly of the prospect that we might all perish. I am certain that one blizzard of a few hours duration would have wiped us out.

Two days up and the top hidden by swirling white clouds, I dug my knife into a crevice to give myself extra purchase in hauling myself up from a narrow ledge. With my body pressed close against the rock, I loosened each hand and foot in turn so that I could flex my cramped fingers and wriggle my stiff toes. Then I reached for the knife handle above me and began to haul on it with my right arm. Suddenly the knife sprang like a live thing, leapt from my hand and flew over my head with the steel singing. I took fresh hold and, digging in with fingers and toes, dragged myself to safety. The knife was gone. There was no sign of it. I felt as though I had lost a personal friend.

Near the summit on the third day the climbing became easier, but we began to doubt seriously whether we could make it. The cold was terrible, eddying mist dropped down about us and lifted, dropped and lifted again. The effects of high altitude were draining from us what slight reserves of stamina we still had. Every step was a fight against torturing lassitude, making one want to sit down and cry with weakness and frustration. I could not get enough air into my bursting lungs and my heart thumped audibly, hammering against my chest. Will-power became a flaccid thing. Any one of us, alone, could have given up thankfully, lay down happily, closed his eyes and drifted into death. But somebody was always crawling on, so we all kept moving. A final refinement of misery was nose-bleed. I tried to stop mine by plugging the nostrils with bits of sacking, but the discomfort of breathing only through the mouth was too much and I removed the plug. The blood poured down into my beard, freezing and congealing there.

We knew we should have to spend the night in this rarefied atmosphere and the knowledge did our spirits no good.

"We must keep going while there's light," Zaro said. "We must try to get over the top before dark."

So we went on and on, painfully, like flies struggling through a pool of treacle. We made long traverses to right and left to avoid the impossible extra exertion of a frontal assault. I do not remember going over the summit. I remember only the point at which I noticed with vague surprise that Zaro, leading, was slightly below me. We climbed again a little and then we knew with certainty the descent had begun.

That night was the crisis of the whole enterprise. On a broad, flat ledge where the snow had drifted and piled, we axed through the hard crust of the surface and dug laboriously through a few feet of snow to make ourselves a barely adequate refuge against the rigours of the night. We had no fire. We were so bone-weary we could have slept literally standing up, but we knew it would be courting death even to attempt to doze.

It was the longest night of my life. We huddled there standing, with our arms about one another. Sleep lay on our lids like a solid weight and I found myself holding my eyes open with fingertips pressed against the eyeballs under my mask. Three times Kolemenos, the arch-sleeper, let his chin sag on his chest and began to snore, and each time we punched and shook him back to consciousness. Each man was his brother's keeper, watching for drooping eyelids and the nodding head. At intervals we would stamp slowly around in a close ring. Even during this grotesque dance I began to swim down into beautiful, velvet sleep, but the American dragged me back by gently cuffing me, pulling my beard and shaking me. There came that awful pre-dawn period when fatigue and cold together combined to set me shivering in an uncontrollable ague from head to foot.

"Let's get going," said someone. "Let's get down to some place where we can breathe again."

Paluchowicz spoke. "I could not last another night like that." He was voicing the thought of us all.

It was barely light, but we broke out and started on our way, Paluchowicz leading and Zaro and I in the rear. Even now I could not convince myself we would make it. Once, around noon, we were marooned for fully an hour when the track of our descent ended abruptly on a foot-wide shelf over a terrible drop. We inched our way back, climbed upwards in our old tracks and tried again in another direction. This time we succeeded, but not without great danger and frequent use of the rope and axe.

In about ten hours of gruelling toil we must have come down about five thousand feet before nightfall. Breathing became easier, morale improved, hopes rose a little again. We dragged on through another depressing, wakeful night and continued the descent the next day until we were able to see the valley below quite clearly.

In the afternoon Zaro said to me, "Do you notice anything peculiar about this valley?"

I looked around. "No," I answered. "Why?"

Zaro pointed to a long ridge thrown out from the main body of the mountain away to the west. "It is a similar formation to the ridge in which we found the shepherd's cave."

I laughed. "You don't think we shall meet another shepherd and his flock?"

"No," said Zaro. "But we might find a cave in which we can get a night's sleep."

We called the others over and suggested swinging away down the ridge to look for a cave. They agreed readily.

The extraordinary feature of this venture was not that, after a couple of hours search, we found a cave. But the cave was indeed a herdsman's winter retreat. Unlike the other, it was untenanted, but there was a stack of brushwood near the entrance and a cached pile of untreated fleeces against the wall at the back, about twelve feet in from the opening. If we had needed a sign that Providence was still on our side, this was it.

Hanging from a peg in the roof was something parcelled in soft lambskin. Someone lifted it down and unwrapped it. Inside was a leg of goatmeat, partly smoked and nearly black. We were too hungry to be fastidious. We decided to get the fire going and cook it.

What a fire that was. We stoked it up until the dancing flames lit up the far corners of the cave. Watching the meat cooking, we thawed out for the first time for weeks. Without the knife we had to do some crude carving with the axe, leaving half the joint to be eaten in the morning and tearing up the rest in strips. Toothless Paluchowicz, without the knife to help him, took longer than the rest of us to eat his portion, but we all managed to take the edge off our hunger.

In this cave, for the only time since we left Siberia, we helped ourselves to another man's belongings. We broke out fleeces from the cache and made ourselves a sleeveless surcoat each. For this I hope we may be forgiven, but our need was great for something which would keep away the mountain cold from our hard-used bodies. We slept the night through in a great communal bed of warm, smelly sheepskins, and when we awoke the day was already a couple of hours old and the fire had long since died out. Hurriedly we replaced the skins which had made the bed, ate the rest of the goatmeat cold, and left.

It was profitless to speculate any further on how near we might be to our journey's end. Not even now were we out of the mountains. The lesser peak we set ourselves to surmount two days after the cave episode was, had we known it, the last outpost of the Himalayas, beyond which the foothills led down into Northern India. I do not remember any of the details of this last climb, but I know we pulled ourselves up the northern face for two days without attaining the height that induced altitude sickness. When we started down the other side the sun was shining and the air was startlingly clear. Far off to the west I could see snow-covered giants which made a modest hill of the eminence on which I stood. Southward the country fell away dramatically. I knew I was looking at India.

In all our wanderings through the Himalayan region we had encountered no other creatures than man, dogs and sheep. It was with quickening interest, therefore, that in the early stages of our descent of this last mountain Kolemenos drew our attention to two moving black specks against the snow about a quarter of a mile below us. We thought of animals and immediately of food, but as we set off down to investigate we had no great hopes that they would await our arrival. The contours of the mountain temporarily hid them from view as we approached nearer, but when we halted on the edge of a bluff we found they were still there, twelve feet or so below us and about a hundred yards away.

Two points struck me immediately. They were enormous and they walked on their hind legs. The picture is clear in my mind, fixed there indelibly by a solid two hours of observation. We just could not believe what we saw at first, so we stayed to watch. Somebody talked about dropping down to their level to get a close-up view.

Zaro said, "They look strong enough to eat us." We stayed where we were. We weren't too sure of unknown creatures which refused to run away at the approach of men.

I set myself to estimating their height on the basis of my military training for artillery observation. They could not have been much less than eight feet tall. One was a few inches taller than the other, in the relation of the average man to the average woman. They were shuffling quietly round on a flattish shelf which formed part of the obvious route for us to continue our descent. We thought that if we waited long enough they would go away and leave the way clear for us. It was obvious they had seen us, and it was equally apparent they had no fear of us.

The American said that eventually he was sure we should see them drop on all fours like bears. But they never did.

Their faces I could not see in detail, but the heads were squarish and the ears must lie close to the skull because there was no projection from the silhouette against the snow. The shoulders sloped sharply down to a powerful chest. The arms were long and the wrists reached the level of the knees. Seen in profile, the back of the head was a straight line from the crown into the shoulders—"like a damned Prussian", as Paluchowicz put it.

We decided unanimously that we were examining a type of creature of which we had no previous experience in the wild, in zoos or in literature. It would have been easy to have seen them waddle off at a distance and dismissed them as either bear or big ape of the orang-outang species. At close range they defied facile description. There was something both of the bear and the ape

228

about their general shape but they could not be mistaken for either. The colour was a rusty kind of brown. They appeared to be covered by two distinct kinds of hair—the reddish hair which gave them their characteristic colour forming a tight, close fur against the body, mingling with which were long, loose, straight hairs, hanging downwards, which had a slight greyish tinge as the light caught them.

Dangling our feet over the edge of the rock, we kept them closely under observation for about an hour. They were doing nothing but move around slowly together, occasionally stopping to look around them like people admiring a view. Their heads turned towards us now and again, but their interest in us seemed to be of the slightest.

Then Zaro stood up. "We can't wait all day for them to make up their minds to move. I am going to shift them."

He went off into a pantomime of arm waving, Red Indian war dancing, bawling and shrieking. The things did not even turn. Zaro scratched around and came up with half-a-dozen pieces of ice about a quarter-inch thick. One after another he pitched them down towards the pair, but they skimmed erratically and lost direction. One missile kicked up a little powder of snow about twenty yards from them, but if they saw it they gave no sign. Zaro sat down again, panting.

We gave them another hour, but they seemed content to stay where they were. I got the uncomfortable feeling they were challenging us to continue our descent across their ground.

"I think they are laughing at us," said Zaro.

Mister Smith stood up. "It occurs to me they might take it into their heads to come up and investigate us. It is obvious they are not afraid of us. I think we had better go while we are safe."

We pushed off around the rock and directly away from them. I looked back and the pair were standing still, arms swinging slightly, as though listening intently. What were they? For years they remained a mystery to me, but since recently I have read of scientific expeditions to discover the Abominable Snowman of the Himalayas and studied descriptions of the creature given by native hillmen, I believe that the five of us that day may have met two of the animals. If so, I think recent estimates of their height as

229

about five feet is wrong. The creatures we saw must have been at least seven feet.

I think that, in causing a deviation of route, they brought our final disaster upon us.

It was about midday that we set off to continue our descent. Everything went well and we made good time. Our spirits were up in spite of our empty bellies. We found an almost ideal cavity among the rocks to spend the night, were greeted by another clear, fine April morning breaking through a thin, quickly-dissipated mist.

Two hours later it happened. Zaro and I had the rope's end belayed around our two stout sticks at the crest of a slope. I was laughing at something Zaro had said about the two strange creatures of the day before. The slope was short and hardly steep enough to warrant the use of the rope, which lay loosely thrown out as a safety line in case Paluchowicz, crawling down backwards on all fours, should slip into an unseen crevice. Behind him were Smith and Kolemenos, well spaced out. All three were astride the limp rope without holding it.

I saw Paluchowicz reach the end of the slope. I turned to Zaro and in that instant saw the rope jerk about the sticks and become slack again. Simultaneously there was a brief, sharp cry, such as a man will make when he is suddenly surprised. Zaro and I swung together. It was a second or two before the awful truth struck me. Smith was there. Kolemenos was there. But Paluchowicz had vanished. Like fools we stood there calling out his name. No one answered. The other two, with their backs to Paluchowicz, did not know what had happened. They had stopped at our first shout and were looking up at us.

"Come back," I called out to them. "Something has happened to Anton."

They clambered back, I hauled in the rope and tied the loose end about my waist. "I am going down to see if I can find him," I said.

I reached the point where, from above, the slope appeared to fall gently away. Zaro took in the slack of the rope and I turned around as I had seen Paluchowicz do. The sight made me catch my breath. The mountain yawned open as though it had been split clean open with a giant axe blow. I was looking across a twenty-

yard gap, the narrowest part of the chasm which dropped sickeningly below me. I could not see the bottom. I felt the sweat
beading out on my forehead. Futilely I yelled, "Anton, Anton!"
I turned and went back, so shaken that I held tightly to the rope
all the way.

They all talked at once. Had I seen him? Why was I shouting?
Where was he?

I told them what it was like down there, that there was no sign
of Paluchowicz.

"We will have to find him," said Kolemenos.

"We will never find him," I told them. "He is gone."

Nobody wanted to believe it. I did not want to believe it
myself. With difficulty we broke a way round to a new point
from which we could look down into the abyss. Then they understood. We heaved a stone down and listened for it to strike. We
heard nothing. We found a bigger stone and dropped that down
and there was still no echo of the strike.

We hung around there a long time, not knowing what to do.
The disaster was so sudden, so complete. Paluchowicz was with
us and then he was gone, plucked away from us. I never thought
he would have to die. He seemed indestructible. Tough, toothless,
devout old Sergeant Paluchowicz.

"All this way," said the American. "All this way, to die so
stupidly at the last." I think he felt it more than any of us. As the
two older men, they had been close together.

Kolemenos took his sack from his back and very deliberately
tore it down the seams. We all stood silent. He put a stone in the
corner and threw it out into space. The stone fell out and the sack
floated away, a symbolic shroud for Paluchowicz. He took his
stick and with the blunted axe chopped an end off and made a
cross and stuck it there, on the edge.

We climbed on down, trying to keep in sight the spot from
which Paluchowicz had disappeared, vaguely hoping we might
find his body. But we never found the bottom of the great cleft
and we never found Paluchowicz.

There were some quite warm days after this and we could
look back and see the majesty of the mountains we had crossed.
We were in terrible need of food and now that the supreme effort
was over we could barely keep ourselves moving. One day we

saw a couple of long-haired wild goats, which bounded off like the wind. They need not have been afraid. We hardly had the strength to kill anything bigger than a beetle. The country was still hilly, but there were rivers and streams and birds in trees.

We had been about eight days without food when we saw far off to the east on a sunny morning a flock of sheep with men and dogs in charge. They were too far off to be of any help to us and were moving away from us, but our hopes rose at the sight of them. Soon we must be picked up. We pulled some green-stuff growing at the edge of a stream and tried to eat it, but it was very bitter and our stomachs would not take it.

Exhausted, walking skeletons of men that we were, we knew now for the first time peace of mind. It was now that we lost, at last, the fear of recapture.

They came from the west, a little knot of marching men, and as they came closer I saw there were six native soldiers with an N.C.O. in charge. I wanted to wave my hands and shout, but I just stood there with the other three watching them come. They were very smart, very clean, very fit, very military. My eyes began to fill and the tears brimmed over.

Smith stepped forward and stuck out his hand.

'We are very glad to see you,' he said.

XXIII

FOUR REACH INDIA

IT WAS HARD to comprehend that this was the end of it all. I leaned my weight forward on my stick and tried to blink my eyes clear. I felt weak and lightheaded like a man in a fever. My knees trembled with weakness and it required real effort to prevent myself slumping down on the ground. Zaro, too, was hunched over his stick, and one of Kolemenos's great arms was drooped lightly about his shoulders. The rough, scrubby country danced in the haze of a warm noon sun. The soldiers, halted but five yards from us, were a compact knot of men in tropical shorts and shirts swimming in and out of my vision.

I dropped my head forward on my chest and heard the voice of Mister Smith. He talked in English, which I did not understand, but there was no mistaking the urgency in the tone. It went on for several minutes. I flexed my knees to stop their trembling.

The American came over to us, his face smiling. "Gentlemen, we are safe." And because we remained unmoving and silent, he said again in Russian, very slowly, "Gentlemen, we are safe."

Zaro shouted and the sound startled me. He threw down his stick and yelled, his arms above his head and fingers extended. He threw his arms about the American and Smith had to hold him tight to prevent his running over to the patrol and kissing each man individually.

"Come away, Eugene," he shouted. "Come away from them. I have told them we are filthy with lice."

Zaro started to laugh and jig inside the restraining arms. Then he had the American going round with him in a crazy, hopping polka, and they were both laughing and crying at the same time. I do not remember starting to dance but there we were, the four of us, stamping round, kicking up the dust, hugging one another, laughing hysterically through the blur of tears, until we collapsed one by one on the ground.

233

Kolemenos lay sprawled out repeating softly to himself the American's words. "We are safe . . . we are safe. . . ."

The American said, "We shall be able to live again."

I thought a little about that. It sounded a wonderful thing to say. All that misery, all that sorrow, the hardship of a whole year afoot, so that we might live again.

We learned from Mister Smith that this was a patrol on exercise which would take us, if we were not too weak to march, a few miles to the nearest rough road where they had a rendezvous with a military truck from their main unit. He had told them that we had come so far a few more miles would not kill us. With the main unit there would be real food.

The patrol produced groundsheets from their packs and rigged up a shelter from the sun. We lay beneath it resting for about an hour. My head throbbed and I felt a little sick. We were handed a packet of cigarettes and some matches. Even more than food just then I wanted to smoke. To handle so ordinary a civilized commodity as a box of matches gave me a warm thrill. The smoke itself was bliss. From somewhere came a big tin of peaches, ready opened, and we dug our fingers in, stuffed them in our mouths and crushed the exquisite juice and pulp from them. We drank water from Army water-bottles and were ready to go.

It seemed to me that none of us could have recalled details of that cross-country trek. The patrol adjusted its pace to our weary shamble and it must have taken about five hours to cover ten miles. Zaro marched with me and we buoyed ourselves up with the pretence that we were getting along at a swinging military pace.

"The heroes' return," Zaro grinned. "All we need now is a band to lead us."

The altogether delightful quality of everything that happened to us at the end of the march was that it required no resolution or decision from us. There was a bumping ride by lorry at that breakneck speed which is the hallmark of Army driving anywhere in the world. We were as thrilled as schoolboys with the trip—our first on wheels since we left the Russian train at Irkutsk eighteen months ago. We were in process of being gathered up and looked after, told what to do, tended, and later, even cosseted. The British took over completely.

I never found out exactly where we were. At that time I did not

234

care. Any guess I might make from perusal of maps could be hundreds of miles out. Smith must have found out, but if he ever told me, the information did not register. I hugged to myself only the great revelation that this was India.

The young British Lieutenant who watched us ease ourselves down over the lorry tailboard was amazingly clean, spruce and well-shaven. I observed him as the American told him our story. His expression as he stood listening in the shade of the trees at the small roadside encampment was incredulous. His eyes kept wandering from Smith to us. He was trying to understand. He put several questions, nodding his head slowly at each answer. I thought how young he looked. Yet, he was about my own age.

The American told us, "He believes me now. He says he will make arrangements for us to be deloused and cleaned up here because he can't take us back to base in this condition. He says he will have to isolate us from his troops until this is done but that we will be well fed and cared for. He says we need not worry."

That night we were given a hot meal that ended with stewed fruit and steamed pudding. I had my first experience of hot, strong, tinned-milk Army tea, lavishly sweetened. We were given cigarettes. We were given first-aid treatment for our torn and bruised feet. And that night we slept secure, wrapped in Army blankets, in a tent.

The novelty, the bustle and the excitement of it all kept me going. There was no time for me to stand still and discover how near to collapse I was. Breakfast the next day absorbed my attention—more tea, corned beef, Australian cheese and butter from tins, unbelievably white bread, tinned bacon rashers and marmalade.

The delousing was a thorough affair. We stripped off all our clothes—the sheepskin surcoats, *fufaikas*, fur waistcoats, caps, masks, padded trousers, sacks and skin gaiters—and piled them in the open. The blankets we had slept in were thrown on top of the heap. Head and body hair was shorn off, bundled and thrust among the clothes. Over the lot they poured petrol and suddenly it erupted into a roaring bonfire, billowing black smoke into the sunny, clear air. Everything went, consumed in flame.

Kolemenos said, "I hope those bloody lice die hard. They have had a good time at my expense."

I turned to him and he to me. Then we were all exchanging looks and the laughter bubbling out of us. We had realised we were seeing one another for the first time—really seeing for the very first time the lines, the set of the mouth, the angle of the chin and the character of the faces of men who for twelve months and four thousand miles had shared the wretched struggle for survival. It seemed the most comical thing that had ever happened to us. I had never thought of what might lie beneath the matted hair, and neither, I suppose, had they. It was like the midnight revelation from some fantastically-prolonged masked ball.

"Why, Zaro," I said, "you are a good-looking man."

"You look all right yourself," Zaro answered.

And Mister Smith was not as old as I had thought him, now that he was shorn of his greying hair. And Kolemenos, in spite of the ravages that marked us all, was as handsome as a big, fine-bodied man could be. We sat there laughing and joking in our nakedness while the fire roared.

Scrubbed clean, our cuts, sores and scratchings anointed, we were made ready for our re-entry into a civilised community. We received white, crisp new underwear, bush shirts, stockings and canvas shoes, and, to top the lot, dashing Australian-type light felt hats. Smith dressed in a leisurely, careful way, but the other three of us hurried through the operation in an enthusiastic race to be first ready. We looked one another over and liked what we saw. We joked about the stark whiteness of our knees.

They drove us away westward. I had a curiously detached feeling about it, like an exhausted swimmer allowing himself to be carried along in a tide race. We came to a military garrison, but I had no chance to look at it. We were immediately lodged in sick quarters.

The Army doctor had been waiting for us. He examined us gravely, eyes narrowed behind thin tortoiseshell spectacles. He nodded his head, thinning on top, in acknowledgment of Smith's answers to terse questions. He was aged about forty, quick-moving, sympathetic behind the professional facade of impersonal efficiency. We needed a lot of care, he told Smith. We needed to take things easy. Recovery might take a long time.

For a few days they kept us there. The doctor dosed us with medicines and pills. We lounged and lay about. We ate most magnificently and were plied with fresh fruit. Kolemenos amused the small staff with his huge appettite. We were allowed to smoke as often as we pleased.

Here it was that we temporarily parted from Smith. He said he was being taken away to see the American authorities. "You three will be taken to Calcutta. Whatever happens I shall see you there."

We shook him by the hand. There didn't seem to be anything we could say.

"Just keep your spirits up," he said. "The doctor tells me we are all going to be very sick before we recover from our trip. But he says that with the proper attention we shall get in a big hospital we should pull through."

I thought we were not as ill as that and said so. I did not appreciate then that I was feeling a quite spurious sense of well-being, that I was a little drunk with the excitement of these wonderful last few days, that the reckoning was yet to come.

He went away from us like a figure slipping out of a dream. Zaro said, "We shall be seeing him in Calcutta," as though India were a small place and Calcutta was just around the corner. It was the way we felt. Everything was taken care of. We were spent forces, content to be carried along. All the hammering urgency and the iron-hard resolution of the last bitter year had drained from us. We were more sick than we knew.

I have small recollection of the journey to Calcutta, except that it was long and tiresome and I was shrouded in black depression. We smoked incessantly.

It was a symptom of our condition, I suppose, that when we were driven in a bus through the teeming, noisy Calcutta streets we were as bright as crickets, pointing out the sights one to the other, almost hysterically good-humoured. I could have persuaded myself then that recovery had already begun. I was being fooled again by the fever of a new excitement.

The bus drove between the tall main gates of a hospital and a medical orderly took Zaro, Kolemenos and me away for a pre-liminary medical examination. At first we were bogged down in language difficulties. After some time it was understood that between us we spoke Russian, Polish, French and German— but no English. Eventually we were interviewed by an orderly

237

who spoke French. They wanted a medical history from childhood, so Zaro told the orderly about our measles and our whooping cough and our operations. It all went down on a set of stiff cards. We were examined by doctors, weighed, measured, given a bath, decked out in pyjamas and tucked in bed in a long ward, Zaro and Kolemenos in adjoining positions on one side and I facing them from directly opposite.

Quite clearly I remember my awakening the next morning, a spotless vision of a nursing sister standing beside my bed laying her strong brown arm against my white one and joking with me until I smiled up at her. Then came the breakfast, of fresh eggs with wafer-thin white bread and butter.

I went back to sleep that morning and dropped into a bottomless pit that stole all mind and recollection from me for nearly a month. I learned all about it later, and it was Mister Smith who gathered the story and told it to me.

They gave me sedatives, they kept a day and night watch on me. Meanwhile Zaro and then Kolemenos went under. At night I screamed and raved in madness. I ran from the Russians all over again, I crossed my deserts and my mountains. And each day I ate half my bread and slyly tucked the remainder under the mattress or in the pillow case. Each day they gently took away my precious little hoard. They talked to me and brought in great white loaves from the kitchens and told me I should never have to worry again. There would always be bread. The assurances meant nothing. I kept collecting bread for the next stage of my escape.

The climax came after about ten days, I was told. After that I was quieter, very weak, exhausted and on the danger list. Kolemenos and Zaro, too, were in a bad way.

But, said the hospital staff, neither of the others matched the performance I put on during the second night of my stay in the ward. I fetched out my saved-up bread, rolled my mattress, bedclothes and pillows and, to their astonishment because they had not believed I had that much strength left, set off staggering under the load for the door. By the time I had rolled my bedding, the night sister had the doctor there. He had said, "Leave him; let us see what he does."

At the door the doctor, the sister and two male orderlies blocked my way. The doctor talked quietly as he would have done to a sleep-walker. I went on. The orderlies held me and I dropped my burden and fought with savage fury. It took all four of them to get me back to bed. I have no memory of the incident.

Four weeks after my admission to the hospital I woke one morning feeling refreshed, as though I had slept the night through dreamlessly and restfully. I could not believe when I was told that my night had been a month long.

Mister Smith came to see us. He looked lean and spruce in a lightweight civilian suit. For a week, he said, he had been close to death. He had been to see me a couple of days earlier but I had shown no signs of recognising him. He had talked to the doctors about us, told them in detail what we had been through.

"You are going to be all right now, Slav," he said. He gestured over to where Zaro and Kolemenos were sitting up in bed and beaming across at us. "And so are they."

One of the soldier patients in the ward wanted to know our names. The American told him but the soldier had difficulty in getting his tongue around the unfamiliar syllables. A compromise was reached. We became Zaro, Slav and "Big Boy".

Our story got round. From other parts of the hospital staff members came along to take a peep at us. The British soldiers in our ward showered us with kindnesses. One of them went round with his hat collecting cigarettes, money, chocolate, little personal gifts, and shared the offering between us.

The American came to see us again later. He gave me a silver cigarette case and some money.

"What are you intending to do when you are better, Slav?"

I told him there was only one course open to me. As a Polish officer I must rejoin the Polish Army.

"Are you sure that is what you want to do?"

"It is the only thing I can do."

"We shall meet after the war, of course. Where shall it be, Slav?"

"In Warsaw," I said. And I wrote down for him the address of my family's house in Warsaw.

"I should like that," he said. "We will meet in Warsaw."

A British officer and a Polish interpreter came to see me. It was a long talk with the characteristics of security interrogation not, however, overstressed. A long catechism about Poland, its people and its politics to test my *bona fides*. Then the Russians and the journey, all over again.

The interpreter returned alone the next day bringing me a gift of half-a-dozen white handkerchiefs and an Indian ivory cigarette-holder. He said transport was being arranged through the British for me to join up with Polish forces fighting with the Allies in the Middle East.

The night before I left, Kolemenos, Zaro and I had a farewell celebration in the hospital canteen.

Mister Smith came to the hospital to see me off on that last day, bringing me a small fibre case in which to pack my few belongings. I had resolved to make the parting from Zaro and Kolemenos as painless as possible. We said goodbye in the ward and the soldiers called out "Good luck" and "All the best, Slav," and things like that. I walked towards the door, Smith ahead of me. Zaro and Kolemenos followed behind. I wanted them to stay where they were but they kept on walking. I turned at the door and big Kolemenos ran forward and hugged me and then came Zaro. And the tears came so that I had to drag myself away. The American walked with me, blowing his nose in his handkerchief.

He rode on the bus with me into Calcutta, where they dropped him off. "Look after yourself, Slav," he said. "And God bless you."

The bus pulled away towards the transit camp where I was to await a troopship for the Middle East. I looked back at him once and he waved.

I felt suddenly bereft of friends, bereft of everything, as desolate and lonely as a man could be.

THE END